CREATING KNOWLEDGE, STRENGTHENING NATIONS

Creating Knowledge, Strengthening Nations

The Changing Role
of Higher Education

Edited by
Glen A. Jones, Patricia L. McCarney,
and Michael L. Skolnik

UNIVERSITY OF TORONTO PRESS
Toronto Buffalo London

© University of Toronto Press Incorporated 2005
Toronto Buffalo London
Printed in Canada

ISBN 0-8020-3856-5

Printed on acid-free paper

Library and Archives Canada Cataloguing in Publication

Creating knowledge, strengthening nations : the changing role of
    higher education / edited by Glen A. Jones, Patricia L. McCarney and
    Michael L. Skolnik.

ISBN 0-8020-3856-5

1. Education, Higher – Aims and objectives.   2. Education,
Higher – Philosophy.   I. Jones, Glen Alan, 1961–   II. McCarney,
Patricia L. (Patricia Louise)   III. Skolnik, Michael L., 1941–

LB2322.2.C75 2005   378'.001   C2004-905979-3

University of Toronto Press acknowledges the financial assistance to its
publishing program of the Canada Council and the Ontario Arts Council.

University of Toronto Press acknowledges the financial support for its
publishing activities of the Government of Canada through the Book
Publishing Industry Development Program (BPIDP).

Contents

**Section 2. Strengthening Nations, Regions, and Cities: Higher
Education and Society**

Foreword: The Role of the University and Basic Research in the New Economy

Robert J. Birgeneau

As it enters the twenty-first century, the University of Toronto, like other major institutions of higher education, faces a world more interconnected than ever before and a world in which knowledge, creativity, and innovation are the essential elements of thriving societies.

Universities have always been keepers and creators of knowledge. They have sought to prepare new generations with the skills, cultural and scientific literacy, flexibility, and capacity for critical inquiry and moral choice necessary to make their own contributions to society. They are well placed, therefore, to respond to the new challenges of educating their graduates for participation in a rapidly changing global economy, and more broadly, for citizenship, not only of their home nations and communities, but of the world.

To consider how universities in the twenty-first century can fully rise to these challenges, the University of Toronto hosted an important symposium entitled 'Creating Knowledge, Strengthening Nations: The Changing Role of Higher Education.' The symposium was held from 30 October to 1 November 2002, as part of the univesity's celebrations to mark its 175th anniversary (King's College, later to become the University of Toronto, was granted its charter by King George IV in 1827. The symposium brought together recognized experts in higher education, senior officials from universities and government, and representatives of international agencies from North America, Europe, Africa, and Asia.

Near the end of the Second World War, in a study entitled, 'The Endless Frontier,' the father of the modern research university, Vannevar Bush, stated: 'New products and new processes do not appear full grown.

They are founded on principles and new conceptions, which in turn are painstakingly developed by research in the purest realms of science.' What those elegant words identify is the indisputable importance of basic research to economic progress – research that takes place in universities. Five decades ago Bush's influential study and its findings delivered to the U.S. government the most succinctly stated rationale for large-scale investment by government in basic research. It touched off decades of accelerated investment by the U.S. government in research universities, and in basic research.

Today, there is little doubt that investment in university-based basic research is in large measure responsible for the phenomenal increase in output of the North American economy over the past five decades. This message, however, requires and deserves regular repetition.

In modern societies, research universities are the principal sources for the creation of new knowledge and, as such, they have a disproportionate impact on the economy. Although the return on investment in basic research is not often immediately apparent, there can be a wholly unforeseen and dramatic return over the long term.

There are numerous cases of investments made in basic research that have later yielded impressive commercial results. The scientific roots of the global positioning system (GPS) provide one example of the impact of basic research on the economy. Many current up-scale cars have navigational devices that can tell you, electronically, exactly how to get from here to there. These units are based on the GPS. In fact, for a few hundred dollars, you can now buy a device that will tell you exactly where you are on earth to within a few metres. This extraordinary technology is entering the popular economy through the high-end car market, and in the next generation of automobiles, every car is going to have one of these onboard. Literally drivers will have no excuse to become lost. Of course, they are also invaluable for sailors, for people who like to trek in the wilderness, and for the military. What are the roots of this extraordinary technology? - Basic science, of course. Importantly, the people who did the basic research had no idea that their fundamental work would underlie this new technology.

The research that made the GPS possible was led by Norman Ramsey and Dan Kleppner. Back in the 1950s, Dan Kleppner was an undergraduate student at Cambridge University in England. One of his professors there believed that if they could determine how to lock an oscillator to a hydrogen atom, they could make a frequency standard, and therefore a time standard that would be better than anything that had been produced before. This effort would require improving technology by a factor of a million, and he reasoned that if it could be done, they could test Einstein's theory of general relativity. They might actually see that a photon's light frequency changes as it comes towards earth. One cannot imagine anything more basic for a scientist than wanting to test Einstein's theory of general relativity.

Kleppner next went to Harvard for graduate school where he met and worked with Norman Ramsey on this idea, and the result of this work was that together they invented the hydrogen maser. For that work, and some other research that he had done, Ramsey received the Nobel Prize. Ramsey and Kleppner's invention was subsequently generalized to caesium clocks and rubidium atomic clocks that allow us to measure time more precisely than anyone had ever imagined.

Kleppner wrote an interesting little piece in *Physics Today*[1] about his experience, and there are several lessons to be gleaned from his account. First, if a researcher went to a funding agency and said, 'I'm going to enable you to sell luxury cars in which you can never get lost, and I'm going to do that by developing a more accurate clock than you could ever imagine,' he or she would be shown the door. Moreover, when Kleppner and Ramsey were doing this research, they could not have imagined the GPS application, because satellites did not yet exist. To conceive of a global positioning system, you needed the entire investment in satellites that now exists. At present there are twenty-four satellites in space for the sole purpose of the GPS.

From basic research in the laboratory to economic impact, a phenomenal technological development was also required, and that is how it always is. You cannot have an impact on the economy unless you have the basic research, but you need basic research, *and* technology, *and* venture capital all coupled together. These are the necessary ingredients that ultimately will provide an economic impact.

A second example concerns the work of a very modest man named Paul Berg of Stanford University, who was responsible for the basic research that led to what we now call *biotechnology*. In 1980, Professor Berg was awarded the Nobel Prize for his efforts. Berg did the basic work on gene splicing of DNA, which immediately preceded the work done by Stanley Cohen of the University of California at Berkeley and Herb Boyers of the University of California at San Francisco. Their work led to the first recombinant DNA clone, and this marked the beginning of the biotechnology revolution.

Berg tells an interesting story about how after he made his discovery, he visited Merck and Company Incorporated – a pharmaceutical company that strongly supported basic research, and one with a wonderful research laboratory in Montreal. It turns out that there was a scientist at Merck Research Laboratories, who was following exactly the same track as Berg, and was in a position to start the biotechnology revolution himself. The trouble was that he ran into a technical difficulty, something you just had to get over when doing this kind of research. But Merck, in spite of being a great corporation and being committed to fundamental research, nevertheless had a time horizon of between twelve and eighteen months on its research projects. As it turned out, that was not enough, and the scientist who might well have created the new field of biotechnology at Merck was ordered to stop and was switched to a project with a shorter time horizon.[2]

The lesson we can take from this is that most often this kind of research can happen only in a university. Accordingly, if we are really going to produce radically new technologies on which new economies are based, it will almost certainly happen in universities. Specifically, universities are the only places that have long enough time horizons to allow researchers to do the kind of research that is *revolutionary*, rather than *evolutionary*. Beyond this is the obvious fact that you cannot make an impact on the economy with just the discovery; you also need technologists and business people with foresight.

An important aspect of the example of biotechnology is that it reveals dramatically the long time frames involved in the transition from basic research to a new industry. There was about a *thirty-year* delay between the establishment of basic research programs in molecular biology in the mid-1950s in some lead universities, to the creation of industries such as Amgen and Biogen in the mid-1980s.

A further example of such fundamental research with remarkable but unexpected commercial results is furnished by the phenomenon that has invaded everyone's lives – the World Wide Web. Experimenters carrying out fundamental research in elementary particle physics at the European nuclear accelerator centre known as CERN needed to find a way to share their data internationally so that, for example, physicists at universities in Canada and the United States could analyse the results in real time. To accomplish this, the CERN scientists and, specifically, Tim Berners-Lee invented the World Wide Web. Roughly a decade later, the result is an entirely new economy – the dotcom universe. I suspect that this, too, was the furthest thing from the minds of the Web's creators. Although the dotcom universe is experiencing reversals these days, there is no doubt about its phenomenal impact on the economy. The lesson is, once again, that this kind of serendipity can only result from research investment that does not have a narrow commercial focus.

We can, however, help to create an environment where such research can flourish and find sponsors. The University of Toronto is currently involved in just such an initiative, an exciting new incubator project called MaRS, for medical and related sciences. We hope that MaRS will become a model in Canada for the forms of cooperation possible between the public and private sectors.

MaRS Discovery District is a not-for-profit corporation with facilities designed to house start-up companies created to develop and market research discoveries. Related businesses and services such as patenting offices, law firms, venture capital offices, and government services would also be part of the complex. MaRS will be unique in North America, because it will combine all the elements of engineering, computer science, and biotechnology. Furthermore, if the stars line up correctly in downtown Toronto, we will have a major incubator facility within walking distance of world-class medical, engineering, and scientific research laboratories. It is difficult to imagine more propitious conditions. The chapter in this volume by John Evans provides insight into this exciting new initiative.

Initiatives such as this, which involve a number of partners, suggest that the future bodes well for research, not only at the University of Toronto, but at universities across the country. Universities, however, face challenges as they begin to engage more fully the institutions that surround them.

One of those challenges concerns the relationship between universities and industry. From a variety of camps, on and beyond campus, we hear the concern that universities must maintain a distance from industry; that they must retain full and absolute academic autonomy.

In this respect, some recent analyses of important pieces of legislation introduced over two decades ago in the United States are revealing. They suggest that there is no evidence that academic autonomy is compromised when universities enter into mutually beneficial and carefully considered relationships with the private sector. This, of course, requires that appropriate safeguards be built into any such agreements.

The transfer of research results from universities to the commercial marketplace for the public benefit – technology transfer – is closely linked to fundamental research activities in universities. The Bayh-Dole Act, introduced in the United States in 1980, was intended to facilitate the transfer of ideas to the market by granting universities the right to own the intellectual property that came out of the research being done by their faculty members and students.

The federal government in the United States spent considerable time and study in the 1960s and 1970s on the issue of policies pertaining to federal patents. One of the primary areas of concern was the perceived lack of efficacy on the part of the federal government in the promotion and adoption of new technologies by industry. In part, this was an issue because there was, at the time, no government-wide policy regarding the ownership of inventions made by government contractors and recipients of federal government grants.

Furthermore, there was a total lack of harmonization among the policies and practices of the many funding agencies. The result was a highly restricted flow of government-funded inventions to the private sector.

Agencies were also reluctant to allow universities and other grantees to possess ownership of inventions. For its part, the government was highly reluctant to give up ownership of federally funded inventions to the inventing organization, with the exception of those rare cases in which individual petitions had wound their way through the lengthy and difficult waiver process. So, instead of ceding ownership of federally sponsored – and owned – intellectual property, the federal government opted to retain title, but make these inventions accessible and available through non-exclusive licences to anyone who wanted to practise them.

Under this policy scenario, industry did not possess exclusive rights to manufacture and sell goods developed under those government-held patents. As a result, companies were less than willing to invest in and develop new products if their competition could just as easily purchase licences for those products and duplicate their manufacture. This state of affairs continued to result in a poor response from industry in licensing government-owned patents. Some legislators felt that this was an unacceptable – and to some extent a wasteful – use of tax money in research, considering that the potential exploitation of that research was simply not being fully realized. In the beginning of the 1980s, there was sufficient political will in the United States to change this course. The result was the Bayh-Dole Act, which permitted universities and small businesses to have the potential to opt for ownership of inventions made under federal funding.

What then can be said of the growing public perception of the hazards of closer relations between university and industry? Recent research on the effect of the Bayh-Dole Act on both Stanford University and the University of California has produced very significant conclusions. Namely, once the university has ownership of intellectual property, there is a tremendously positive impact on the transfer of basic science and technology from the universities to the private sector and then to the economy, thereby creating a marvellous number of jobs.

What troubles people in this instance is that this growth in emphasis on technology transfer might possibly have a negative effect on universities. In fact, the overwhelming evidence in the research-intensive universities in both Canada and the United States is that this has not happened. Indeed, if you look at the pattern of basic research in the United States before 1980, and the pattern of basic research after 1980, it has not changed one iota. So, the process of technology transfer has in no way blemished the purity of basic research, at least in the leading institutions.

Another notable finding of the study was that, although the Bayh-Dole Act gave ownership of intellectual property to universities, it did not change the character of university-industry relationships. It just added to the richness and fullness of their impact on the economy.

Another challenge faced by research-intensive universities pertains to the increasing complexity of society's expectations of our work, including the tension produced by the need to be both an institution of the world and an institution of the local community. These expectations pertain to our students and graduates as well as our faculty.

This means that as a public research university in Canada our responsibilities at the University of Toronto are more complex, for example, than those of many leading private universities in the United States. Because such small, highly selective institutions have applicant pools that reach beyond regional and national boundaries, they possess no equivalent obligations to their local communities. This is one of the greatest challenges generated by the twin forces of internationalization and globalization – but one that requires all institutions to remain reflective and responsive: the obligation to be global in our orientation, while at the same time serving the needs and expectations of our surrounding communities.

The chapters in this book address these challenges and offer new insight into the evolving multiple and complex roles for higher education in the coming decades. The contributors to this volume were central to our symposium celebration, held at a critical turning point in our evolution and success in the new global economy, and their papers published here offer thoughtful reflections and guidance on the changing role of higher education.

NOTES

1 Daniel Kleppner, 'Where I Stand,' *Physics Today* (Jan. 1994).
2 E. Press and J. Washburn, 'The Kept University,' *Atlantic Monthly* (March 2000).

Acknowledgments

The editors gratefully acknowledge the financial assistance for publication support provided by the International Development Research Centre in Ottawa. In addition, the Office of the Vice-President, Research and International Relations at the University of Toronto and the Steering Committee for the Symposium were instrumental in bringing together the researchers that have contributed to the volume. Finally, we would like to thank Hyla Levy, Department of Political Science at the University of Toronto, for her generous editorial work in the preparation of the manuscript.

CREATING KNOWLEDGE, STRENGTHENING NATIONS

Introduction

Glen A. Jones, Patricia L. McCarney, and Michael L. Skolnik

In these early years of the twenty-first century, institutions of higher education are having to confront the complex transformations currently taking place in the economic, political, scientific, and social climate. The university's response to the external challenges represented by a knowledge-driven, global economy is increasingly contested, with a view to better balancing the economic purpose of higher education with its cultural, moral, and intellectual purposes.

This volume seeks to deepen the analysis of this balance and improve understanding of higher education as advancing not merely economic growth and entrepreneurialism but also strategic societal goals of equity and redistributive justice. It is in this broad-based context of 'strengthening nations' that the changing role of higher education is situated.

Our objective in this chapter is to introduce and explicate a number of the core themes and issues that are interwoven through the analysis and discussion of these complex goals and relationships. We begin by highlighting a number of the basic tensions that underscore this discussion, and how these tensions have been taken up by scholars located in different fields with different discourses, traditions, and operating within the boundaries of different disciplines. We then turn to the three sections of the book and analyse the key themes that run through each section.

Many of the tensions associated with defining or redefining the role of higher education in contemporary society involve questions of balance. Balancing the economic versus non-economic objectives of higher education, for example – a long-standing tension seen throughout the past century – is here examined within the contextually different framework posed by globalization and privatization. Even though universities are commonly viewed as essential institutions in the increasingly global, knowledge-based economy, this new role is not being supported as in the past by sustained levels of public investment in higher education. In many countries, declining or at best stable levels of public investment mean that public higher education can no longer assume that it will receive protection by government from market competition. As a result, universities have been repositioning themselves in terms of their relationship to the state and industry, and assuming the role of key players in a global economic system where new knowledge and highly skilled human resources are perceived as the fuel of economic development.

The resulting tension is one between those who celebrate the 'entrepreneurial university' and those lamenting the new alignment between the university and the business community as undermining the civic responsibility of the university and its freedom of speech, leading to curtailment of critical inquiry. However, recognition of the complexity in the relationship between research and practice, and the growing sensitivity to equity and ethical issues, provides an important context for theorizing about the role of the university in contemporary industrial society. Here, the complex transformations currently taking place in the scientific community provide a critical backdrop for evaluating this tension. The two most recent waves of technological change, first, information and communications, and more recently, biotechnology and genomics, force us to re-assess the nature of these tensions and to re-evaluate the university-industry relationships of late.

In other words, the ruggedness of this new scientific terrain cautions us to take a step back and re-assess the older linear model in which research undertaken in a university provided useful information for industry subsequently to exploit. This volume addresses the need to understand the precise functions that universities perform in contributing to economic growth and development, and offers insight into a more complex, multifaceted, and interactive model deemed essential for the effective relationship between the university and industry.

Moreover, in recognizing the complexity of the relationship between research and practice in the physical and life sciences, a growing sensitivity to equity and ethical issues relating to new technology is witnessed. As the chapters in this volume show, these changes provide an important context for theorizing about the role of the university in contemporary industrial society. It is here that university research in the humanities and social sciences is vital. This volume thus advances a particular vision of the university, as one that highlights not merely economic growth and entrepreneurialism but also strategic societal goals of equity and redistributive justice. The world's truly great universities have a responsibility to organize themselves internally in such a way as to protect fundamental science, research, and teaching, while devising external relationships that enable external partners to capture, develop, and exploit university research for the benefit of the whole society.

The symposium that gave rise to this book reflects these tensions and undercurrents in higher education and its contribution to the economies of nations. The papers published in this volume open new debates on the policies governing and affecting the role of universities. The authors introduce challenges for institutions of higher education themselves, for firms engaged in the knowledge economy, and for governments concerned with creating new policy levers for the higher education sector.

It is also important to note that these issues and tensions have been taken up by scholars and practitioners who are located in different academic fields and in very different positions within the expanding network of relationships associated with the changing context already described. Many important contributions to this debate have been made by scholars in the academic field of higher education. This is an extremely heterogeneous, interdisciplinary field of scholarship, but at its core is a focus on analysing higher education phenomena, and therefore the boundaries of the field are frequently defined in terms of the boundaries of the higher education sector. At the same time, complementary issues and research activities have been taken up by scholars located in other parts of the academy. Political scientists have become increasingly interested in government policy activity designed to strengthen the knowledge creation and/or dissemination infrastructure implied by the transition to the knowledge economy. A range of interdisciplinary scholarship has focused on issues of economic development in global and national terms, with particular emphasis in recent years on social, cultural, and economic development at the level of the region and the city. Others have focused their attention on the study of research and issues of knowledge creation and consumption.

There has been an apparently natural tendency to create focused discussions of specific themes that emerge from one of these areas of scholarship. In contrast, the organizers of the University of Toronto symposium made a strategic decision to invite leading scholars representing a variety of field and discipline perspectives. In the editorial process we have attempted to be selective, not only in terms of the overall scholarly quality of individual contributions, but also in terms of maintaining a balance of contributions from different areas of scholarship.

We have organized the chapters into three complementary sections. The first, entitled 'New Pressures, New Roles: The Changing Context for Higher Education,' focuses on broad challenges and changes associated with higher education. The second section focuses attention on issues related to the role of higher education in relation to society, with particular emphasis on its role in strengthening nations, regions, and cities. The third section focuses on issues related to knowledge creation and dissemination. The boundaries between these sections are obviously artificial and arbitrary, but underscoring the chapters in each section are a number of extremely important issues and themes.

New Pressures, New Roles: The Changing Context for Higher Education

The first section of this volume presents a group of chapters that discuss broad changes in the context and environment of higher education. A central theme is that significant social and economic transformations are challenging what some might view as the traditional role and position of universities in society, in arguing that these institutions need to understand and find ways of addressing these important but complex challenges.

Many of these new pressures are captured by use of the term 'globalization' or 'global economy' by four of the five authors in the titles of these chapters. Much of the research literature and discussion of globalization in higher education has focused on the economic dimension of this notion, and one might conclude that this growing body of literature has become increasingly bifurcated between those who view the movement towards economic globalization as inevitable, and therefore focus on the necessity of institutional reforms, and those who view globalization as an unnecessary evil where economic interests have displaced broader social, human, and democratic concerns. The latter argue in favour of resistance, while the former frequently assume that resistance is futile.

To some extent all five of the authors represented in this section take a middle path, although they frame their understanding of these new pressures in quite different ways, and offer quite different arguments. At the same time, there are a number of common themes, noted by two or more of the authors, and reviewing these themes can provide a foundation for exploring the nuances and contradictions associated with the changing context of higher education.

A common assumption running through all of these chapters, for example, is that there is no such thing as *the* university in terms of a standardized and universal institutional form. 'University,' as the term is used in this discussion, is best understood as an umbrella label for what are, in reality, a myriad of institutional forms organized in quite different ways in order to address quite different social, political, and economic goals. An obvious reason for these differences is that, as Peter Scott notes, in his chapter, the 'idea of the university has developed alongside the idea of the state': the higher education reforms of nineteenth-century Europe were inseparably linked to the rise of nationalism and the nation state, just as twentieth-century reforms were frequently linked to the development of the welfare state. Universities did continue to share common broadly defined goals and functions, but they were national institutions designed and funded to serve national interests. These distinct national models were frequently exported through European colonialism, or, as Ruth Hayhoe notes, in her chapter, freely adapted by such countries as China, Japan, and Thailand, based on the assumption that the university could play a major role in modernization. However international the scope of their activities, or the origins of their faculty and students, universities were, and are, national and/or regional institutions.

A second common theme is the central role of the university in the movement towards a knowledge-based economy. The university is being repositioned in terms of its relationship to the state and industry because it is now viewed as a key player in a global economic system where new knowledge and highly skilled human resources are perceived as the fuel of economic development. 'The new importance of higher education,' to use David Bloom's phrase from his chapter, has also come to imply increased pressure on universities to respond to market needs and to strengthen their capacity to contribute to regional and/or national economic development through research and teaching. As several authors note here, while universities are commonly viewed as essential institutions in the increasingly global, knowledge-based economy, this new role is supported by flat, and in many countries, declining, levels of public investment in higher education. Many governments have reduced or shifted the nature of higher education funding mechanisms. This is based on the assumption that increasing market influences in higher education will stimulate competition and increase the level of responsiveness to market needs. According to James Duderstadt, in his chapter, 'public higher education can no longer assume that public policies and investment will shield them from market competition.'

A third common theme is a logical extension of the first two: different institutions in different national contexts are differently positioned to address the challenges, problems, and opportunities represented by the global economy. Eva Egron-Polak and David Bloom both focus attention on inequities between developing and developed nations in terms of the capacity to respond to these new pressures. Universities in the developed world have struggled to respond to increasing demands for higher education in the face of decreasing government support. These challenges must be viewed as modest, however, in comparison with the pressures faced by their peers in the developing world. Duderstadt notes that there are at least thirty million people in the world who are qualified but cannot find a space in a university.

The authors differ in terms of how they understand and frame the challenges ahead. Bloom argues for a prioritization of investment in and attention to the expansion of higher education in the developing world. He suggests that globalization is exposing a fundamental contradiction in the approach of many international organizations and national governments 'where, on the one hand, education is said to be essential, and on the other, the most advanced type of education is neglected.' His is not a call to reform higher education in response to the needs of international market forces, but rather an argument in favour of recasting higher education in terms of its role in increasing the pace of development while avoiding the pitfalls of globalization. For Bloom, higher education reforms can contribute to broader social goals, including the eradication of extreme poverty and hunger and ensuring universal primary and secondary education. These reforms should include facilitating cross-institutional networking, the adoption of new teaching methods, and the expansion of liberal education. Bloom argues that the core issue is one of implementation, and he suggests that urgent attention much be given to both the 'technical and political aspects of reform.'

Egron-Polak begins by asking whether universities are actors or spectators in the face of the new pressures associated with the global economy. It soon becomes clear that she is raising an extremely complicated series of questions related to 'finding a balance between the pressures to internationalize academically and the need to remain an active player in the globalized system.' While Bloom focuses on system-level reforms. Egron-Polak focuses on the issues and questions that institutions must address if they are to avoid becoming little more than passive subjects to external economic pressures.

In a similar vein, Duderstadt frames the issue in terms of the university's response to the external challenges represented by a knowledge-driven, global economy. He focuses on four major challenges: the skills race, the markets, technology, and global sustainability. He argues that the discussion of how to transform the university to address these challenges must focus on a series of important issues. It should begin, according to Duderstadt, with a reconsideration of 'values of the university that should be protected and preserved during a period of change.' It should recognize the increasing importance of diversity in higher education. It should consider issues of subsidiarity and autonomy, whether the institution has the organizational independence necessary to respond to a rapidly changing environment, and the degree to which citizens and governments continue to view higher education as a public good. Like Egron-Polak, Duderstadt notes that universities are only one component of a broader network of institutional types that form the higher education sector. He emphasizes the importance of revisiting the distribution of roles and responsibilities among institutions through creative alliances along both local or regional and international spheres. Although raising different questions, both authors argue that perhaps the most difficult challenges facing universities involve their need to be proactive, to develop what Duderstadt refers to as 'the capacity for change' that will allow institutions to make strategic choices.

Scott's analysis of the pressures facing universities in the context of globalization frames the issues in a very different way. Acknowledging that much of the debate over globalization has focused on its conceptual association with economic liberalism, he argues that many of the greatest challenges and pressures facing the university may be a function of the social-cultural dimension of this phenomenon. His contribution to the scholarly discussion of globalization and higher education is to refine, if not redefine, our understanding of this term by focusing both on the implications of the globalization of the right, traditionally characterized by the movement towards market liberalization, the knowledge economy, and mass culture, and the globalization of the left, 'the world-wide movements of resistance to market liberalization and its political and cultural effects.' The real challenge to the university, in Scott's view, involves internal and external pressures associated with the social and cultural aspects of these changes. The internal challenge relates to changes in institutional structures and practices associated with overlaying the notion of an entrepreneurial university on the traditional university (Clark 1988), although Scott does not view the former as superseding the latter. The challenge involves working out the relationship between these two forms, and reconfiguring institutional practices in light of this new balance. The greatest external threat to the university is posed by 'truly alternative knowledge organizations' that challenge traditional notions of scientific excellence and objectivity. The impact of this cultural revolution can be felt in changes in student culture and mentality as a new generation learns to 'navigate a de-centred world and live multiple lives,' in changes in how and where knowledge is generated, and in challenges to the traditional communicative culture of the university.

In many respects Hayhoe's chapter provides a wonderful example of the challenges and pressures that Scott discusses under the rubric of 'cultural revolution.' However, her focus on these challenges is in terms of understanding their roots in context-rooted historical and epistomological phenomena. Framing her analysis in terms of the 'dialogue among civilizations,' Hayhoe discusses how a series of experiences and development activities led her to develop a particular interest in reflecting on the very different situations of women in academia in the West and China. The contrasting stories of struggle by women for entry and acceptance in these two civilizations illuminates the importance of understanding the extraordinary differences in culture and epistomology that underscore knowledge systems. Hayhoe argues that women have played a special role in engaging in this conversation of difference, this dialogue across civilizations, that is 'contributing to a transformation of the knowledge patterns once so entrenched in Western universities.' Hayhoe and Scott frame their respective contributions in entirely different theoretical foundations. Yet, there are remarkable similarities in terms of how these scholars understand the nature of the complex transformations that are currently taking place.

It is interesting to note that none of the contributors to this volume discuss the implications of the events of 11 September 2001 to our understanding of globalization and the changing context of higher education. Most of the chapters were written shortly after the 2001 attacks and long before the controversial initiatives that would eventually result in the American-led invasion of Iraq in 2003. Some of the changes associated with these events may have dramatic implications for higher education, including the shifting role of the state as the guardian of national security, new limitations on the cross-national flow of knowledge and knowledge workers, and shifts in the delicate balance of regional (local) and global interests. It is still too early to know where these changes are leading. Nevertheless, there can be little doubt that the implications of these events and shifts will require additional research and analysis.

Strengthening Nations, Regions, and Cities: Higher Education and Society

In the chapters that form Section 2 of this volume the role of higher education is examined in varying local, regional, national, and global contexts. The relationship between research and the innovation process is now understood to be more complex than public policy discussions have heretofore suggested. A framework of analysis that embodies the institutional and interpersonal linkages of universities, firms, and governments, and better addresses the specific properties of knowledge generated by researchers engaged in each, is now required if we are to better understand the innovation process. This is true at varying levels in the system, from local city to global contexts.

In an address to this symposium given by Maureen O'Neil, president of the International Development Research Centre, and included at the start of Section 2, it is argued that for the effective progress of development globally, the promotion of higher education is dependent on the promotion of good governance. O'Neil argues that 'where civil and political rights are suppressed, higher education cannot thrive.' Her address testifies to the intimate interaction between higher education and open, responsible government. O'Neil contends that by simply measuring the value of higher education in instrumental terms, which correlates graduates with economic performance, we fail to capture the more intrinsic benefits of higher education as both a private and a public good.

This theme is taken up in the chapter by Michael Skolnik, where the balance between the economic and non-economic objectives of the university is examined in recent historical and current perspectives. Skolnik presents a comparative overview between the 1960s and our own period, times when the literature on higher education and the policy environment reflect an 'unbridled enthusiasm over the contribution of higher education to economic growth.' In this comparative context, Skolnik examines the relationships between the university and non-university sectors of post-secondary education. He suggests that the dualism often associated with the categories of higher education – knowledge for its own sake versus knowledge for practical ends – does not fully explain the current realities of the higher education field. Furthermore, Skolnik argues that such boundaries falsely compartmentalize human beings into their vocational selves and their other selves. In deepening the analysis of the balance between economic versus non-economic objectives of higher education, he argues that the contextual differences between the 1960s and today, posed by globalization and privatization, require greater reflection on the contested roles of higher education, with a view to better balancing the economic purpose with the cultural, moral, and intellectual purposes of higher education.

Higher education is to be understood as advancing not merely economic growth and entrepreneurialism but also strategic societal goals of equity and redistributive justice in the argument made by George Subotzky in his chapter. During the political transformation of the 1990s, higher education was seen in South Africa as a policy lever to overcome the ravages of apartheid. Universities were to have played a crucial role in building a new society and in contributing towards the national development priorities of the new democracy. Subotsky contends that this policy position has been constrained by 'the hegemony of the global, market-oriented, neo-liberal discourse' and that the dominance of the single market model in South Africa has produced its higher education equivalent – the entrepreneurial university. In making his argument Subotzky examines, in depth, the higher education reform policy in South Africa since the mid-1990s and its outcomes.

The challenges confronting the field of higher education in India are reported in the chapter by Ramamurthy Natarajan. Like many countries of the developing world, India is responding to the global challenges posed by the rapidly changing field of information technology (IT) and is developing new policy directions. Natarajan addresses the role of technical education, in particular, and the Indian experience to date, in strengthening the system of higher education so that it can raise the country's IT profile and help it to play a central role in the knowledge economy.

David Wolfe takes a step back from the idea that universities are central to the emerging knowledge-based economy and cautions us on the need to understand the precise functions that universities perform in contributing to economic growth and development. Wolfe critically examines how universities contribute to economic growth specifically in regional economic clusters. He suggests that universities perform two vital functions: as generators of new knowledge through their leading-edge research activities and as trainers of highly qualified labour. Both of these, when integrally linked, provide the essential infrastructure from which regional economic clusters can develop. Wolfe demonstrates why spatial proximity matters in a knowledge-based economy. In discussing the relation between the codified and tacit dimensions of knowledge, he suggests that tacit knowledge is locally embedded; that makes spatial proximity important in the development of economic clusters. He argues that it is a mistake to view the primary purpose of universities as spinning off research results into new products and firms. While this can assist in the growth of cluster development, Wolfe suggests that this transformation of research findings into commercial products is too narrow a focus for universities and that the research and teaching functions of universities remain essential.

The connection of universities to their locality is a theme taken up by Beth Savan, in her chapter. She examines different models of partnerships between university researchers and the community. Unlike many of the chapters in this volume, Savan's work does not address the economic nature of university research, but rather examines the more social aspects of the campus-community relationship, profiling one community-based research project at Innis College in the University of Toronto that is an attempt to respond to community needs.

In her chapter, Patricia McCarney tracks the recent evolution of the study of global cities. She argues for the importance of situating universities and the role of higher education in an analysis of global cities. Likewise, in examining the literature on higher education, McCarney concludes that the spatial location of universities in cities is too often overlooked as a crucial context for the consideration of innovation. This dual examination points to strong resonance between global cities and higher education and the need to improve understanding on this emergent and vital relationship. Just as universities are often celebrated as engines of economic growth in the knowledge economy, and as essential contributors to a nation's competitiveness in the global economy, so also are cities defined in similar terms: cities are typically termed a nation's engine of growth, and cities are regarded as the new global actors competing in the global economy. Convergence is also seen in the criticisms of these positions. The tension, for example, between those who celebrate the entrepreneurial university and those lamenting the new alignment between the university and the business community – as undermining the civic responsibility of the university and its freedom of speech, leading to curtailment of critical inquiry – is echoed in a dualism in global cities. Similarly, cities, too, are facing the dual challenge of being globally competitive while also meeting the demands of their citizens, thus struggling to reconcile the domains of public versus private interests in the city. Both the universities and the cities in which they reside are alike in that they engender civic tolerance, democratic values, and civilizing forces. In other words, McCarney argues, there is much to be gained on a policy terrain that has a better understanding of this essential relationship between universities and their cities.

Creating Knowledge: New Challenges and Roles

A number of the chapters in this collection speak of *new* challenges and *new* roles for higher education. Regarding an institution that has been in existence as long as the university, there may be room for argument as to whether some of the apparent challenges facing it today and the ways that it responds to those challenges are actually new, or merely variants of its past experience. Insofar as the latter might be the case, the experience in question likely would date back only to the late nineteenth century. For it was only then that the intentional production of knowledge that would have useful application for a nation's economic development became a substantial element in the mission of the university. Unthinkable as it seems in today's context, the industrial revolution in the eighteenth century began outside the universities and was largely ignored by them. However, as noted by Harold Perkin, historian of higher education, 'industrial society, nevertheless, eventually recreated the university in its own image (Perkin 1991, 183).'

Industrial society has changed since the late nineteenth century. Accordingly, the university's relationship to it has changed in ways that are reflected in the chapters in Section 3. Whereas the dominant industries where research was fuelling change were once metallurgy, chemicals, and textiles, our authors identify the two most recent waves of technological change as being, first, information and communications, and more recently, biotechnology and genomics. These areas have been a major focus of recent university-industry relationships. Three of the chapters in this section (those by Daar and Singer, Evans, and Stiller) focus specifically on the role of the university in regard to the production and application of knowledge in the broad area of health, biotechnology, and genomics.

Two other important changes in industrial society that occurred over the last part of the twentieth century are the recognition of the complexity in the relationship between research and practice and the growing sensitivity to equity and ethical issues relating to new technology. As the chapters in this volume show, these changes provide an important context for theorizing about the role of the university in contemporary industrial society.

Calvin Stiller chairs the Canadian Medical Discoveries Fund. In his chapters, he describes how the older linear model – in which research undertaken in a university provided useful information for industry subsequently to exploit – has given way to a more complex, multifaceted, and interactive model for the effective relationship between the university and industry. He argues that the new dynamic interface between the university and industry is more like a network in which the whole university is 'present, excellent, engaged, and renewed.'

Louis Tornatzky elaborates on the components of this dynamic interface. Tornatzky draws upon case studies of twelve universities in the United States that were judged by a diverse panel of experts to be leading institutions in regard to partnering with industry. He reports that a characteristic of these 'best-in-class' institutions is that they are actively involved in all or most domains of practice. These domains include the following: industry research partnerships, technology transfer, entrepreneurial development, industry-focused education and training, career services and placement, formal partnerships with state or regional economic development organizations, and use of industry input in campus programs. Tornatzky also noted a high degree of coordination and communication across the university with respect to the various external initiatives in which the university is involved.

Stiller and Tornatzky look at these relationships largely from the vantage point of the university. John Evans presents an examination of the Medical and Related Sciences (MaRS) Discovery District. MaRS is an example of a particular newly developing network for fostering commercialization of research from the perspective of the whole cluster of constituent entities. This new cluster is located in a part of Toronto in proximity to a major university, several hospitals and scientific and medical research facilities, Canada's major financial district, and the government of the Province of Ontario. Consistent with the ideas about the relationship between research and innovation in the Stiller and Tornatzky chapters, MaRS is presented by Evans as 'an attempt to achieve the benefits of a cluster as defined by Porter and Martin through geographic co-location of businesses, financial, and academic enterprises that feed on each others' ideas and experience.' In addition to the importance of the generation of new knowledge and the training of highly qualified labour that Wolfe emphasizes in his earlier chapter, Evans highlights the role of venture capital in the development of successful economic clusters. He argues that initiatives like MaRS are particularly important to Canada because the country has lagged behind other industrialized countries, particularly the United States, in regard to catching new waves of technological innovation.

The potential contributions of university research in the physical and life sciences, like those anticipated in the MaRS project, have been the focal point in government agendas for innovation. Shirley Neuman argues that university research in the humanities and social sciences is also vital. She offers many examples of what is gained thereby, including a better understanding of the innovation process; an understanding of how technology shapes areas other than technology; an exploration of the interaction between learning and innovation; and learning how policy and regulatory regimes that are intended to foster innovation actually work.

Besides their potential for contributing to national economic development, the new technologies bring with them serious issues of equity and ethics. The social sciences and humanities offer important expertise for examining those issues. For example, one equity issue raised in this book is the gap between those who have the benefit of the new IT and those who do not: The revolution in information technology may be seen as a democratizing force insofar as it has vastly increased access to knowledge for large numbers of people; however, the widening digital divide between those who have this access and those who do not is a cause for concern. The difference in access to the benefits of new technology is particularly great between economically advanced countries and developing ones

Life expectancy is another examples. In Canada it is about eighty years and rising, while in several countries in sub-Saharan Africa it is expected to be less than thirty years in 2010. Abdallah Daar and Peter Singer assert, in view of this fact, that the greatest challenge for the future is 'to bridge the gap between what we know we can do and what needs to be done.'

In the context of that challenge, Daar and Singer describe a university-based initiative, the Canadian Program in Genomics and Global Health (CPGGH). The primary goal of the CPGGH is to harness genomics and biotechnology in the service of global health equity and thus help bridge the divide between developed and developing countries. This is a global social goal, in contrast to a national economic one, which is the focus of many of the other chapters. Nevertheless, the CPGGH embraces a model of sustained, multi-faceted engagement with a variety external agents that is similar to the one favoured by Evans, Stiller, and Tornatzky. The CPGGH is concerned with the fields of science and technology. It is located within the University of Toronto's Joint Centre for Bioethics, and it reflects the personal commitments of its founders. The CPGGH has devoted particular attention to ethical issues in the applications of research in biotechnology and genomics.

The kind of external engagement by the university that is the focus of the chapters by Evans, Daar and Singer, Stiller, and Tornatzky could be seen alternatively as flowing from, or implying, a particular vision of the university. The way that Daar and Singer explicate this vision is by suggesting that in the future the world's truly great universities will need to emphasize three 'I's': innovation, interdisciplinarity, and internationalism. The other chapters referred to in this paragraph concentrate on two of the I's, innovation and interdisciplinarity, but in apparent awareness of the international dimension, they do so within the context of globalization. Stiller puts the latter two I's together in his discussion of literature that describes the shift from traditional, discipline-based university research (so-called Mode 1) to multidisciplinary research with a focus on application (Mode 2).

It is important to note also that all our authors are sensitive to the implications of this type of shift in orientation for the university's traditional values. With that concern in mind, Stiller describes a new social contract between society and its universities, in which it is the responsibility of the universities to organize themselves internally in such a way as to protect fundamental science, research, and teaching, while devising external relationships that enable external partners to access, develop, and exploit university research for the benefit of the whole society. Citing a Government of Canada document, Neuman calls attention to a similar vision in which universities would more aggressively contribute to innovation in Canada – including, in her view, through research in the social sciences and humanities – in return for long-term government commitment to the knowledge infrastructure that makes such research possible.

Common to all three sections of this volume is an attempt to describe the various types of responses that universities in different parts of the world are making to the external challenges of an increasingly knowledge-driven, global economy. In addition to describing these experiences, most of the chapters examine the way that the tension between serving society's economic goals and maintaining attention on the university's broader cultural, moral, and intellectual purposes is being handled. In addition, many of the authors offer analyses of the factors that lead universities to respond in one way or another to the external challenges, as well as speculation about the longer term ramifications of these developments for both universities and the societies around them.

Although all of the chapters at least hint at the public policy options involved in rethinking the centuries-old and continually evolving relationship between society and the universities, several authors address such policy options and their implications quite explicitly, including a few that present the broad outlines of a new social contract that those authors suggest is appropriate for the knowledge society of the early twenty-first century. In summary, the contributions to this volume range from detailed description of universities' responses to external challenges and expectations related to their knowledge- creation potential, to analysis and interpretation, to consideration of implications for public policy and university practices.

REFERENCES

Clark, Burton R. (1998). *Creating Entrepreneurial Universities*. Oxford: Elsevier Science.

Perkin, Harold. (1991). History of Universities. In Phillip G. Altbach, ed. *International Higher Education: An Encyclopedia*, vol. 1. New York: Garland, pp. 169–204.

New Pressures, New Roles: The Changing Context For Higher Education

CHAPTER 1

Raising the Pressure: Globalization and the Need for Higher Education Reform

David E. Bloom

Higher education and globalization have combined to influence the lives of individuals and societies for many centuries. In 1193, a Hungarian nobleman named Miklos left behind the mountains of Transylvania to become the first student to officially register at Oxford University. In the sixteenth century, in Santo Domingo and Mexico, the Spanish introduced universities to the Western hemisphere. More recently, the Humboldt University in Berlin, established in 1810 and known as the 'mother of all universities,' marked the first attempt to combine an all-round humanist education with research. Its founder, Wilhelm von Humboldt, wrote, 'The university teacher is no longer teacher and the student no longer merely a pupil, but is rather engaged in research in which he is led and supported by the professor. University teaching not only enables an understanding of the unity of science but also its furtherance' (as cited in 'Studying at the Humboldt-University' n.d.) The Humboldt model was quickly mimicked across the world and is now the norm in many universities in developed countries.

The past few decades, however, have intensified pressure on universities to respond to global integration. The unprecedented speed of globalization has turned a piercing spotlight onto each country's systems and institutions of higher education. Those countries whose universities and colleges can adapt to the rapidly changing economic, political, and social climate will have much greater prospects of success.

In much of the developing world, higher education systems are poorly equipped to cope with this increasing pressure. Other development priorities, such as development of infrastructure, health, and the drive for universal basic education, are in greater demand, and few poor countries have enough money to cover those. Higher education, moreover, is a long-term investment – the benefits to society do not accrue in the short term. The benefits of investment in education, its expansion, and its quality, therefore, are less apparent from a political perspective. Making the case for investment in higher education requires vision and leadership. Many of the organizations most directly involved with formulating education policy for the developing world, however, have failed to recognize fully the value of higher education. Organizations like the World Bank, driven for many years by a narrow and ill-founded belief that advanced education provides a lower return on investment than does basic schooling, have directed their funds towards the latter at the expense of the former.[1] As the World Bank itself has recently acknowledged (2002, xxiv–xxv): 'Much of the support provided by World Bank tertiary education projects was piecemeal ... The Bank was rarely able to offer the type of long-term comprehensive support for tertiary education that is required for successful reform and effective institution building.'[2] In turn, governments in many developing countries, and particularly those post-colonial governments that saw universities as preserves of the imperialist elites, have allowed their higher education systems to drift, while focusing their efforts instead on the drive for basic schooling.

Globalization is exposing this contradiction – where, on the one hand, education is said to be essential, and on the other, the most advanced type of education is neglected – as being fundamentally inappropriate to the needs of developing countries. As this chapter will argue, globalization is exerting new pressures on higher education. These pressures both magnify the benefits of higher education reform and reduce its costs. The argument rest on three main points:

1 Higher education is essential to promoting economic growth and sustainable human development.
2 In a globalizing world, devoting more resources to the higher education sector must be given higher priority. Reform is urgently needed.
3 Implementation of higher education reform requires deeper attention. The harsh realities of the field must be considered at the same time as policy design.

The New Importance of Higher Education

Making the Most of Globalization ...

Globalization refers to the process whereby countries become more integrated, mainly via movements of goods, capital, labour, and ideas.[3]

Figure 1.1. Higher education gross enrolment ratios vs globalization ranking

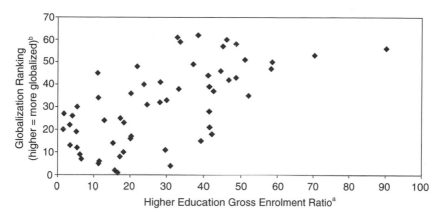

^a The higher education gross enrolment ratio is the total number of students in higher
education divided by the population of the age group that typically enrols in higher education institutions.
^b For the globalization ranking, values are plotted with numbers opposite from their pub-
lished form, to create a more intuitive chart.

Globalization has considerable potential to boost economic well-being
and human welfare. Those countries that have benefited from the opening up of international trade and investment channels and, to a lesser
extent, the more limited opening up of labour markets, have seen significant improvements in living standards. As well as North America,
parts of Australasia, and Western Europe, formerly poor regions such as
East and South-east Asia have made rapid strides in recent decades,
largely as a result of international trade and investment.

Globalization also brings with it controversy. Not all regions have benefited from its spread. Many, indeed, have experienced declines in living
standards as the gap between rich and poor countries has grown. Even in
some countries that have done well, economic growth has often been
accompanied by environmental degradation, the effects of which are felt
both within and beyond national borders. Figure 1.1 shows a cross-coun-
try scatterplot of the higher education gross enrolment ratio in versus the
globalization ranking of sixty-two countries. The ranking index takes into
account a country's international activities in the political arena, technology, personal interaction, and economic interaction (Kearney 2003).[4]
The higher education enrolment rates are taken from UNESCO's Divi-

sion of Statistics, from 1999 online data (for 1995). The most salient feature of this scatterplot is the positive correlation between a country's globalization ranking and its higher education enrolment ratio (with a correlation coefficient of 0.64); this is consistent with the proposition that there is a connection between higher education and globalization.[5]

Testing and estimating the strength of the causal pathways between higher education and globalization is beyond the scope of this chapter. Instead, a central contention here is that higher education has considerable potential to make an impact on both the positive and negative aspects of globalization. As well as stimulating economic growth, higher education can put countries in a better position to arrive at informed decisions about how to manage global integration and negotiate solutions to their problems. For example, as Jan Sadlak has noted (1998, 106), universities are playing a more prominent role in responding to the challenges posed by globalization, as they increasingly influence social and economic affairs in modern society and no longer just mirror them.[6] This section will examine how higher education can help developing countries thrive as a result of globalization. The next section will discuss how it can also help countries steer clear of the downside of globalization.

The leadership and knowledge inculcated by good higher education can enable a country to derive maximum benefit from its entry into the global market for good and services. At a company level, plugging into global business networks requires a familiarity with how they work and with how companies within them thrive. Being able to make good business decisions and adapt to new, and changing, conditions is essential. Efficiency and innovation are also rewarded. At the economy-wide level, successful integration requires appropriate negotiating skills to secure access to markets and the kind of governance that removes obstacles to trade. Many countries that have done well with exports in recent years, and in particular the East Asian 'tigers,' have benefited greatly from strong systems of higher education. These have been instrumental in nurturing necessary skills.

Countries with highly educated populations can also benefit by attracting foreign capital. India, for example, has taken advantage of both higher education and globalization to build up its software industry. In Bangalore, major foreign firms, including IBM, Intel, Microsoft, Oracle, and Sun Microsystems, attracted by India's supply of computer graduates, have set up software development centres or established links with local companies. Economic growth in the area has been dramatic.

Higher education can also enable countries to benefit from the third major aspect of globalization – the global movement of labour. Currently, movement of labour is perhaps the most restricted aspect of globalization. It is also the most controversial. Many of the best graduates produced by developing countries are lured abroad as soon as they leave college. This makes arguing the case for investment in higher education politically more difficult. Nevertheless, the movement of labour is likely to continue to increase until countries become richer,[7] and governments with vision would do well to attempt to capitalize on this trend. In the case of higher education, this may involve teacher exchanges, where teachers in a developing country move abroad temporarily to learn new teaching methods and expand their knowledge. Students, too, can benefit from a period of study abroad, and society can benefit from the new skills they acquire. Strengthening higher education systems, by improving facilities and pay and cultivating a more stimulating working environment, may act as a powerful motivation for academics to return after a time abroad. Stronger higher education systems and institutions may also attract foreign academics and students, from developed and other developing countries. The vexing phenomenon of 'brain drain' can thus be turned, to some extent at least, into a more positive 'brain exchange.'

The global movement of labour from which higher education can benefit is enormous. According to a 2002 U.N. reports, there are now approximately 175 million people living outside of their native country – twice the number in 1975. Most of these migrants live in Europe (56 million), Asia (50 million), and Northern America (41 million).[8] 'Social remittances,' that is, the experiences, attitudes, habits, and aspirations that migrants acquire abroad, and convey to their home countries, can be important to developing countries, and are especially likely to come about as a result of higher education exchanges.[9] Financial remittances are also a natural, and often a significant, source of benefit to developing countries.

The fourth key aspect of globalization is the movement of ideas. Teacher and student exchanges are one way developing countries can take advantage of the world's rapidly increasing flow of knowledge. Use of new technology is another. Globalization has both facilitated, and been facilitated by, advances in information and communications technology. These advances have dramatically increased the speed at which new ideas are brought to fruition. Knowledge and access to knowledge have become vital determinants of national wealth (Bloom et al. 2003).[10] So far, however, the developed world has had a virtual monopoly on the production of knowledge. Rich countries, home to 15 per cent of the world's population, are responsible for over 90 per cent of patents granted (Oxfam n.d.; Singh n.d.). They are also responsible for the vast majority of Nobel Prize winners (see Developing Countries and the Nobel Prize, below). Higher education, by giving students skills to gain access to and implement ideas and technologies developed elsewhere, can be a critical instrument for helping developing countries to narrow the gap.

... and Avoiding Globalization's Pitfalls

Higher education is vital for steering clear of the potential drawbacks of globalization. The United Nations Millennium Development Goals (MDGs) address many of these drawbacks. But, while higher education has an obvious part to play in helping countries to achieve these goals, it receives no mention either as a goal in itself or as a means to achieving the goals. This is a potentially damaging omission.

The first of the MDGs – eradicating extreme poverty and hunger – is reliant largely on economic development and measures to reduce poverty. Neither, of course, is easy to achieve. Macroeconomic policies to promote growth, for example, include controlling inflation and government budgets, reforming tax policies, and planning local and national government spending. Efforts to reduce poverty by promoting social development include measures to employ technological advances to improve health and implementing microfinance programs to empower poor people to set up and grow businesses. Institutional reform, aimed at combating corruption, increasing efficiency in the public sector, and decentralizing the responsibilities of the state, may also be required. Although by itself it will neither promote economic development nor reduce poverty, higher education can make a major contribution to equipping people with necessary skills and knowledge. Higher education, thus, is a necessary component of a country's overall strategy.

The next U.N. goal – ensuring universal primary and secondary education – can also be furthered by higher education.[11] If increased quantity of education is to be matched by improved quality, effective teacher training systems will be necessary. Post-secondary learning has a natural role to play in producing knowledgeable and more highly skilled teachers.

By educating women in the skills needed to hold positions of power, higher education also has a role to play in working towards the third goal – women's empowerment. The latter is a very complex aim, and both technical skills and political will (in, for example, ensuring access to education for women and drawing up gender equity laws) will be needed. Women's empowerment is reliant on improved reproductive and maternal health.

Reducing child mortality and improving maternal health are the fourth and fifth development goals. Improvements in both areas will be made easier if shortages of well-trained medical personnel are overcome.

Advanced medical training will also facilitate progress towards the sixth goal – combating HIV/AIDS and other infectious diseases. Reversing the loss of environmental resources – the next goal – is heavily reliant on changes in the behaviour of both individuals and companies. Environmental degradation can be reduced by well designed taxation and incentive policies to discourage pollution and carbon dioxide emissions. Among many other knowledge-driven initiatives, research into alternative energy sources, or at least the acquisition of the skills to adapt the research done by others, will be in valuable in helping developing countries to improve their living standards in an environmentally sustainable way.

All of the above requirements for achieving the U.N.'s MDGs are closely linked to educational achievement, and most particularly to the skills in development and application of knowledge that higher education produces. The international development community must begin to recognize these links. Unfortunately, the World Summit on Sustainable Development, for example, which was held in Johannesburg in August 2002, made but limited mention of the role of tertiary schooling in development. It appears that the World Bank's new, more enlightened approach has yet to catch on elsewhere.

Higher education, then, offers significant opportunities for developing countries to benefit from the process of globalization. As the next section will discuss, however, existing systems of higher education in many developing countries are ill-equipped to take advantage of these opportunities and their benefits.

The Need for Reform

In much of the developing world, the delivery of higher education is woefully unsuited to the demands of globalization. Existing systems satisfy neither the requirements of the global labour market nor domestic social and economic needs. Missed opportunities abound. We highlight three of them here.

One of the many opportunities globalization is fostering is the increasing tendency for people to burrow out of the confines of their own institutions and link up with others elsewhere to develop knowledge and solve problems. Michael Gibbons (1998), director of the Science Policy Unit at the University of Sussex, has described a new form of knowledge production, which is gaining prominence at the expense of traditional methods of working. In the new model, instead of working purely within the bounds of their specialist subjects with people with similar skills and knowledge from their own institutions, today's knowledge producers are what Gibbons calls 'socially distributed.' Because of the rapid expansion of knowledge, most of the information required to solve a problem inevitably lies elsewhere. Universities – the traditional guardians of knowledge development – are therefore forced to link up with other institutions of higher education as well as with non-educational institutions, which may be drawn from industry, business, government, or elsewhere. These networks of expertise, which 'bubble up like molasses on the stove' as intellectual resources shift from 'area to area, problem to problem, grouping to grouping,' can trigger innovation and thus economic development.

Very few developing countries are making the most of this opportunity. Cross-institutional and cross-border networks, which offer great promise for promoting scientific innovation appropriate to the needs of developing countries, are few and far between. One exception is South Africa's University of Cape Town.[12] That university has established strong links with other African institutions, in Botswana, Kenya, Tanzania, Uganda, Zambia, and Zimbabwe, as well as with several universities in the developed world. Students attending Cape Town from the Southern African Development Community region are charged local rather than international fees. The university's International Academic Programs Office oversees programs such as the University Science, Humanities, and Engineering Partnerships in Africa (USHEPiA) program. With the help of funds from international donors, USHEPiA encourages collaboration among African universities 'to develop a network of African researchers capable of addressing the developmental requirements of sub-Saharan Africa.' Postgraduate fellowships, 'sandwich' courses (in which an overseas component falls in the middle of a longer program of study), lecturing exchanges, and joint research projects are some of the tools for bringing this about. In 2001 a series of workshops, on 'Applying Biotechnology to Poverty in Africa,' brought together experts from across the region to assess how to apply biotechnology to health equity and food security. The university web site gives no examples of practical successes from the program, but even promoting dialogue between institutions and countries is a step in the right direction.[13]

Neglect of liberal schooling is another opportunity missed in developing countries. These countries could gain great benefit from the expansion of liberal education. In a globalizing world, the broad-mindedness inculcated by a good liberal schooling is becoming increasingly important to countries' ability to cooperate with others. A good liberal education also encourages people to question and challenge conventional thinking. As Thomas Jefferson once observed in a letter to John Adams, it can therefore increase the fluidity of an economy by raising the value society places on merit rather than on status or wealth at birth: 'Worth and genius would thus have been sought out from every condition of life, and completely prepared by education for defeating the competition of wealth and birth for public trusts' (Jefferson 1813).

Liberal education is particularly important in a globalizing world. As well as encouraging an attitude of looking beyond private goods to the improvement of society as a whole, liberal education promotes tolerance and appreciation of other cultures and attitudes. As Bloom and Rosovsky have noted, 'in an increasingly interconnected world, empathy with other cultures can encourage both peaceful relations and productive business and cultural interaction' (2003, 20).

In the developing world, examples of successfully implementing liberal education are scarce. The liberal arts university set up by the Bangladesh Rural Advancement Committee (BRAC) is one of very few explicit attempts to reap the benefits of liberal schooling. BRAC designed its curriculum after researching the needs of local employers, students, and parents. According to a report by the World Bank's Task Force for Higher Education and Society, 'BRAC wanted to ... ensure not only financial viability through good initial enrollment rates, [but also] that the university's graduate stream would prove attractive to prospective local employers; this, in turn, would link back to maintaining enrollment on an ongoing basis' (2000, 85). Research found that local employers placed a high value on graduates who could think analytically and communicate clearly. The ability to take the initiative on tasks was also much sought after.

There is no standard general education curriculum, nor should one be advocated. For example, South Africa should not blindly adopt a North American model. Rather, it should take lessons learned elsewhere and adapt them to the needs of South African society. Fortunately, the communications advances that have accompanied globalization make such lesson learning and adaptation considerably easier.

The benefits of cross-institutional networking and liberal education will be greatly enhanced by improved teaching methods. Globalization offers new opportunities to adapt teaching methods from elsewhere, but so far many developing countries have failed to capitalize on this. The rapid growth of the knowledge economy means that new technologies are continually making old ones obsolete. At the same time, old skills quickly become less useful. This means that workers need to be able to acquire new proficiencies if they are to thrive. Currently, higher education in developing countries does not equip students with this flexibility. Instead of rewarding creativity and curiosity, a focus on old-fashioned rote learning places a premium on memory alone.

Although technological development pressures systems of higher education to adopt more interactive teaching methods, it also offers the potential for coping with this pressure. Curriculum designers, for example, can learn from curricula developed elsewhere. Teachers can access online lesson plans and, by virtue of both the increased mobility of labour brought about by globalization and the boom in communications technology, learn new teaching methods from their counterparts in other institutions and overseas. Students, too, can work with colleagues studying elsewhere to solve problems and develop knowledge. Cross-institutional working, liberal education, and new teaching methods, together, offer great opportunities for the system of higher education in a developing country. Outlining the problems and suggesting ideas for solving them, however, is the easy part. Implementing these ideas, as the development community has consistently demonstrated, is the real challenge.

Implementation

As in other areas of international development, many sensible ideas have been suggested for higher education reform, but examples of successful implementation are far less plentiful. Three issues – curriculum reform, brain drain, and distance learning – highlight some of the difficulties of implementing new higher education policies. If institutions of higher education in developing countries are to produce graduates capable of participating and competing in our emerging global society, curriculum reform will be necessary. Existing curricula are often out of date and ill-suited to the demands of twenty-first century society. Curriculum reform, however, is usually tackled as if it were purely a technical problem rather than a political one. This can greatly jeopardize its chances of success.

Curriculum reform is often impeded by a failure to take into account the views of key stakeholders. Current faculty members often feel most threatened by curriculum reform, so it is essential to involve them in the process from an early stage. As the BRAC example shows, consulting local employers and the students themselves can also have benefits – by pooling external perceptions of how a curriculum should be designed, reformers can ensure that courses are relevant to society's goals.

Pakistan is emerging as one of the developing world's pioneers of higher education reform. Pakistan, thus, provides an interesting model for managing the complex process of curriculum reform, and indeed for managing reform in general (British Council, 2002). The Pakistan Higher Education Task Force (PHETF) is an independent group composed of representatives from academia, business, civil society, and a U.S.-based Pakistani think tank. PHETF has pursued a deliberate and innovative policy of employing 'social entrepreneurs' to kick-start the reform process. In this entrepreneurial model, instead of attempting to garner support from all sides before embarking on reform, the PHETF has focused on co-opting small numbers of promising and proactive individuals who will take the initiative in their small part of the system. Seeking out what they describe as 'strategic points of entry,' they attempt to make small changes that will trigger larger ones. At the same time, by creating and promoting early success stories, they work to enlist wider support. This model makes it possible to set reform in motion without the support of government or even of the broad academic community. In Pakistan, the momentum generated eventually won over both, and the government established a Higher Education Commission in 2002, along with a substantial increase in funding for higher education. The Pakistani model is clearly not universally applicable, but it does highlight the importance of drawing in critical stakeholders from across the societal spectrum if reform is to succeed.

The controversial issue of brain drain is another example of good ideas being thwarted by inattention to the practical issues of implementation, and of the importance of addressing the political obstacles to reform. Knowledge has become a valuable commodity in today's globalized world. This has led to an increase in demand for higher education, as students realize that an academic degree is becoming a minimum qualification for a successful career. However, highly educated students are attractive targets for foreign firms and governmental agencies. This has led to concerns over brain drain, which have complicated the political case for higher education. Many have argued that the rewards of developing countries' investment in higher education accrue largely to the developed countries that lure the best talent away. As with curriculum reform, the political issues around brain drain must be considered at the implementation stage.

The migration of students does not have to be a bad thing for a country. The improvements in communications technology and reductions in transport costs that have accompanied globalization allow links with those who have moved abroad to be established and nurtured. The Colombian Network of Researchers and Engineers Abroad (Red Caldas), for example, has members in twenty-three countries. These members, who are mainly science and engineering graduates, collaborate, largely through e-mail, to develop the scientific knowledge that Colombia needs. Twinning with universities abroad has also brought benefits to some. Malaysia's Sepang Institute of Technology (SIT), for example, is twinned with Adelaide University.[14] SIT students in the program take the same courses and receive the same degree or certificate as their counterparts in Adelaide. Professors from Australia share knowledge with those in Malaysia to ensure that course quality is maintained. Students therefore receive a developed world education without leaving behind their homes in a developing country. SIT, meanwhile, gains prestige from its association with one of Australia's top universities. Adelaide benefits by accepting some students from Malaysia into its own programs, and by strengthening links between Australia and one of its key trading partners.

As well as the political aspects of reform, technical aspects must also be considered at an early stage. Distance learning is facilitated by improvements in technology, and offers an effective means of increasing access to higher education. Distance learning gives an opportunity to those who cannot afford to leave home to study at a far-off institution – women who cannot or do not wish to leave home are likely to derive particular benefit. The Internet offers a promising avenue for the expansion of distance learning. Although few developing countries have widespread access to telephone lines, the development of wireless communications technology may help some to leapfrog this stage. The Grameen Trust, a Bangladeshi non-governmental organization (NGO), has set up an Internet centre in the village of Mirzapur. It uses a wireless link to connect to the Internet via the NGO's headquarters in Dhaka (BBC 2002). The centre, which also acts as a local Internet service provider to local businesses and community groups, is reportedly very popular with students, who use it to browse the Web and send e-mail. The World Bank, too, is promoting distance education via its Global Distance Education-

Net.[15] In Mexico, Tec de Monterrey runs the Virtual University, with more than 80,000 students. Courses span the range from basic literacy (for some students coming from the poorest sectors of Mexican society) to professional training.[16] Another prominent example of success stories in the arena of distance learning is the University of Phoenix, in the United States. With an enrollment of nearly 230,000 students from forty countries, and some on-campus presence as well, the university has successfully focused on reaching working adults who are seeking higher education.

Distance learning by itself is no panacea, however. A good education should involve social interaction with other students and discussions with those delivering a course. Online meeting places can contribute to interaction to some extent, but several distance-learning institutions in developing countries have also recognized the value of personal contact. The University of Zambia, for example, invites all distance learners to the main university's campus during the summer vacation. Zimbabwe Open University arranges monthly face-to-face meetings with tutors in its regional centres (British Council 2002).

Finally, it is important to note that the divide between developed and developing countries is growing. This is making reform of higher education and its application to development goals all the more pressing. A short two years after its 1998 World Conference on Higher Education, UNESCO noted that the spread of information technology had led to the strengthening of elites in many countries – elites whose access to technological resources is diminishing societal cohesiveness.[17] Greater social inequalities are making the problems of higher education more difficult to solve (Kearney 2001).

Urgent consideration of both technical and political aspects of reform then is essential. Reform in Pakistan is still at an early stage, but the example is a promising one, because it shows what can be done even from unpromising beginnings. Political leadership and the vision to successfully make the case to the public for investment in higher education is highly desirable, but if strategic entry points can be found, reform is possible even in its absence. Whether reformers come from the upper or lower echelons of the political spectrum, however, they will benefit from devoting the same amount of time and energy to the obstacles and consequences of implementation strategies as to policy design. One cannot work without the other. The challenges for reformers in a developing country are great and new, but the speed of globalization leaves no time for delay in embarking on reform.

Developing Countries and the Nobel Prize

A glance at the distribution of Nobel Prize winners (see Table 1.1) confirms the notion that innovations and new knowledge production stem disproportionately from developed countries. Developing countries now account for 80 per cent of the world population (less in the past, of course), but only about 5 per cent of all Nobel Prizes were awarded to citizens of developing countries. More than half of those were in the fields of literature or peace – crucial and deservedly celebrated areas of human endeavour, but not good measures of knowledge production. Of the nine prizewinners from developing countries who won in the fields of chemistry, physics, or physiology, six were working in an institution in a developed country when they received their prize (see Table 1.2), as were two of the corresponding fourteen winners from the former Soviet Union and Eastern Europe.

Of course, it may be said that the awarding of Nobel Prizes has been tainted by political considerations and that the judges' criteria emanate from a Western view of what is significant. This may be a valid point. However, it is clearly not of a scale that affects these results. Regarding the Western view of what advances are prize-worthy, we must note that developed countries are, in the most common (if, perhaps, nevertheless narrow) use of the term 'developed,' precisely those that have been able to take advantage of advances in Western science and technology. As scores of countries pursue various aspects of development, most of them realize that they need to develop the ability to engage in or at least capitalize on Western science.

Finally, it is perhaps worth noting that the proportion of Nobel Prizes that have gone to nationals of developing countries has increased slightly over time. In every year through the 1970s, the share varied greatly, but was always 6 per cent or less, whereas in the 1980s and 1990s, it was 9 per cent and 12 per cent, respectively – mirroring to some extent the change in overall population shares during the twentieth century.

Appendix: United Nations Millennium Development Goals and Targets

Goal 1: Eradicate extreme poverty and hunger

- Halve, between 1990 and 2015, the proportion of people whose income is less than $1 a day.

Table 1.1 Nobel Prize winners by field and level of development of the country of which they are nationals[a]

	Chemistry	Economics	Literature	Peace	Physiology or Physics	Medicine	Total
Developed[b]	139	50	79	70	157	175	670
FSU/EE[c]	3	1	10	3	8	3	28
Developing	2	1	10	18	4	3	38
TOTAL	144	52	99	91	169	181	736

Source: Author's calculations, based on information available at: http://www.nobel.se/search/nationalities.html, as of January 2003.

[a] The Nobel Foundation tracks winners by nationality, not by the country in which the work was done; some winners are counted twice – either because they have won twice or because they have dual nationality. One winner was stateless. Organizational winners are not included

[b] Countries are considered 'developed' if they currently fall into the 'high-income' group as defined by the World Bank.

[c] 'FSU/EE' means former Soviet Union and Eastern Europe; data include pre-revolutionary Russia.

Table 1.2 Developing country Nobel Prize winners in the sciences

Field	Year	Recipient	Nationality	Institution of major affiliation
Chemistry	1970	Luis Leloir	Argentina	Institute for Biochemical Research, Buenos Aires, Argentina
	1999	Ahmed Zewail	Egypt and United States	California Institute of Technology, Pasadena, United States
Physics	1930	Venkata Raman	India	Calcutta University, Calcutta, India
	1957	Chen Ning Yang	China	Institute for Advanced Study, Princeton, NJ, United States
	1957	Tsung-Dao Lee	China	Columbia University, New York, United States
	1979	Abdus Salam	Pakistan	International Centre for Theoretical Physics, Trieste, Italy; Imperial College of Science and Technology, London, United Kingdom
Physiology	1947	Bernardo Houssay	Argentina	Institute for Biology and Experimental Medicine, Buenos Aires, Argentina
	1951	Max Theiler	South Africa	Rockefeller Foundation, New York, United States
	1984	César Milstein	Argentina and UK	MRC Laboratory of Molecular Biology, Cambridge, United Kingdom

- Halve, between 1990 and 2015, the proportion of people who suffer from hunger.

Goal 2: Achieve universal primary education

- Ensure that, by 2015, children everywhere, boys and girls alike, will be able to complete a full course of primary schooling.

Goal 3: Promote gender equality and empower women

- Eliminate gender disparity in primary and secondary education preferably by 2005 and in all levels of education no later than 2015.

Goal 4: Reduce child mortality

- Reduce by two-thirds, between 1990 and 2015, the under-five mortality rate.

Goal 5: Improve maternal health

- Reduce by three-quarters, between 1990 and 2015, the maternal mortality ratio.

Goal 6: Combat HIV/AIDS, malaria, and other diseases

- Have halted by 2015 and begun to reverse the spread of HIV/AIDS.
- Have halted by 2015 and begun to reverse the incidence of malaria and other major diseases.

Goal 7: Ensure environmental sustainability

- Integrate the principles of sustainable development into country policies and programs and reverse the loss of environmental resources.
- Halve, by 2015, the proportion of people without sustainable access to safe drinking water.
- By 2020, to have achieved a significant improvement in the lives of at least 100 million slum dwellers.

Goal 8: Develop a global partnership for development

- Develop further an open, rule-based, predictable, non-discriminatory trading and financial system (includes a commitment to good governance, development, and poverty reduction – both nationally and internationally).

- Address the special needs of the least developed countries (LDCs). (Includes: tariff and quota free access for LDC exports; enhanced program of debt relief for heavily indebted poor countries and cancellation of official bilateral debt; and more generous official development assistance for countries committed to poverty reduction.)
- Address the special needs of landlocked countries and small island developing states (through Barbados Programme and 22nd General Assembly provisions).
- Deal comprehensively with the debt problems of developing countries through national and international measures in order to make debt sustainable in the long term.
- In cooperation with developing countries, develop and implement strategies for decent and productive work for youth.
- In cooperation with pharmaceutical companies, provide access to affordable, essential drugs in developing countries.
- In cooperation with the private sector, make available the benefits of new technologies, especially information and communications.

Source: Available http://www.undp.org/mdg/abcs.html as of 23 August 2004.

NOTES

The author thanks Henry Rosovsky for helpful discussions and Larry Rosenberg, Helena Turner, and Mark Weston for valuable assistance. An early draft of this paper was presented at the October 2002 University of Toronto symposium, 'Creating Knowledge, Strengthening Nations: The Changing Role of Higher Education,' held in honour of the 175th anniversary of the founding of the university. The author also thanks the participants in the symposium for helpful discussions.

1 For critical assessment of the rate of return approach, see: *The Task Force on Higher Education and Society* (2000), Chapter 2, 'Higher Education and the Public Interest'; David Bloom and Jaypee Sevilla (2003 forthcoming), David Bloom and David Canning (2002); and Nancy Birdsall (1996).
2 The World Bank has recently revised its approach to higher education. *Constructing Knowledge Societies: New Challenges for Tertiary Education* (2002) acknowledges the new importance of higher education in a globalizing

world. The bank's president, James Wolfensohn, launching a report on higher education by the Task Force on Higher Education and Society, signalled this shift in thinking: 'Primary and secondary education ... are not enough. You have to have the centers of excellence and learning and training if you're going to advance the issue of poverty and development in developing countries ... This is not a world which doubts the need for higher education. It's a world which, in the practical sense, accepts that higher education is an essential part of the creation of opportunity for people in development, for people who are poor, to give them an opportunity in a meritocratic framework but also as a national need if the countries are to compete on a global basis' (Wolfensohn 2000).

3 Bloom and Brender (1993) have discussed how developing countries will benefit, via global integration, from having a rising share of the world's labour force. Bloom and Noor (1997) found that increased trade, much more than the movement of labour, accounts for the growth of a regional labour market.

4 The top three countries in the ranking are Ireland, Switzerland, and Sweden. The bottom three are Iran (the least globalized), Saudi Arabia, and Venezuela. Note that the index includes particularly few countries in sub-Saharan Africa.

5 The scatterplot does not, by itself, permit us to infer whether causality runs from higher education to globalization, globalization to higher education, or both. Nor does it permit us to infer whether there is any causal link between higher education and globalization, as the correlation may arise as a result of one or more 'lurking variables' that independently affect globalization and higher education enrolment.

6 Sadlak was then chief of the section for higher education policy and reform at UNESCO, in Paris.

7 Emigration, which is very low when countries are extremely poor (as people lack the resources to travel), tends to increase in the early stages of development before levelling off as incomes between sending and receiving countries converge (Irresistible Attraction 2002).

8 The wall chart *International Migration 2002*, issued by the United Nations Population Division, is available at http://www.un.org/esa/population/publications/ittmig2002/press-release-eng.htm

9 For more on social remittances, see Levitt (2001).

10 The importance of knowledge production, and therefore of higher education, in promoting economic growth in Asia is addressed in Bloom, Rosenberg, Steven, and Weston (in press).

11 David E. Bloom and Joel Cohen (2002) address some of the links between pre-tertiary and higher education.

12 Details are available at http://www.uct.ac.za/
13 The value of universities working together should not be confused with recent moves within the World Trade Organization to open up higher education to trading as if it were any other service. Philip G. Altbach (2001) explains why such a move would be harmful to universities in developing countries and to the countries themselves.
14 Details are available at http://www.sit.edu.my/nne/articles/2001/feb/star180201t.htm
15 Details are available at http://www1.worldbank.org/disted
16 Details are available at http://www.ruv.itesm.mx/portal/principal/qs/
17 Nevertheless, information and communication technologies are important for developing countries. See Bloom, Weston, and Steven (in press).

REFERENCES

Altbach, Philip G. (2001). Why Higher Education Is Not a Global Commodity. *Chronicle of Higher Education* 47(35): B20.

BBC News Online. (2002, 14 Oct.). Net Reaches Bangladeshi Villages. Retrieved 2003 April 10, from http://news.bbc.co.uk/1/hi/technology/2249597.stm.

Birdsall, Nancy. (1996). Public Spending on Higher Education in Developing Countries: Too Much or Too Little? *Economics of Education Review* 15(4): 407–19.

Bloom, David E., and Adi Brender. (1993). Labor and the Emerging World Economy. *Population Bulletin* 48(2): 1–39.

Bloom, David, and David Canning. (2002). Rates of Return on Investments in Education: Reconciling Micro and Macro Estimates. Paper presented at the American Academy of Arts and Sciences, Cambridge, Massachusetts, July.

Bloom, David E., and Joel Cohen. (2002). Education for All: An Unfinished Revolution. *Daedalus* (Summer): 84–95.

Bloom, David E., and Waseem Noor. (1997). Is an Integrated Labor Market Emerging in East and Southeast Asia? In Duncan Campbell, Aurelio Parisotto, Anil Verma, and Asma Lateef, eds., *Regionalization and Labour Market Interdependence in East and Southeast Asia* New York: St Martin's Press, pp. 15–39.

Bloom, David E., Larry, Rosenberg, David, Steven, and Mark Weston (in press). Liberalization, Economic Growth and Sustainable Human Development in Asia: Learning from the Miracle Workers. In Manuel R. Agosin, David E. Bloom, Georges Chapelier, and Jagdish Saigal, eds., *Solving the Riddle of Globalization and Development.* London: Routledge.

Bloom, David E., and Henry Rosovsky. (2003). Why Developing Countries Should Not Neglect Liberal Education. *Liberal Education* 89(1): 16–23.

Bloom, David E., and Jaypee Sevilla. (in press). Should There Be a General Subsidy for Higher Education in Developing Countries? *The Journal of Higher Education In Africa.*

Bloom, David E., Weston, Mark, and David, Steven, (in press). Continental Drift: Globalization, Liberalization and Sustainable Human Development in Sub-Saharan Africa. In Manuel R. Agosin, David E. Bloom, Georges Chapelier, and Jagdish Saigal, eds., *Solving the Riddle of Globalization and Development.* London: Earthscan.

British Council. (2002). *From Peril to Promise: How Higher Education Can Deliver.* Report on the British Council / World Bank higher education seminar, Bath, U.K., March. Retrieved 8 April 2003 from www.tfhe.net.

Gibbons, Michael. (1998). Speech delivered at the World Conference on Higher Education, UNESCO, Paris, Oct.

Irresistible Attraction. (2002). *Economist,* 31 Oct. Retrieved 16 April 2003 from http://www.economist.com

Jefferson, Thomas. (1813). The Natural Aristocracy. Letter to John Adams. Monticello, 28 Oct. Retrieved 10 April 2003 from http://www.tncrimlaw.com/civil_bible/natural_aristocracy.htm.

Kearney, A.T. (2003). Foreign Policy Magazine Globalization Index 2003. *Foreign Policy,* Jan./Feb. Retrieved 8 April 2003 from http://www.foreignpolicy.com/wwwboard/g-index.php.

Levitt, Peggy. (2001). *The Transnational Villagers.* Berkeley: University of California Press.

Oxfam. (n.d.). Genetically Engineered Food Will Not Feed the World. Retrieved 8 April 2003 from www.oxfam.org.hk/english/campaigns/food_hunger/geneng_food.shtml.

Sadlak, Jan. (1998). Globalization and Concurrent Challenges for Higher Education. In Peter Scott, ed., *The Globalization of Higher Education.* Buckingham, England and Philadelphia, PA: Society for Research into Higher Education and Open University Press, pp. 314–19.

Singh, A. Didar. (n.d.) Electronic Commerce: Issues for the South. Working paper for the South Centre. Retrieved 8 April 2003 from http://www.   south-centre.org/publications/ecommerce/ecommerce-09.htm.

Studying at the Humboldt-University in Berlin. (n.d.) Retrieved 8 April 2003 from http://www2.rz.hu-berlin.de/ethno/english/departm/humboldt.htm

Swenson, Craig. (2002). New Models for Higher Education: Creating an Adult-Centered Institution. Paper prepared for the conference 'Globalisation: What Issues Are at Stake for Universities?' at the Université Laval, Quebec, Canada, Sept.

Task Force on Higher Education and Society. (2000). *Higher Education in Developing Countries: Peril or Promise?* Washington, DC: World Bank.

Wolfensohn, James. (2000). Launch of the Higher Education Task Force
    Report, Washington, DC., 1 March. Transcript retrieved 9 April 2003 from
    http://www.tfhe.net/resources/launch_transcript.htm
World Bank. (2002). *Constructing Knowledge Societies: New Challenges for Tertiary
    Education.* Washington: World Bank.

CHAPTER 2

The Opportunities and Threats of Globalization

Peter Scott

Universities may be surprised by the impact of globalization – not because it will be greater than expected and, therefore, stretch to the breaking-point the university's capacity for adaptation; nor because it will be smaller than expected and, therefore, globalization will be a more limited catalyst for change; but because universities may look in the wrong direction and, therefore, be caught off their guard. Instead of being essentially a techno-market phenomenon, leading to a proliferation of virtual, corporate, or for-profit 'universities' (which can ultimately be controlled and contained within more plural higher education systems), globalization may present itself as a socio-cultural phenomenon, which subverts the codes of rationality, the communicative culture, the ethical (and 'expert'?) foundations of the academy – or, alternatively, enriches and enlarges its intellectual possibilities. This, revisionist perhaps and certainly counterintuitive, account of the impact of globalization on higher education is the theme of this chapter.

It is certainly ironic, and it may be significant, that the university, which has a legitimate claim to be regarded as the oldest international institution, an institution indeed that predates in its primeval form the nation state, has been slow, even reluctant, to engage with globalization. Despite the internationalist rhetoric in which university leaders frequently indulge, and despite the evidence of very real international collaboration between universities, especially in research, globalization typically has been perceived by universities as a turbulent and threatening 'other.' The potential inclusion of higher education in the World Trade Organization's General Agreement on Trade in Services (GATS), currently excluded under the 'public services' exemption, has led to fears that 'academic' values will be subordinated to 'commercial' ones if higher education is redefined as a global knowledge industry. The European Universities Association (EUA), the Association of Universities and Colleges of Canada (AUCC), the American Council on Education (ACE), and the Council for Higher Education Accreditation (CHEA) produced a joint statement that voiced these fears and urged their respective governments not to enter into further commitments to liberalize trade in educational services (AUCC et al. 2001). This essentially conservative stance taken by higher education towards GATS is apparently at odds not only with higher education's long history of 'universal' values and international collaboration, but also with its projected future as the centrepiece of a global knowledge society.

Not all higher education leaders and not all universities shrink from globalization. There are some who embrace globalization as a potential catalyst of change, and relish the prospect of the 'market' university which they regard, not necessarily accurately, as an inevitable outcome of the impact of globalization on publicly oriented, if not publicly funded and controlled, higher education systems. Global alliances of typically research-intensive universities, such as 'Universitas 21,' have emerged, albeit in loosely coupled (and ineffective?) forms. Individual universities have taken bold initiatives to embrace the global future. For example, the Massachusetts Institute of Technology announced in 2001 that it intended to make many of its teaching materials freely available on the World-Wide Web. But it would be fair to characterize the mainstream university response to globalization as ranging from reluctant acknowledgment that globalization is an inescapable phenomenon likely to overturn many of the existing assumptions about the aims and organization of universities to a determination to resist its alleged corruption of the university's core academic and public purpose values.

The reluctance of higher education to embrace globalization is a puzzle that demands explanations. There are several available. One is that globalization has become closely associated with economic liberalism, which is regarded as a threat not only to core academic values (because it emphasizes instrumentalism, and consequently vocationalism, at the expense of idealism, and so liberal education and scientific curiosity) and also to the resource base of public higher education systems (because economic liberalism tends to undermine the welfare states within which such systems have flourished). A second explanation is that free-market globalization, which higher education perceives as a threat, cannot be regarded simply as a higher or more intensive form of internationalization, to which most universities are committed (both as a rhetorical discourse and also as a practical resource as they compete to increase their share of the, often lucrative, flows of international students). Globalization is a turbulent and invasive phenomenon, which potentially allows world markets, brands, and cultures to override nation-state politics and 'local' traditions; internationalisation, on the other hand, can be regarded as a benign expression of harmonious cooperation between nation states and of equitable economic and cultural exchanges (Scott 1998).

A third explanation, of course, is that globalization is a problematic and contested phenomenon. Alongside the familiar globalization of the right, market liberalisation and mass-media culture, there is a globalization of the left, the world-wide movements of resistance to market liberalization and its political and cultural effects. Both have their distinctive global signifiers; the dress and behaviour of anti-globalization protestors in Seattle, Washington, Prague, and Genoa are as familiar and predictable as the iconic brands of so-called Coca-Cola culture. Indeed, it can be argued that the globalization of the left predated the globalization of the right. Greenpeace and other environmental movements had already emerged strongly in the 1970s – a decade or more before the full-blown development of market liberalization, which did not really get into its stride until the 1980s and gathered pace in the 1990s.

Moreover, globalization for-and-against has come to replace the old fractures in society between left and right, proletariat and bourgeoisie, liberal and conservative. It is the new politics – in very many ways. For example, the inevitabilities of market liberalization, attributed to globalization, have been taken to invalidate the postwar welfare state with its mixed public-private economy, commitment to social justice, and espousal of public-service values. The emerging tensions between the United States and the European Union can be attributed to different approaches to the impact of globalization on public policy. Either way the distinction between international and domestic politics has been – almost – abolished. Even the 'war on terrorism,' the next cold war, may reflect the clash between two globalizations – one real (in the sense of being market-led) and secular; the other ideal (or, pejoratively, fundamentalist) and religious.

Globalization and the Knowledge Society

These complexities help explain why people involved in higher education apparently feel so ambivalent about globalization – and also perhaps why, although globalization can hardly claim to be a new phenomenon, its current form is perceived to be so different and so unsettling. There has been a world economy since at least the sixteenth century (actually, of course, for much longer, because to date the beginning of the world economy from the expansion of European empires is to betray an indefensible Eurocentricity). International trade as a proportion of total economic activity reached a peak in the early twentieth century. In this sense the economy is less global than it was almost a century ago. There have also been 'world' societies, such as the Roman or Chinese empires – not literally so in terms of their geographical reach but actually so in terms of their culture and mentality. Certainly, by the nineteenth century a fully developed world economy, and also a self-confident (even arrogant) 'world' culture based on the secular, liberal, and individualistic values of the West, existed.

The reasons for the excitement generated by, and even the obsession with, globalization at the end of the twentieth and beginning of the twenty-first centuries – although that world economy has become more intrusive (although not in every sense) while that self-confident 'world' culture has fractured – are by no means as obvious as the flow of political and media commentary would suggest. One reason has already been discussed – the degree to which arguments about globalization have substituted for the traditional left-right discourse of politics. But a second, more substantial, reason is that the forms of globalization now being experienced feel different from (and perhaps more alien than) older forms of world economy and world culture. There are two main clusters of attributes of twenty-first-century globalization that may help to explain why it is perceived in this way.

The first is the acceleration of all those trends, many well-established for several decades, associated with the idea of a 'knowledge society' – which itself has been progressively redefined (see Albrow and King 1990; Castells 1996–9; Stehr 1994). Daniel Bell's essentially technocratic vision (1960, 1973) of a society that had grown out of ideological conflict has been superseded by darker visions of anomie and risk. The regular rhythms of the mechanical age, dominated by the forces of production (and, also, of classical Weberian bureaucracy, whether state or corporate) are being replaced by the irregular and even chaotic rhythms of the electronic age, dominated by the forces of consumption and of the de-construction of traditional institutions – and privatization, which will be discussed later in this chapter. The results are everywhere – round-the-clock round-the-globe financial and other markets are only the most obvious.

There are three dimensions of this general acceleration. The first is technological and refers to the remorseless rise of information and communication technologies. This has made an enormous impact on every aspect of our lives – from leisure (such as computer games), through management systems (which allow us to manipulate massive datasets), to the overall configuration of production and consumption. But this technological revolution has been accompanied by a cultural revolution – which itself has many dimensions. One is new patterns of social interaction, of which the mobile phone is the most ubiquitous example; equally significant is the rise of 'virtuality' and highly sophisticated visualization techniques. Another is the dominance of global brands such as Nike or Coca-Cola. The third dimension of acceleration, of course, is the wider dominance of the 'market' and the application of 'market' discourse to non-commercial domains. Some years ago Francis Fukuyama (1993) heralded the 'End of History.' Philip Bobbitt (200) has recently developed the idea of a 'market state' as the successor to the nation (and welfare) state. Some dismiss this worship of the 'market' as a temporary aberration. Others fear that it runs deeper and that there may be a more fundamental incompatibility between acceleration, combining increasing volatility with more intense innovation, and the regularity (rationality?) principles on which the welfare state is based.

The second cluster of attributes that help to explain why the contemporary phenomenon of globalization feels so different can be summed up in a single word – uncertainty. Alongside the knowledge society has grown up the 'risk society' (Beck 1992). Contemporary society is a remorseless producer of uncertainties – about individual identity, about social affinities, about gender roles, and of course, about jobs and careers. These uncertainties cannot be reduced, much less eradicated, because they are derived from the processes of acceleration and innovation. Instead, they must be accommodated and internalized – either by accepting that we live for the moment, in a kind of 'extended present' or through the elaborate protocols designed to 'manage' risk that are characteristic of the so-called audit society (Power 1997). Globalization is part of this wider uncertainty. But globalization is doubly implicated: first, as a generator of uncertainties, but second as a response or even resistance to them. As has already been pointed out, anti-globalization campaigners are themselves part of the phenomenon they oppose; not only do they employ the most sophisticated technologies (and techniques) of global communication, but they have created their own global discourses, styles, and even brands.

The Impact of Globalization on the University

The history of the university, as with many other histories, is mis-remembered. The historical record demonstrates that the idea of a university has developed alongside the idea of the state – first the princely state, then the dynastic state, later the nation (and welfare) state. Most universities were established as acts of deliberate policy by states. The very few that predated the formation of states have been decisively remoulded by state action (for example, in Britain Oxford and Cambridge were subjected to successive royal commissions during the nineteenth century and subsequent reform). The development of its most classical form, the Humboldtian university (see Introduction to this volume), was part of a wider project, the modernization of the Prussian state after its humiliating defeats in the wars with Napoleon. The origins of the land-grant universities in the United States, another highly influential model for the modern university, can be traced to an act of Congress designed to promote agricultural improvement. If the nineteenth-century university was aligned with the formation of modern, expert, and professional, society, the twentieth-century university was aligned as closely with the development of the welfare state. To the extent that universities have pursued internationalist agendas, it has often been in pursuit of national agendas – for example, to increase a particular nation's share of the market in international students, for diplomatic or commercial reasons; or to relieve the burden on its own taxpayers, by charging international students high fees. This helps explain why, despite their internationalist rhetoric and their universalist aspirations, universities have hesitated to launch, or re-brand, themselves as 'global' institutions.

If it is accepted that universities are fundamentally national institutions (because, until recently, the idea of the nation and the idea of modernity – and of science – were closely entwined), globalization poses three immediate threats:

- The first threat is to the exclusive privileges granted to universities by the state – as the providers of higher education (and the credentials necessary to gain access into the professions and, more widely, to occupy elite positions in society). It is the preservation – or not, as the case may be – of these privileges which is at the heart of the debate about GATS. Under conditions of globalization it becomes increasingly difficult to square the circle, to treat universities in their national context as essentially public-service institutions while encouraging or even obliging universities to represent themselves as market organizations in an international context.

- The second threat is to traditional patterns of governance in higher education. Even when universities are not directly state institutions, they are still governed according to public-service norms (which include a high degree of institutional and academic autonomy). For example, university boards and councils are still typically regarded as having predominantly fiduciary responsibilities, with presidents (or vice-chancellors) and other senior managers, or senates, determining the strategic drive (Bargh et al. 1996). However, if universities are to be redefined as entrepreneurial institutions within a global 'market,' current arrangements for governance may be regarded as increasingly anomalous.

- The third threat is to the funding of higher education, which is still predominantly derived from public sources. This is certainly true in Europe, but also largely true in north America, where the overall contribution of privately funded institutions is often exaggerated (largely, perhaps, because of the high profile of 'Ivy League' universities in the United States). As the welfare state struggles to preserve core services – for example, in basic education, health, and social security – universities may find that their current funding base is increasingly eroded. In some countries, notably Britain since the election of a (New) Labour government in 1997, there have been efforts to define a 'third way' between public and private sectors which emphasizes the public-private partnerships particularly in relation to the funding of public services. The autonomy traditionally enjoyed by universities, and their consequent semi-detachment from state bureaucracies, have made them especially vulnerable to these new experiments in 'semi-detachment' (in other words, reduced availability of state subsidy). The upward pressure on tuition fees in 'state' universities is perhaps an example of this phenomenon.

In discussions of the likely impact of globalization on higher education most attention has been focused on the first dimension – the information and communications technology (ICT) revolution, global brands, and the dominance of the 'market.' But the other, cultural, dimension is equally important, and both must be given equal weight. Typically there are two responses to the first dimension of the impact of globalization on higher education, and these can be described as Mode-1 globalization. The first is that universities must become more self-reliant and more entrepreneurial, with significant consequences for their governance, management, and funding. Typically this has taken the form of more aggressive approaches to the recruitment of international students and development of global partnerships, greater emphasis on the commercialization of research (and, in particular, on its – profitable – dissemination and on technology transfer and consultancy services), and on the development of stronger managerial cultures and infrastructures to control and direct these new activities. However, such changes are only partly attributable to the impact of globalization; they are also responses to more challenging national environments.

The second response is that universities are likely to have to confront and/or compete with rival knowledge organizations. These organizations fall into two main categories, although it is not clear that the first category – so-called borderless education and 'virtual' universities (Middlehurst 2000) – can properly be regarded as rival knowledge organizations. Perhaps it is more accurate to regard them as extensions of the drive towards more entrepreneurial forms of the university itself. Certainly, this first category of organizations is not such a serious threat to traditional universities as is sometimes argued – for the following four reasons.

1 As has just been pointed out, universities are likely to be significant players in borderless education; and they may be the actual sponsors of 'virtual' universities, although probably in association with other partners, such as mass-media organizations and IT companies. Also much of the intellectual content will be derived from academic and other staff employed by universities (although they may need to ensure that their policies on intellectual property are sufficiently robust to take account of this new and more open environment). Universities cannot – easily – be a threat to themselves.

2 To the extent that other knowledge organizations become involved, their emphasis will be on delivery mechanisms and marketing strategies, not on what would be regarded as the core academic enterprise of devising new teaching programs. And, of course, these alternative organizations are unlikely to become engaged at all in research. Consequently, they are unlikely to become direct competitors. Instead, a division of labour is more likely to develop in cartelized structures, with universities providing core 'content' and their mass-media or other partners providing the marketing and delivery 'wrap-rounds.'

3 Only a limited number of subjects are suitable for delivery through

borderless education, or virtual, methods – principally, computer science (in terms of ICT applications rather than basic design) and business and management. Many other subjects are (still) more culturally specific – which may be evidence of the limits of globalization. Therefore, the extent to which borderless education is new, except in its delivery techniques, is open to question. Publicly funded higher education has always faced competition – for example, from 'night schools' or language schools. The existence of such institutions may actually have stimulated the demand for higher education, not least by providing employment opportunities for university graduates. The issue is whether the novelty of ICT-powered delivery – and, in particular, its ability to transcend temporal and spatial constraints – is sufficiently powerful to shift the balance of power from traditional to borderless institutions.

4 The fourth reason is the lessons of the dot com collapse. Virtuality, by itself, is not sufficiently attractive – whether in the commercial or educational arenas. But online delivery, combined with more traditional methods, can be highly effective. A good example is medical education, where simulation and visualization techniques are well developed. But the need for hands-on clinical experience is still as great as ever. Indeed, it is possible to argue that the potential of ICT-powered delivery may actually enhance the position of traditional universities. Blending online delivery with face-to-face education on campus (or in a near-campus environment) mainly serves to enhance the latter, while attempts to use face-to-face education as an adjunct to largely online delivery have proved to be more problematic. For example, summer schools operated by the Open University in Britain have operated largely at the symbolic level by building student networks and mimicking rituals of academic socialization rather than contributing directly to student learning.

The second category – corporate and for-profit 'universities' – can more accurately be regarded as rival organizations. Even here, however, the degree of rivalry can be overstated. First, the threat they pose to the traditional university may have been exaggerated, for some of the same reasons. Corporate and for-profit 'universities' are focused on marketing and delivery, not educational content (and certainly not research). They are most effective in a narrow range of culturally neutral subjects. Some corporate universities are essentially contrived brands – although perhaps the university should be flattered that they have 'stolen' its brand name. Despite the publicity generated by the University of Phoenix, for examples, it poses little threat to traditional universities in core areas such as research, high-status professional training such as law or medicine, or elite undergraduate education. Second, there is evidence that as profits have been squeezed and competition has intensified (both of which, incidentally, may be aspects of globalization), companies have tended to down-size, re-define, or even close down their corporate universities. Their reaction has often been to concentrate on their core business, outsourcing non-core activities. Unless companies are research and development (R&D) intensive or need to place a special emphasis on people development (perhaps to underpin a service-oriented and customer-focused corporate culture), the activities grouped under corporate-university labels are likely to be identified as non-core. It is logical, therefore, for them to outsource to specialist providers such as universities, especially for cutting-edge research and consultancy and development of high-level skills.

The Real Challenge of Globalization

The greatest impact of globalization on the university may be felt in other, less obvious, ways. The first is inside the university, in terms of the reconfiguration of institutional structures and reform of operating practices. The radical challenge posed by globalization to the traditional culture of the university may be at the root of the ambivalence towards globalization apparent in large parts of higher education. The second is outside the university. But the threat will not come from new kinds of 'university' – corporate, virtual or for-profit – that seek to provide university-like services to students and research-users in a more efficient and customer-friendly fashion. It will come from truly alternative institutions that seek to challenge the core values of the traditional university.

One of the most substantial challenges to the traditional university, therefore, may be the entrepreneurial university within, although it is probably a mistake to over-sharpen this distinction (Clark 1998). It is misleading to suggest that there is a dialectical relationship between the traditional university and the entrepreneurial university, or that one organizational paradigm is being superseded by another. The relationship between these two forms is much more subtle and much less dramatic. It is apparent in many different ways – internationalization (with or without the profit motive uppermost) balanced by greater emphasis on regional (and local) engagement; the proliferation of research institutes that sit outside traditional faculty and departmental structures; and the drive to widen participation (because the university is not only becoming entrepreneurial but more socially engaged). This 'challenge from within' is also apparent at the level of systems. One of the primary motives for the 'Bologna process,' the drive to create a common European higher education area, is the desire to make European universities more competitive in relation to American higher education, even though this requires substantial and perhaps unwelcome modification of the traditional structure of courses and degrees in many European systems.

The challenge from without, from truly alternative knowledge organizations, may be even more radical. In the past decade new social movements have emerged which to a significant extent have taken over from traditional political movements. Examples include campaigns to defend the environment or to promote sustainable development, the women's movement in its many forms – and, of course, opponents of market-led globalization. These movements are often very sophisticated in terms of their knowledge bases and their use of global media. Yet they may also pose a radical challenge to traditional notions of scientific excellence, and even of scientific objectivity, to which the university is bound. They espouse alternative knowledge traditions – which once could be dismissed as merely 'local' but now, in an age of globalization, demand to be heard around the world. And globalization gives them voice. The consequences may be both benign and threatening. An example of the former is the widespread but lazy assumption that globalization will reduce cultural and linguistic diversity by promoting a secular, mid-Atlantic, Anglophone culture. On the contrary, new communication and publication technologies have dramatically affected the economies of scale in academic publishing and therefore make publishing in minority languages much more viable. At the same time globalization has provided the means for minority languages and minority cultures to establish global coalitions to resist the hegemony of the predominantly Anglophone and free-market 'West.' An example of the darker consequences of globalisation's capacity to empower the disempowered is the challenge posed by organizations that use 'Western' technologies (including all the paraphernalia of the knowledge society and globalization) to attack 'Western' values.

This is why the second aspect of globalization – globalization as a cultural revolution, the producer of uncertainties (but also, of course, innovations), and the generator of risks (but also of creativity). The impact of this second form of globalization on the university may be even more dramatic than the impact of the more familiar globalization of ICT, global brands, and market liberalization. There are three ways in which its impact may be felt.

1 As a consequence of this cultural revolution, students come to the university with a new temperament, culture, and mentality. Fundamentally, they have learned to navigate a de-centred world and live multiple lives. They come to higher education with more diverse forms of preparation, which are no longer the hallmark of the 'non-standard' student. As a result, they sometimes resist socialization into traditional forms of academic culture. Their commitment to participating in a (largely) holistic intense linear learning experience can no longer be assumed. The Balkanization of the university curriculum may be a reaction to their more episodic and fragmented engagement. Their attitudes to work and careers – and even to social and personal relationships – are also very different. What matters now are not elite or professional careers, which are either not available or occupy at best half the span of working life, but exposure to and immersion in a 'graduate culture' which confers meaningfulness and identity through other means than work.

2 The impact of Mode-2 globalization is not confined to higher education; it also extends into the life-world of research. Knowledge is now generated in much more heterogeneous environments where producers, users, and brokers mingle promiscuously, and where experts in neatly regulated 'scientific communities' no longer hold sway. Knowledge, as a result, has become not simply more highly contextualized – for example, in terms of growing emphasis on its potential applications – but also more intensely reflexive, with the results, first, that controversy and contestation now play much more significant roles in knowledge production and, second, that it is important to (try to) grasp the implications, as well as the applications, of research (Gibbons et al. 1994; Nowotny et al. 2001). This has major implications for universities as research producers, because their privileged status has tended to be eroded. But it also has major implications for universities as teaching institutions, because of the proliferation of, and competition between, alternative knowledge traditions, and also because of the wider social and cultural impacts of two or three generations of mass higher education.

3 Most fundamentally, globalization is producing a revolution in 'communicative culture.' Universities have developed a particular 'com-

municative culture' – cerebral, 'objective,' codified, and symbolic – a culture summed up in a single word *logos*, which embraces mathematics and the natural sciences just as much as, and perhaps more than, the traditional humanities. Yet globalization promotes a different kind of 'communicative culture' – visual, intuitive, volatile, 'subjective' – in which distinctions between the intimate and the domestic and the official, the public, and the corporate have been eroded. Intimacy and virtuality coexist under conditions of globalization – with untold effects for traditional forms of scholarly and scientific discourse. Although this other 'communicative culture' has not been entirely absent from the university in its broadest sense (for example, it has been espoused and practised in art schools and music conservatories), it has been very much on the fringes of traditional academic culture. Perhaps a role reversal is imminent.

Universities will have to come to terms with this radical democratization, this wider social distribution, of knowledge generation – just as they will have to engage with new kinds of students and with new 'communicative cultures.' All these things are consequences of globalization – which are at least as important as the potential challenge of borderless education or corporate universities.

REFERENCES

Albrow, Martin, and Elizabeth King, eds. (1990). *Globalisation, Knowledge and Society*. London: Sage.

Association of Universities and Colleges of Canada (AUCC), American Council on Education (ACE), European Universities Association (EUA), and Council for Higher Education Accreditation (CHEA). (2001). Joint Declaration on Higher Education and the General Agreement on Trade in Services. Geneva, September.

Bargh, Catherine, Peter Scott, and David Smith. (1996). *Governing Universities: Changing the Culture?* Buckingham: Open University Press.

Beck, Ulrich. (1992). *Risk Society: Towards a New Modernity*. London: Sage.

Bell, Daniel. (1960) *The End of Ideology: On the Exhaustion of the Political Ideas of the Fifties* (with *The Resumption of History in the New Century*, 2000). Cambridge: Harvard University Press.

– (1973). *The Coming of Post-Industrial Society*. London: Heinemann.

Bobbitt, Philip. (2002). *The Shield of Achilles: War, Peace and the Course of History*. London: Allen Lane.

Castells, Manuel. (1996–9). *The Information Age: Economy, Society and Culture.* 3 Vols. Oxford: Blackwell.

Clark, Burton. (1998). *Creating Entrepreneurial Universities: Organisational Pathways of Transformation.* Oxford: Pergamon Press for the International Association of Universities.

Fukuyama, Francis. (1993). *The End of History and the Last Man.* Harmondsworth: Penguin.

Gibbons, Michael, Camille, Limoges, Helga, Nowotny, Simon Schwartzman, and Martin Trow. (1994). *The New Production of Knowledge: The Dynamics of Science and Research in Contemporary Societies.* London: Sage.

Middlehurst, Robin. (2000). *The Business of Borderless Education.* London: Committee of Vice-Chancellors and Principals.

Nowotny, Helga, Peter Scott, and Michael Gibbons. (2001). *Re-Thinking Science: Knowledge and the Public in an Age of Uncertainty.* Cambridge: Polity Press.

Power, Michael. (1997). *The Audit Society: Rituals of Verification.* Oxford: Oxford University Press

Scott, Peter. (1998). Massification, Internationalization and Globalization. In Peter Scott, ed. *The Globalization of Higher Education.* Buckingham: Open University Press.

Stehr, Nico. (1994). *Knowledge Societies.* London: Sage.

CHAPTER 3

Universities in the New Global Economy: Actors or Spectators?

Eva Egron-Polak

The title of this chapter is formulated as a question. Indeed, the complexity and interconnectedness of many of the issues and trends changing the landscape of higher education mean that there are far more questions than firm answers facing the leaders of higher education. Furthermore, the answers found are rarely clear-cut or applicable everywhere. Of course, universities are both actors and spectators in the new global economy. In other words, they both drive the changes taking place and are subject to the forces that are transforming our world. But unless we probe further, this acknowledgment does not get us very far in the search for the most appropriate role for universities in a world that is increasingly globalized.

A Broad Topic

The role of universities in the new global economy is a vast topic and one which can be analysed from several perspectives. It invites us to look at the 'big picture' even if we all know that universities face vastly different circumstances between and within different regions and countries in the world. These differences exist even among the members of a national university organization such as, for instance, the Association of Universities and Colleges of Canada (AUCC) with its ninety-two or more institutions. Looking at the nearly 650 members of the International Association of Universities (IAU), from Kabul University in Afghanistan, which rejoined the association in 2002, to the University of Zimbabwe, and passing through the University of Toronto or Université Claude Bernard in Lyon, for example, the diversity of situations and contexts is truly astounding.

Universities are only one set of actors even within the educational universe. They are part of an increasingly diversified higher education sector, and their unique role now needs to be examined and defined in the context of the other institutional contributions in education, training, and research. It must be underlined that it is precisely the wider and more comprehensive societal role of universities and their contribution to the public good that defines their specific nature in this new landscape.

The increased and often almost exclusive focus on the university as a driver of economic development can threaten that specificity by undermining some of the basic values for which the university stands and which it is expected to uphold and pass on. This is not to say that universities do not play a major role in local and regional economic development, particularly in the South. There too, however, the broader contributions that universities make to society must be recognized, encouraged, and protected. The search for alternatives and new paths to sustainable development are important in all regions of the world and require graduates who have benefited from a broad-based, general education that has helped them to develop the analytical capacities and soft skills so needed in a world full of complexity and contradiction. This was a key message of *Higher Education in Developing Countries: Peril and Promise*, a report produced by the International Bank for Reconstruction and Development (World Bank, or IBRD) and UNESCO's task force, completed in the late 1990s (World Bank and IBRD, 2000). The World Bank's own latest strategy, entitled *Constructing Knowledge Societies*, now underlines the social and public role and broad societal benefits of tertiary education. Some of these benefits are greater social cohesion, improved health, better basic and secondary education, democratic participation (World Bank 2002, 77–81).

While taking the macro view, caution must be exercised in trying to understand the role of universities in the new Global economy. The assumption that there *is* a new global economy also requires some caveats, since many of the least developed countries (LDCs), in particular, are not integrated into this global economy, whether new or old, on an equal footing. The gaps that exist between developing and developed nations are said to be widening, and many would argue that globalization of an increasingly knowledge-based economy may even exacerbate this reality.

Internationalization or Globalization of Higher Education?

The International Association of Universities (IAU) has for some time focused on the internationalization of higher education on the one hand, and the impact on higher education, of the forces of globalization, on the other. This is fitting because IAU's existence and mandate for more than fifty years have rested on the premise that international cooperation among universities and, more recently, internationalization of higher education, offer solid paths towards better quality and stronger universities, in a more just and peaceful world. It can be argued that today globalization of the higher education sector is radically changing even the way universities are internationalizing by creating a new and complex dynamic. The full extent of the changes that globalization of higher education may bring is still largely unpredictable and may remain so for some time. But already the debate is raging about both the threatening or negative aspects, as well as the positive opportunities that greater globalization of the sector may offer.

Indeed, higher education is both a major driver of economic growth through its teaching and research functions, and simultaneously is itself increasingly considered to be an economic sector. Viewed as a sector, it is quite huge, representing millions of dollars or Euros in each country and billions internationally. Considered part of the service sector of the economy, it is being exchanged and, within the World Trade Organization (WTO) perspective, being traded. As this sector continues to globalize, many argue that here, too, we must be aware that those who are doing the globalizing may reap its benefits, while those who are being globalized may be subject to far less positive consequences.

All of us are searching for a better understanding of the interconnected forces that are transforming societies – forces of a technological, economic, political, and social nature. In this search, very broad but often undefined concepts such as globalization, knowledge society, sustainable development, public good, and even internationalization have become shorthand in our higher education discourse in the past few years.

Yet, to really explore what is happening and to do so in an international context, with the intercultural and linguistic dimensions adding complexity to the layers of meaning, it is critical to start by articulating what we mean by the words we use and unbundling how some of these concepts fit together. Even if we may not all agree, at least the areas of disagreement will become clearer, and that too is essential for dialogue and better understanding.

Internationalization of Higher Education

Definitions of internationalization in higher education abound.[1] The one most commonly used views internationalization as a proactive effort on the part of universities to embrace their universal nature by opening their curriculum, research, classrooms, and networks to the world. It means introducing an international and intercultural dimension into how we teach and what we learn, what we expect from our faculty members, and whom we hope to attract to our classrooms, laboratories, and as partners in our research projects. In short, it is a process-oriented and comprehensive definition that views the university as a whole. It is also a fairly introverted process, in that the transformation taking place is internal, even though some if not most of the means used to achieve it are internationally interactive.

The extent to which universities have taken this approach seriously is debated widely. For some, university internationalization is often not much more than 'high octane rhetoric' used by higher education leaders (Scott 1998, 111). It is true that university rhetoric often appears to take these institutions' international nature as a given. However, in the past fifteen years or so, internationalization has been adopted as a strategic goal, and pursued through specific policies and actions at every level, in many universities in Europe, North America, and elsewhere. While national surveys to confirm this have been taken in several countries including Canada, IAU is undertaking a first global survey of its members to examine to what extent this is true elsewhere.

The prominence given to internationalization has been, in large measure, the result of an acceleration of economic globalization, which, in turn, was greatly facilitated by an explosion of information and communications technologies (ICT). In that respect, internationalization can be viewed as an initial response to these trends by universities and other higher education institutions throughout the 1990s. Many among them opened international relations offices, designed new exchange and collaborative programs, institutionalized their international research networks, and began, in earnest, to pay attention to how they exposed their students to the shrinking outside world which required such exposure and understanding.

The main characteristics of this process include an emphasis on academic mobility and two-way exchanges of both students and faculty, international research projects and networks, more academic courses integrating an international perspective, and a greater emphasis on how international cooperation projects, particularly with universities in developing countries, are mutually enriching for all participants. Internationalization in this sense has an academic and cultural rationale first, with an entrepreneurial dimension present, but more or less in the back seat.

Globalization and Higher Education

Change is rarely linear or sequential, and the globalization of higher education as a sector of the economy is taking place simultaneously with its internationalization, in response to some of the same external forces, manifesting itself in similar actions but with somewhat different institutional motivations and consequences. The processes of internationalization and globalization of higher education are complementary but different, and their respective impacts are rather difficult to untangle. To attempt to do so is, however, essential, especially for policy-making to reinforce the positive and diminish the negative impacts.

Globalization of higher education is perhaps easier to demonstrate through examples than by definition. In this process, higher education is viewed as a service sector of the economy, with some of its institutions acting globally much like large multinational firms. They are delocalizing, franchising, exporting places by importing students, designing global marketing strategies to increase these exports, selling consulting services, setting up profit centres which generate revenues for further development, and building international alliances and networks. Universities are capitalizing on their brand-name recognition, and entire countries are doing so in order to protect their overseas market share, as is the case for the United States, Australia, the United Kingdom, and to some extent Canada, which have so far enjoyed the lion's share. Other countries are just entering the scene and want to win a share of that education market. Here we see the governments of Germany, the Netherlands, and France, among others, elaborating major initiatives to enhance the attractiveness and visibility of their institutions of higher education so that they can occupy part of this global market space.

This process, too, is about retaining excellence and strength in higher education. Some would say it is about survival in the context of the following external factors:

1 The reality of a knowledge-based economy in which producing, disseminating, adapting, using, and applying knowledge are the key factors of economic growth and competitiveness;
2 Declining real per student funding from public sources, despite the overall growth of the sector and in direct contrast to the rhetorical importance given to knowledge and higher education by governments;
3 An increasingly regionalized but also globalized labour market, and of course,
4 The ICT revolution.

All of these factors act as push-pull levers on individual institutions and on the system as a whole. In the knowledge-based economy, global demand for higher education is steadily growing. Some telling statistics are provided in Alison Wolf's recent book entitled *Does Education Matter?* (2002, 3–5). She indicates that in 1999, the total number of students (at all levels) in the world was more than 1.1 billion, representing 20 per cent of the world's population. The most important fact, though, is that this represents a 90 per cent increase since 1970. For higher education, UNESCO data allow her to estimate a total of 88 million students world-wide, the vast majority of them in publicly funded universities. Further-more, these enrolment numbers are still far from meeting the demand for higher education, so further expansion is likely.

In fact, Denis Blight, former head of the International Department Program (IDP) in Australia, estimated several years ago that in Asia alone, the demand for higher education would grow by 48 million stu-dents between 1995 and 2020. This he equated to a need for 37,000 new university places each week.[2] John Daniel, then vice- chancellor of the Open University in the United Kingdom, writing in *Mega Universities and Knowledge Media,* published in 1996, estimated a global need for one new university per week. What other sector of the economy projects this kind of growth in demand?

This growing demand for higher education is coupled with an almost chronic funding crisis in public higher education. Perhaps the most dra-matic case of this has been the United Kingdom since the 1980s, although in almost all countries in the Organization for Economic and Cultural Development (OECD), per student funding as a percentage of gross domestic product (GDP) per capita, has been declining (Wolf 2002). For most governments, there is an expectation that university funding must become more diversified. In some systems this means an increasing share of the costs covered by students. In other systems, par-ticularly where tuition remains free, these reductions are to be met by efficiency gains, streamlining, and increased revenue generation. The result more generally has been a growing and fierce competition for funds, for faculty who will attract research funds, for students, and for service contracts for training and consultancies, in short, competition for a share of the education and training market at home and increas-ingly worldwide. The entrepreneurial aspect has moved from the back seat to share the front of the bus.

A second consequence has been an explosion of new private provid-ers of higher education, both 'not for profit,' and 'for profit', in many higher education systems, whether these systems are predominantly publicly funded or whether they already have a private higher education sector. Even within countries where higher education remains part of the public sector, commodification of higher education is becoming a reality. The inclusion of trade in educational services in the General Agreement on Trade and Services (GATS) is the starkest example of this new reality, but by no means the only one.

The regional and even global labour market, particularly for academics, researchers, and scientists, and for students as well, is another key facilitator of the globalization of higher education. Projections for teacher and faculty shortages in countries such as Canada, the United States, and elsewhere, as well the competition for other professionals, for example, in the health care field, are giving rise to policies to retain, attract, and import highly qualified people. The concept of brain drain is now used in the context of intra-OECD competition for the best brains. In fact, it could be said that it has been dusted off and now serves as a lever to stimulate R&D investment in several countries. Yet, these policies to strengthen and thus increase the attractiveness of the research environment in universities, in particular, may also have a debilitating impact on countries and regions where the brain drain has already been a reality for some time. The World Bank indicates that in 1990, 75 per cent of all emigrants from sub-Saharan Africa and 75 per cent of all those from India were holders of tertiary education qualifications (World Bank 2002, 15).

The European Union offers a good example of such 'import' strategies. In both its educational programming, such as with the renowned ERASMUS program, and in the research field with the sixth framework program's Marie Curie grants, the EU is planning to launch well-funded, worldwide opportunities to allow non-EU students and scientists to come to European institutions. The likelihood that some of these individuals extend their stay in the host country is fairly high, in light of the conditions that are being proposed, even if the EU is categorical in its commitment to do as much as possible to prevent this. Their programs are designed with incentives for return, but these may prove insufficient when a scholar's or graduate student's scientific career is considered in the long term.

The fourth and final factor needs no real elaboration. The application of ICTs to teaching and learning, which have caused a real explosion of distance education and e-learning opportunities, coupled with the other factors mentioned, creates totally unprecedented transformations in the higher educational scene within nation states and at the transnational level. The now widely used term 'borderless education' is appropriate not only for cross-border or international delivery of education by means of traditional in-class methods. ICTs applied to education also remove the frontiers imposed by time and physical distance. The dual development, through ICTs, of new 'virtual' or e-learning institutions, and technology-enhanced learning opportunities offered by almost every traditional university, add new potential for globalizing the system for all higher education actors.

The cumulative effect of these globalizing factors on the systems and institutions of higher education means that to varying degrees they have become characterized by increasing diversification of types of institutions, programs, delivery channels, and students or clients, greater privatization, and perhaps most importantly by the highly competitive nature of the environment. Internationally, other countries are viewed in terms of market potential rather than as partners whose academics may bring new insights into a discipline or research project and who add an international dimension to the work. In this process, instruction in English is a real asset since it makes programs accessible to many more individuals. There is not much concern that the use of English may be a threat to cultural diversity and a factor for homogenizing the education on offer.

It must be noted that the internationalization and globalization of higher education are not mutually exclusive, nor do they represent opposing poles on a continuum. Often they are indistinguishable, and the promotion of one can strengthen the occurrence of the other. Yet, they do differ in goals and long-term results. For this reason, it is crucial not to use these terms as interchangeable and to probe continuously for a better understanding of their underlying assumptions and rationales.

The realm of globalization is the marketplace; its motor is most often, if not always, economic, and it is fuelled by competition. Institutions build alliances within and across systems and strive to fill a niche more than to fulfil a need. It can be argued that internationalization as defined above is less market-oriented and depends more on policies and incentives that are academic rather than economic in nature. For this reason, internal transformation, cooperation, two-way exchange, and partnerships predominate in these relations.

Both trends are present worldwide in today's systems of higher education. Both are having a very dynamic influence on systems and institutions of higher education. Both are profoundly changing the domestic and international landscape, giving rise to many new programs and courses, providers, new delivery mechanisms, and new kinds of linkages and networks among institutions of higher learning and also with the business community.

The challenges ahead are many. One priority must be finding the appropriate balance between the pressures to internationalize academically and the need to remain active as a player in the globalized system. This requires finding ways to ensure that the potential negative impacts, such as homogenization, exclusion of some individuals or parts of the world from the opportunities offered by this new dynamic, and excessive commodification and privatization of higher education, are countered by the political will to recognize the contribution of higher education to the public good and by policies that promote international cooperation and capacity building rather than increased exports. At the same time, it is becoming apparent that in this world of globalized higher education, a new infrastructure is needed for sharing information, for collective advocacy, and for identifying and addressing gaps such as adequate quality assurance and regulatory mechanisms to protect the learners. Increasingly, it is argued that this regulatory policy infrastructure needs to be developed by the higher education community working collectively rather than by the market working through WTO rules and the trade regime.[2]

As actors and spectators in both internationalization and globalization processes, and mindful of the different impact actions have whether we are actively driving the process or are relatively passive subjects to its consequences, universities may need to ask themselves some of the questions proposed below, as they develop international initiatives. These may be helpful in advancing the analysis of the longer term and unintended impacts of internationalization and globalization of higher education. These questions include the following:

- Will the planned project or program improve the quality of education and research opportunities at home and abroad?
- Will it improve access? If so, for whom? Will it enrich and broaden the educational offer? Will the research planned be relevant to local needs?
- Recognizing the need to generate revenue, has the appropriate balance been struck between the entrepreneurial and academic rationale for the international actions? When are the choices of research networks and projects being made?
- Will the planned project promote or even be mindful of cultural and linguistic diversity?

- When working in partnership with others in other countries, will the project contribute to or undermine the development of the local institution or the higher education system, more broadly?
- Will the quality of the work done internationally be as high as at home?
- Will the initiative contribute or diminish the trend towards commodification of education and its logical extension that sees education as part of the international trade in services?
- Are we working in the spirit of cooperation or competition? And in either case, are we on a level playing field with our foreign colleagues?

Whether as actors or as spectators in the new global economy, universities have a tremendous responsibility towards society to continue to search for answers and to find the appropriate balance between the various and often contradictory forces pulling at them. IAU, too, can play a role in collaboration with regional and national university organizations in Europe, Africa, North America, and elsewhere, to build this new international infrastructure that will help ensure that many reap the benefits of a strong system of global higher education.

NOTES

1 For a full discussion of the definition of internationalization, see, among others: J. Knight, *Internationalization: Elements and Checkpoints.* CBIE Research no. 7 (Ottawa: Canadian Bureau for International Education, 1994); J. Knight and H. de Wit, 'Strategies for Internationalisation of Higher Education: Historical and Conceptual Perspectives,' in H. de Wit (ed.), *A Comparative Study of Australia, Canada, Europe and the United States,* (Amsterdam: European Association for International Education, 1995) Van der Wende, *Internationalizing the Curriculum in Dutch Higher Education* (The Hague: Nuffic, 1996).

2 D. Blight, 'Partnership in International Education: Tautology or Oxymoron? (1997) cited in 'Trading Public Good in the Higher Education Market,' F. Newman, and L. Couturier, in the *Observatory on Borderless Higher Education,* (www.obhe.ac.uk), Jan. 2002.

3 For suggestions and arguments in this direction, see E. Egron-Polak, 'Ethical and Policy Considerations of Worldwide Marketing of Higher Education,' presented at ACA Seminar on Marketing Education Worldwide, 2002; D. Van Damme, 'Higher Education in the Age of Globalization,' in *Globalization and the Market in Higher Education* (Paris: IAU/UNESCO, 2002); G. Breton, 'De l'internationalisation à la globalisation de l'enseignement supérieur,' pre-

sented at conference *Globalization: What Issues are at Stake for Universities?* at Laval University, Quebec, 2002.

REFERENCES

Daniel, J.S. (1996) *Mega-Universities and Knowledge Media: Technology Strategies for Higher Education.* London: Kogan Page.

Scott, P. (1998). *The Globalization of Higher Education.* The Society for Research into Higher Education., Buckingham: Open University Press.

Wolf, A. (2002). *Does Education Matter?,* Harmondsworth: Penguin.

World Bank (Internatiolnal Bank for Reconstruction and Development; IBRD), Task Force on Higher Education and Society. (2000). *Higher Education in Developing Countries: Peril and Promise.* Washington, DC: author.

World Bank. (2002). *Constructing Knowledge Societies: New Challenges for Tertiary Education.* Washington, DC: author.

CHAPTER 4

Universities, Women, and the Dialogue among Civilizations

Ruth Hayhoe

The United Nations declared 2001 the Year of Dialogue among Civiliza tions. The purpose of this designation, as elaborated on a special website, is as follows: to 'emphasize that the present globalization process does not only encompass economic, financial and technological aspects, but must also focus on human cultural, spiritual dimensions and on the inter- dependence of mankind and its rich diversity' (http://www.unesco.org/ dialogue2001). UNESCO sees this dialogue as 'an essential stage in the process of human development that is both sustainable and equitable. It humanizes globalization and lays the basis of an enduring peace, by nur- turing conscience and a common basis for human existence, rooted in history, heritage and tradition' (http://www.unesco.org/dialogue2001).

This call to dialogue presents a significant challenge to universities, given the dominance of certain patterns of knowledge and approaches to epistemology in the university's traditions. This chapter will explore ways in which women scholars in the university community may contrib- ute to overcoming the constraints of these patterns, and stimulate active participation in dialogue. Two experiences over the past decade gave me a sense of the particular qualities women scholars could bring to such a dialogue. One related to a major project of development with the Cana- dian International Development Agency (CIDA) and the second to preparations for the United Nations World Congress on Women held in Beijing in 1995.

Between 1989 and 2001, I was involved in two major CIDA projects sup- porting a number of normal universities or teachers universities in

China, in graduate studies and research. The projects began as standard development projects, offering academic and professional support from Canadian universities. They soon shifted, however, from a focus on development to dialogue, as Canadian partners became aware of all that could be learned from China's rich educational traditions and experience. As more and more women scholars became involved on both sides over the years, and took up much of the leadership, it became evident that women scholars were particularly skilful in cross-civilization dialogue. This, in turn, caused us to reflect on why women tended to be comfortable with a fairly high degree of flexibility over knowledge definitions and approaches to research collaboration across highly divergent academic cultures. Could it have something to do with women's historical experience over the past millennium in relation to the university and other institutions of higher learning?

The second experience that stimulated some probing into the comparative history of women in higher education was the lead-up to the historic United Nations Congress on Women held in Beijing in 1995. We became involved in some of the preparatory work for the congress, particularly making it possible for North American feminist scholars and activists who were working to set the agenda to meet with Chinese women scholars visiting Canada under our project. It soon became evident that the concerns and issues were quite different in China and North America, and we realized there were many reasons for this. As scholars of higher education, we wanted to reflect on whether historical differences in the relation of Chinese and Western women to the modern university might shed some light on this.

This chapter thus has two main parts. The first is a comparative historical overview of women in the academy in China and the West. It identifies both commonalities in women's experience and differences over a long period. It also looks at the approaches women have brought to fundamental questions of epistemology on both sides of the globe, and how these approaches positioned them in relation to the development of universities throughout the twentieth century. The second part provides some illustrations of women's approach to knowledge issues in the dialogue among civilizations. It employs results from six contributions by women to a conference volume that arose from our work with the mentioned CIDA development project, and shows now development had quickly transformed itself into dialogue, and the approaches that women brought to this dialogue.

Women and the Academy in the West and China:
A Historical Overview

One of the European women intellectuals whose reputation has enjoyed a remarkable resurgence in recent years is Hildegard of Bingen, the medieval abbess and nun. She wrote scholarly treatises on cosmology, ethics, and medicine, and corresponded with popes and rulers on a wide range of subjects (Newman 1998). Before the founding of European universities, in the twelfth century, women had been active in scholarship and spiritual leadership through organizations such as nunneries, abbeys, and religious schools. Once the university was founded, however, women were excluded from formal participation in the world of higher learning, resulting in what one scholar has depicted as a 'world without women' (Noble 1992) in European universities over a period of seven centuries. It was not until the nineteenth century that women began their long and arduous struggle to be accepted in modern universities, first as students, then as professors, ultimately as deans and presidents. One pair of woman scholars has described this process as 'storming the tower' (Lie and O'Leary 1990), a phrase that gives some sense of the intensity of the effort and energy called forth in this historic process.

There was little, if any, interaction between Chinese and European scholarly communities in the early medieval period. Nevertheless, it is fascinating to note that women became excluded from the academy in China in precisely the same century as in Europe, that is, the twelfth century. In the European context, David Noble has explained how this was linked to the adoption of celibacy by the Christian clergy in Europe of the time, and to the ways in which early universities were dominated by members of the clergy, as both teachers and students. In the Chinese context, a different set of dynamics led to the exclusion of women from higher learning. During China's Tang dynasty (698–907 CE), women had been able to take an active part in religious and scholarly life, under the liberalizing influence of Buddhism, which had been introduced from India. Buddhist nunneries provided a context for women's scholarship, as well as religious leadership (Tsai 1981), and the aesthetic life of the period was characterized by images of women dancing and participating freely in a range of social activities.

The decline of Buddhist influence and the emergence of neo-Confucianism in the early Song dynasty changed the context for women's education in some important ways. In the twelfth century, the great neo-

Confucian scholar Zhu Xi established a revised canon for scholarly study, entitled the *Four Books and Five Classics,* which was to dominate both the official institutions associated with the imperial examination system and the non-formal academies for 800 years, until the abolition of the traditional examination system in 1905 (Miyazaki 1976). This dominant pattern of scholarship laid down clearly prescribed duties and study tasks for women within the family, and strongly discouraged independent roles for women, including those within Buddhist institutions (Birge 1989).

This intriguing coincidence in the timing of women's exclusion from academic institutions and the world of scholarship provides a point of commonality in the historic struggle of women in China and the West. The subsequent development of scholarly knowledge in European universities, and the emergence of modern science in the sixteenth and seventeenth centuries, however, had few parallels in China. Furthermore, the standing and status of European universities in the global community in the mid- to late nineteenth century, the period in which Western women began their long struggle for acceptance in the university, was completely different from that of China's modern universities, which were established at a time of national humiliation and defeat. These differences in historical context made for a different kind of struggle, and a different set of epistemological resources for the struggle.

Let me begin this train of thought on the Western side. Universities have tended to determine what kinds of knowledge are given high status and set the standards as to what is valued and important. With the emergence of modern science in the seventeenth to the nineteenth centuries, the tremendous productivity and effectiveness of using the scientific method in solving many kinds of problems became more and more evident. Thus, the idea of each of the modern disciplines constituting a value-free, objective science, operating entirely in the cognitive realm of knowledge, has tended to dominate the university's culture (Weiler 2001). Knowledge in the social sciences and humanities has been held to the same standards of scientific objectivity and detachment, as well as of statistical rigour and quantitative forms of evidence and proof. In his influential essay, 'Science as a Vocation,' Max Weber spoke of this as a kind of 'disenchantment of the world,' which he saw as inevitable yet deeply regrettable (Weber 1967, 155).

Women have been particularly sensitive to other ways of knowing, recognizing that only some dimensions of reality can be caught in this objectivist cognitive framework. The West may have made enormous contributions to human civilization through the discoveries and applications of modern science. Yet, these discoveries have also brought many problems in the realms of the environment, health, family life, social cohesion, and what women probably worry most about – conflict and war. Women have been particularly open to forms of wisdom and knowledge available in other civilizations that could contribute to the solution of some of these unintended consequences of progress.

Only after women had overcome formidable barriers to their equal participation in university life as students and professors were they able to analyse the predominant patterns of knowledge. Only then could they develop a feminist critique of the epistemological tenets that had tended to dominate university disciplines. Scholars such as Sandra Harding (1986, 1987, 1991) and Carolyn Merchant (1980) have demonstrated the linear and mechanistic character of the university's rationalism. They have questioned its espousal of a dualism of facts and values as a solution to the need for freedom of scientific inquiry. They have challenged the university's commitment to objectivity and the resultant isolation of the subject from the objects under scrutiny. They have called attention to the university's embrace of metaphors drawn from the mining of natural resources and the subjugation of 'irrational' forces in nature. They have worked to build new approaches to knowledge that could move beyond the one-dimensional approach of positivist scientific methodologies. These concerns have also been picked up by some male scholars in the academy. Bruce Wilshire (1990) identified a 'moral collapse' in the American university. Mark Schwehn (1993) has depicted university members as 'exiles from Eden' because of its inadequacy in dealing with spiritual knowledge. These challenges to the once dominant knowledge orientation of the university have been important for the emergence of genuine dialogue across civilizations.

American sociologist Elise Boulding began to consider issues of global dialogue more than a decade ago. In her book entitled *Building a Global Civic Culture* (1988), Boulding illustrates the possibilities of an integrative and multidimensional approach to knowledge. She identifies four aspects of knowledge which she considers vital to the development of a global civic culture – the cognitive, the affective, the intuitive, and the aesthetic:

'The *cognitive* faculty assists the individual in utilizing and integrating new information into existing mental frameworks and in developing criteria for evaluating new information. Proficiency in the *affective* faculty is apparent when individuals are able to negotiate their personal wants with others in their environment, when they develop empathic identification with others or when they are able to reveal disciplined, intentional behaviour in the face of a diversity of choices. Maturation of the individual's *intuitive* capabilities finds expression in her/his ability to "tune into signals from the natural and social environment which do not lend themselves to verification by empirical procedures"' (Boulding 1988, 100).

Finally, 'the development of an individual's *aesthetic* expression ... may facilitate communication between and among global citizens from different countries, as artistic expression can be employed to supplement written communication.' (Boulding 1988, 98).

Perhaps one reason for women being particularly active in pioneering these integrative forms of knowledge goes back to their centuries of exclusion from European academia. They are less bound to the views of knowledge that have dominated the university, since these were originally developed by an all-male world of scholarship. They are more easily able to balance cognitive approaches to knowledge with the affective, intuitive, and aesthetic in ways that make possible greater openness to other cultures and civilizations.

Nevertheless, an immense effort was required for this 'storming of the tower' that has created space for women's ways of knowing. After all, women began their long struggle to gain acceptance into the university precisely at the time when the European model of the university was viewed as an essential accoutrement to modernization around the world. It was imposed on many societies under conditions of colonialism or imperialism, but it was also freely chosen by other societies as an essential institution in their modernizing efforts. The latter was true of Japan, China, and Thailand, among others (Altbach and Selvaratnam 1989). The establishment of modern universities around the world in the late nineteenth and early twentieth centuries took place in a time of supreme confidence in the achievements of those sciences which had been nurtured by a male world of scholarship in the European context.

Here the contrast with the historical experience of Chinese women is particularly striking. Western women struggled to gain entry to a triumphant institution which was being emulated around the world in the late nineteenth century, Chinese women struggled to enter newly established universities in China, where a completely different mood prevailed. Chinese scholars and political leaders were experiencing a profound sense of humiliation in an international environment so threatening that it was not clear whether China would survive as an independent nation. There were deep regrets at the failure of classical Chinese scholarship and traditional knowledge institutions and the necessity of their abolition. Many of the progressive male scholars who led the newly developing universities were sympathetic to women, feeling that women's experience of oppression in traditional Chinese society gave them a particular capacity to understand the deep chagrin that came with the recognition of China's lowly status in the world of nations. (Chen 1928, 366–8; Hayhoe 1999, 264).

If the conditions of their entry into modern higher education were different, less a storming of the tower than the building of a wholly new type of higher education institution on Chinese soil, the patterns of knowledge which Chinese women confronted were also less alien. It is true that modern Chinese universities borrowed many of the features of the modern disciplines that had developed in the West. There was a particular emphasis on the physical sciences, engineering, agriculture, and medicine, which were seen as essential to modern nation building. Considerable attention was also given to social sciences such as economics, sociology, anthropology, political science, and psychology (Hayhoe 1993). Undergirding this transplanted set of modern disciplines were traditional patterns of knowledge, which were holistic and integrative. China's dominant scholarly culture of Confucianism had allowed space for cognitive, aesthetic, affective, and intuitive forms of understanding, and it had never become bound to a narrow positivistic epistemology (Ding 1995). It had been supportive of scientific innovation and indeed fostered an extremely successful traditional science, admired even in Europe, up to the sixteenth and seventeenth centuries (Blue 2001; Maverick 1946).

At this point a fascinating puzzle emerges. On the one hand, Confucian forms of learning were more open to women's ways of understanding, and more supportive of an integrative and holistic way of looking at human problems than were the patterns of European universities. On the other hand, dogmatic forms of state Confucianism utilized by successive dynasties to legitimate their rule were as absolute in the exclusion of women as the traditional universities of Europe. Chinese women had never been allowed to take part in the traditional civil service examinations, nor had they been able to study in non-formal academies. Yet once these institutions had gone, the patterns of knowledge and approaches to epistemology that continued to nurture scholarly lives in newly established universities were more supportive of women than the forms of rationalism and positivism that were so deeply rooted in the culture of European universities. The struggle of modern Chinese women has thus been a different struggle, and the cultural and intellectual resources which they are able to bring to global dialogue are rooted in a very different civilization.

The recent surge of interest in Confucianism on the part of American philosophers has highlighted the androgynous ideal of scholarship in Confucian tradition, in contrast to the privileging of male approaches to philosophy in the European tradition (Hall and Ames 1998, 79–100). There is a suggestion that men and women in East Asia, whose approach to scholarship is rooted in Confucian tradition, are likely to embrace a multifaceted approach to knowledge and an openness to forms of dialogue that include moral, affective, and aesthetic understanding, as well as cognitive.

With the development of women's studies in China, there has also been a rethinking of some aspects of Chinese history, including the roles of women writers, teachers, and poets in periods such as the late Ming, the fifteenth and sixteenth centuries (Koh 1995). Rather than seeing women mainly as victims who suffered exclusion from mainstream social and educational institutions, it shows women as agents of their own destiny, and explores how they managed to create their own world of scholarship and pedagogy within the broad parameters of Confucian thought. Chinese women have also developed their own critical views of the modern disciplines introduced from the West in recent years, in one case contrasting the openness of anthropology to cultural difference and in-depth inquiry with the precision and dryness of positivist sociology (Chen 1994).

There may thus be historical reasons that women scholars in universities around the world are likely to be particularly active in fostering dialogue among civilizations. They are aware of the limitations of the academic discourse arising from the disciplines of knowledge established in European universities in the nineteenth century. These disciplines and their associated discourses were introduced to most parts of the world under the compulsion of a worldwide movement towards modernization. However, women's historical struggle for equal access to these modern universities took place in different sociocultural contexts, and women scholars have been able to draw upon differing cultural traditions and differing visions of how the university's knowledge patterns might be transformed.

Women's Voices in the Dialogue of Civilizations

In this second section of the chapter I return to the experience described earlier of collaboration with universities in China, which involved joint research, doctoral training, and institutional development. As part of our move from development to dialogue, we organized a major conference in 1992 under the title 'Knowledge across Cultures.' We invited senior scholars from China, India, and the Arabic world, as well as various Western countries, to present their views. Scientists, historians, and educators shared reflections on 'some of the fundamental critiques of knowledge and modernity in the Western context that have arisen from within and as a result of Eastern perspectives and critiques' (Hayhoe et al. 1993, v). The conference volume was published in both English and Chinese in 1993, and then republished in Hong Kong in 2001, with more than half of the papers updated for this revised version in honour of the United Nation's Year of Dialogue among Civilizations. The voices of women scholars in this volume illustrate some of the qualities I have described above in women's ways of knowing.

Let me begin with Ursula Franklin, a distinguished professor emeritus of metallurgy at the University of Toronto. Her metallurgical studies led her to investigations of ancient Chinese bronzes, going back to the sixteenth century BCE, which were remarkably advanced from a scientific point of view. Her attention went beyond pure scientific investigation to explore what could be known about Chinese society. She discovered patterns of the organization of labour and production that were remarkable for their time and expressed a right way of moral and practical conduct, or the Confucian *li*. From this basis Franklin then went on to do pathbreaking work on technology as a system of social instructions, and the social and cultural implications of modern technology. She thus suggests that technology must be understood in its social and cultural context and cannot be simply transferred across social and cultural boundaries as neutral or universal sets of rules or principles. Technology as a way of working together carries with it implicit knowledge, on which the cohesion of communities and cultures depends (Franklin 2001, 248).

A second woman contributor, Samiha Sidhom Peterson, a sociologist from Egypt, focuses her study on processes of knowledge transfer, involving national and international aid agencies such as UNESCO, USAID, and others, in the area of basic education for all. Peterson directs attention to the four layers or levels at which knowledge transfer is negotiated – the international, national, organizational, and individual. She shows how, at each level, the people involved in formulating, adopting, and implementing policy are deeply influenced by their own values and beliefs, and these have a kind of filtering effect on the knowledge that is transferred. She illustrates this by reference to policy debates at the international level, indicating a range of different views of development.

At the national level, Peterson explains how commitment to basic education in Egypt has moved from education for all to excellence for all in
the forms of educational development and teacher education undertaken, reflecting the values of those leading this international initiative
at the national level. She goes on to consider the cultural context of the
bureaucratic organizations at the national level whose members interact
with international agencies, and finally the individuals responsible for
the implementation of these educational policies right down to the local
level (Peterson 2001).

A third woman contributor, Verna Kirkness, a member of a First
Nations Community in Canada and former director of the First Nations
House of Learning at the University of British Columbia, focuses on the
interaction between students from First Nations backgrounds in Canada
and the university, distinguishing between a concept of 'coming to the
university' and 'going to the university.' The expectation that these
young people will be totally assimilated to the university's culture is associated with 'coming to the university,' while the students themselves
bring a different set of expectations in 'going to the university.' Students
hope to be able to contribute valuable insights and forms of understanding from their own oral traditions and the spiritual heritage of their people, to gain respect, and engage in reciprocally beneficial dialogue with
students and faculty of the mainstream. Kirkness's contribution opens up
vistas of the enrichment that could be brought to some of the disciplines
of knowledge in the university, at both the national and international
level, if it were open to respecting and integrating into discussion and
debate this wealth of understanding from a distinct community. (Kirkness and Barnhardt 2001).

On the other side of the globe, Renuka Narang writes about her pioneering work at the University of Mumbai in developing a program of
extension education for rural women. The program involves university
students in teaching, mentoring, and literacy work. The university itself
is one of India's oldest and most prestigious, with a very high national
standing, and a sophisticated network of international contacts. By giving students university level credit for their work with rural women, and
requiring them to keep a diary of all that they learn in this process, the
university promotes awareness of indigenous roots of knowledge in rural
India. This makes it possible for the university to embrace the challenges
and opportunities of globalization, while at the same time strengthening
its roots in India's own indigenous cultures, and exposing its students to
real life opportunities for exploring those roots (Narang 2001).

This project in India fits closely with the call of Lu Jie, a senior woman professor at Nanjing Normal University in China, for strengthening of the indigenous character of Chinese pedagogy. Lu Jie has done extensive work in rural education in China, and she sees how crucial it is for Chinese educators to root their thinking in China's rich traditions of pedagogy. Thus, the many external theories and ideas flowing in through the open door of recent years can be successfully integrated into China's own highly developed educational culture. Her longer term aspiration is for Chinese educational thought and achievements to contribute to world pedagogy, and she sees China's social transformation over the past two decades as a component of worldwide modernization. What makes it different from Western experience is the speed of the transformation and the fact that two types of transformation are taking place in tandem, from agricultural to industrial society, and from industrial to post-industrial, resulting in a situation where Chinese people 'have to make choices in the complicated context of a situation somewhere between tradition and modernity, modernity and post-modernity' (Lu 2001, 250).

Finally, Zahra Al Zeera, a woman scholar from Bahrain provides an incisive overview and commentary on four paradigms in Western social sciences, beginning with positivism and going on to three emergent paradigms – postpositivism, critical theory, and constructivism. She points to an 'invisible string' linking them all together, and rooted in the Aristotelian principle of 'either or.' Drawing upon the great Islamic philosophers Ibn Sina and Al Ghazzali, she develops an Islamic paradigm of social knowledge which links body, mind, and soul in one integrated self, and enables both individual and society to advance to higher stages of being. Al Zeera suggests that 'grounded theories at universities in Islamic countries should be based on an Islamic paradigm ... which will have the capacity to encompass the wholeness of human beings as well as the wholeness of society and life in general. This will help to overcome the fragmentation and polarization of individuals and society, which is the task of holistic, integrated knowledge' (Al Zeera 2001, 59).

These reflections by women from Canada, Egypt, China, India, and Bahrain illustrate certain features of women's ways of knowing that are supportive of dialogue across civilizations, and that are contributing to a transformation of the knowledge patterns once so entrenched in Western universities. They include the following: an openness to indigenous and local knowledge, and a recognition of the importance of strengthening local knowledge in face of globalization and the kinds of homogenization it brings; a tendency to privilege the subject, the person as knower, and to create a balance between objective canons of knowledge and subjective understanding; a commitment to integrating different disciplinary approaches into a holistic understanding of problems and issues; and finally, a profound sensitivity to spiritual knowledge and recognition of its vital place in human development and the health of the environment. These points about women's ways of knowing bring us back to the opening quotation from the United Nations Web site on the dialogue among civilizations: the call to focus on 'human cultural, spiritual dimensions and on the interdependence of [hu]mankind and its rich diversity.'

REFERENCES

Al Zeera, Zahra. (2001). Paradigm Shifts in the Social Sciences in the East and West. In R. Hayhoe and J. Pan, eds. *Knowledge across Culture: A Contribution to Dialogue among Civilizations*. Hong Kong: Comparative Education Research Centre, University of Hong Kong, pp. 55–74.

Altbach, P., and V. Selvaratnam, eds. (1989). *From Dependence to Autonomy: The Development of Asian Universities*. London: Kluwer.

Belenky, M.F, B.M.,Clinchy, N.R. Goldberger, and I.M. Tarule. (1986). *Women's Ways of Knowing*. New York: Basic Books.

Birge, Bettina. (1989). Chu Hsi and Women's Education. In W.T. de Bary and J. Chaffee, eds. *Neo-Confucian Education: The Formative Stage*. Berkeley: University of California Press, pp. 325–67.

Blue, Gregory. (2001). Chinese Influences on the Enlightenment in Europe. In R. Hayhoe, and J. Pan, eds. *Knowledge across Cultures: A Contribution to Dialogue among Civilizations* . Hong Kong: Comparative Education Research Centre, pp. 277–88.

Boulding, Elise. (1988). *Building a Global Civic Culture: Education for an Interdependent World*. New York: Teachers College Press.

Chen, Dongyuan. (1928). *Zhongguo funu shenghuoshi* [A History of Women's Lives]. Shanghai: Commercial Press.

Chen, Yiyun. (1994). Out of the Traditional Halls of Academe: Exploring New Avenues for Research on Women. Translated by S. Katherine Campbell. In Christina Gilmartin, Gail Hershatter, Lisa Rofel, and T. White, eds. *Engendering China*. Cambridge, Mass.: Harvard University Press, pp. 69–79.

Ding, Gang. (1995). The Shuyuan and the Development of Chinese Universities in the Early Twentieth Century. In R. Hayhoe and J. Pan, eds. *East-West Dialogue in Knowledge and Higher Education*. New York: M.E. Sharpe, pp. 218–44.

Dronke, Peter. (1984). *Women Writers of the Middle Ages*. Cambridge: Cambridge University Press.

Franklin, Ursula. (2001). Art, Technology and Knowledge Transfer. In R. Hayhoe, and J. Pan, eds. *Knowledge across Cultures: A Contribution to Dialogue among Civilizations.* Hong Kong: Comparative Education Research Centre, pp. 243–8.

Hall, David L., and Roger T. Ames. (1998). *Thinking from the Han: Self, Truth and Transcendence in Chinese and Western Culture.* Albany: State University of New York Press.

Harding, Sandra. (1986). *The Science Question in Feminism.* Ithaca, NY: Cornell University Press.

– (1987). *Feminist Epistemology: Social Science Issues.* Bloomington: Indiana University Press.

– (1991). *Whose Science? Whose Knowledge? Thinking from Women's Lives.* Ithaca, NY: Cornell University Press.

Hayhoe, R. (1993). Chinese Universities and the Social Sciences. Minerva 31(4): 478–503.

– (1999). *China's Universities 1895–1995: A Century of Cultural Conflict.* Hong Kong: Comparative Education Research Centre, University of Hong Kong.

– and J. Pan, eds. (2001). *Knowledge across Cultures: A Contribution to Dialogue among Civilizations.* Hong Kong: Comparative Education Research Centre, University of Hong Kong.

– H. Briks, A. Gordon, R. Kybartas, J. Moes de Munich, F. Moody, J. Pan, E. Synowskis L. Wilson, I Winchester, and W. Zhony eds. (1993). *Knowledge across Cultures: Universities East and West.* Toronto: OISE Press; and Wuhan: Hubei Education Press.

Huntington, Samuel P. (1993). The Clash of Civilizations? *Foreign Affairs* 72(3): 22–49.

Kirkness, Verna, and Ray Barnhardt. (2001). Respect, Relevance, Reciprocity and Responsibility. In R. Hayhoe, and J. Pan, eds. *Knowledge across Cultures: A Contribution to Dialogue among Civilizations.* Hong Kong: Comparative Education Research Centre, pp. 75–92.

Koh, Dorothy. (1995). *Teachers of the Inner Chambers: Women and Culture in Seventeenth Century China.* Berkeley: University of California Press.

Lie, Suzanne Stiver, and Virginnia O'Leary. (1990). *Storming the Tower: Women in the Academic World.* New York: Kogan Page.

Lu, Jie. 2001. On the Indigenousness of Chinese Pedagogy. In R. Hayhoe, and J. Pan, eds. *Knowledge across Cultures: A Contribution to Dialogue among Civilizations.* Hong Kong: Comparative Education Research Centre, pp. 249–54.

Maverick, L.A. (1946). *China: A Model for Europe.* San Antonio, Tex.: Paul Anderson.

Merchant, Carolyn. (1980). *The Death of Nature: Women, Ecology and the Scientific Revolution.* San Francisco: Harper and Row.

Miyazaki, Ichisada. (1976). *China's Examination Hell: The Civil Service Examinations of Imperial China.* New York: Weatherhill.

Narang, Renuka. (2001). Social Justice through Non-Formal Education and University Extension Education: An Indian Case Study. In R. Hayhoe, and J. Pan, eds. *Knowledge across Cultures: A Contribution to Dialogue among Civilizations.* Hong Kong: Comparative Education Research Centre, 259–68.

Newman, Barbara. (1998) 'Sybil of the Rhine': Hildegard's Life and Times. In B. Newman, ed. *Voice of the Living Light: Hildegard of Bingen and Her World.* Berkeley and Los Angeles: University of California Press, 1–29.

Noble, David. (1992). *A World without Women: The Christian Clerical Culture of Western Science.* New York: Alfred Knopf.

Peterson, Samiha Sidhom. (2001). Development as Transfer of Knowledge: A View from Egypt. In R. Hayhoe, and J. Pan, eds. *Knowledge across Cultures: A Contribution to Dialogue among Civilizations.* Hong Kong: Comparative Education Research Centre, pp. 229–42.

Schwehn, Mark. (1993). *Exiles from Eden: Religion and the Academic Life in America.* New York: Oxford University Press.

Tsai, Kathryn. (1981). The Chinese Buddhist Monastic Order for Women: The First Two Centuries. In Richard Guisso and Stanley Johannesen, eds. *Women in China: Current Directions in Historical Scholarship.* Lewiston, NY: Edwin Mellen Press, 1–20.

Weber, Max. (1967). 'Science as a Vocation.' In H.H. and C. Wright Mills, eds. *From Max Weber: Essays in Sociology.* New York: Oxford University Press, pp. 129–56.

Weiler, Hans. (2001). Knowledge, Politics and the Future of Higher Education. In R. Hayhoe, and J. Pan, eds. *Knowledge across Cultures: A Contribution to Dialogue among Civilizations.* Hong Kong: Comparative Education Research Centre, pp. 25–44.

Wilshire, Bruce. (1990). *The Moral Collapse of the University: Professionalism, Purity and Alienation.* Albany: State University of New York Press.

CHAPTER 5

The Future of Higher Education in the Knowledge-Driven, Global Economy of the Twenty-first Century

James J. Duderstadt

Clearly, we live in a time of very rapid and profound social transformation. We have been living through the transition from a century in which the dominant human activity was transportation to one in which communications has become paramount, from economies based upon cars, planes, and trains to one dependent on computers and networks. We are shifting from an emphasis on creating and transporting physical objects such as materials and energy to knowledge itself, from atoms to bits; from societies based upon the geopolitics of the nation state to those based on diverse cultures and local traditions, and from a dependence on government policy to an increasing confidence in the marketplace to establish public priorities.

Today, we are evolving rapidly into a post-industrial, knowledge-based society, a shift in culture and technology as profound as the shift that took place a century ago when our agrarian societies evolved into industrial nations (Drucker 1994). Industrial production is steadily shifting from material- and labour-intensive products and processes to knowledge-intensive products. A radically new system for creating wealth has evolved that depends upon the creation and application of new knowledge. In a very real sense, we are entering a new age, an *age of knowledge*, in which the key strategic resource necessary for prosperity has become knowledge itself – educated people and their ideas (Bloch 1988). Unlike natural resources, such as iron and oil, that have driven earlier economic transformations, knowledge is inexhaustible. The more it is used, the more it multiplies and expands.

Knowledge can be created, absorbed, and applied only by the educated mind, and therefore, schools, in general, and universities in particular, will play increasingly important roles as our societies enter this new age. In a sense, knowledge is the medium of the university. Through the activities of discovery, shaping, achieving, transmitting, and applying knowledge, the university serves society in a myriad of ways: educating the young, preserving our cultural heritage, providing the basic research so essential to our security and well-being, training our professionals and certifying their competence challenging our society, and stimulating social change. But the age of knowledge will substantially broaden the roles of higher education. Erich Bloch, former Director of the U.S. National Science Foundation, stated it well when he noted, 'The solution of virtually all the problems with which government is concerned: health, education, environment, energy, urban development, international relationships, economic competitiveness, and defense and national security, all depend on creating new knowledge – and hence upon the health of our universities' (Bloch 1988).

The Challenges of a Knowledge-Driven, Global Economy to the University

The list of the challenges and opportunities presented by the age of knowledge to higher education could (and did) fill a book (Duderstadt 2000). Let me here focus only on four themes: (1) the skills race, (2) markets, (3) technology, and (4) global sustainability.

The Skills Race

Ask any public leader today about priorities, and you are certain to hear concerns about education and the skills of the workforce. The National Governors' Association of the United States has stated: 'The driving force behind the 21st Century economy is knowledge, and developing human capital is the best way to ensure prosperity' (National Governors Association 2001).

Today, a college degree has become a necessity for most careers, and graduate education becomes desirable for an increasing number. In the United States, a growing population will necessitate some growth in higher education to accommodate the projected increases in the number of traditional college-age students (estimated at 14 per cent over the next decade). But even more growth and adaptation will be needed to respond to the educational needs of adults as they seek to adapt to the needs of the high performance workplace. Some estimate this adult need for lifelong learning at the university level will become far larger than that represented by traditional 18- to 22-year old students (Dolence and Norris 1997).

Our universities face more fundamental educational challenges than simply growth in the demand for higher education. Both young, digital-media savvy students and adult learners will likely demand a major shift in educational methods, away from passive classroom lecture courses packaged into well-defined degree programs, and towards interactive, collaborative learning experiences, provided when and where the student needs the knowledge and skills. The increased blurring of the various stages of learning throughout one's lifetime – K–12, undergraduate, graduate, professional, job training, career shifting, lifelong enrichment – will require a far greater coordination and perhaps even a merger of various elements of our educational infrastructure.

The traditional roles of the university revolve around the core of teaching and scholarship: we educate the young, seek truth and create knowledge, propagate our culture and values from one generation to the next, sustain the academic disciplines and the professions, and constructively criticize our societies. At the core, our activities are characterized by critical thinking, analysis, moral reasoning, and judgment. But today, much more is asked of our universities. Beyond teaching and scholarship in the academic and professional disciplines, our universities are heavily involved in utilitarian roles such as technology transfer, health care, entertainment, national defence, and economic and international development. There is an increasing tendency for society to view the university as an engine for economic growth through the generation and application of new knowledge. There has been a shift in emphasis within the university away from simply distributing and analysing knowledge, that is, 'teaching' and 'scholarship,' to creating and applying knowledge, to activities such as 'innovation,' 'creativity,' and 'entrepreneurship.'

The growing and changing nature of the needs for higher education has triggered strong economic forces. Our societies ask us to do ever more, but they are not always increasingly generous in their support of these activities. In many nations there is a declining priority for public support of higher education in face of other social priorities, such as the health care needs of an ageing population. In the United States, traditional sources of public support for higher education, such as state appropriations or federal support for student financial aid, have simply not kept pace with the growing demand. This imbalance between demand and available resources is aggravated by the increasing costs of higher education, driven as they are by the knowledge- and people-intensive nature of the enterprise, as well as by the difficulty educational institutions have in containing costs and increasing productivity. Put another way, the current paradigms for conducting, distributing, and financing higher education may not be able to adapt to the demands and realities of the times.

Markets

Market forces also act on our colleges and universities. We generally think of higher education as a public enterprise, shaped by public policy and actions to serve a civic purpose. Society, however, seeks services such as education and research; and academic institutions must compete for students, faculty, and resources. In the past, most colleges and universities served local or regional populations. There was competition among institutions for students, faculty, and resources – at least in the United States. But the extent to which institutions controlled the awarding of degrees (credentialling) gave universities an effective monopoly over advanced education. Today, all of these market constraints are being challenged. The growth in the size and complexity of the post-secondary enterprise is creating an expanding array of students and educational providers. Rapidly evolving information and communication technologies are eroding geographical constraints. New competitive forces such as virtual universities and for-profit education providers enter the marketplace to challenge credentialling.

The weakening influence of traditional regulations and the emergence of new competitive forces, driven by changing societal needs, economic realities, and technology, are likely to drive a massive restructuring of the enterprise of higher education. From our experience with other restructured sectors of the economy, such as health care, transportation, communications, and energy, we could expect to see a significant reorganization of higher education, complete with the mergers, acquisitions, new competitors, and new products and services that have characterized other economic transformations. More generally, we may well be seeing the early stages of the appearance of *a global knowledge and learning industry*, in which the activities of traditional academic institutions converge with other knowledge-intensive organizations such as telecommunications, entertainment, and information service companies (Peterson and Dill 1997).

It is important to remember that most of our institutions of higher education were the result of public policy and public investment through actions of governments at the national and regional level (Zemsky 1997; Zemsky and Wegner 1998). These policies, programs, and commitments were driven by strong social values and a sense of national and regional priorities. Yet today, in the United States and many other nations, public leaders are increasingly discarding public policy in favour of market forces to determine priorities for social investment. Public higher education institutions can no longer assume that public policies and investment will shield them from market competition.

The market forces driven by increasing demand for higher education and unleashed by technology are very powerful. If they are allowed to dominate and reshape the enterprise of higher education, we could well find ourselves facing a brave new world in which some of the most important values and traditions of the university fall by the wayside. As we assess these emerging market-driven learning structures, we must bear in mind the importance of preserving the ability of the university to serve a broader public purpose.

Technology

As knowledge-driven organizations, colleges and universities are greatly affected by the rapid advances in information and communications technology. Modern digital technologies such as computers, telecommunications, and networks are reshaping both our society and our social institutions. These technologies have vastly increased our capacity to know and to do things and to communicate and collaborate with others. They allow us to transmit information quickly, linking distant places and diverse areas of endeavour in productive new ways. They allow us to form and sustain communities for work, play, and learning in ways unimaginable but a decade ago.

Information technology has the capacity to enhance and enrich teaching and scholarship. It also, however, poses certain threats to our colleges and universities. We use powerful computers and networks to deliver educational services to anyone, any place, and anytime, and we are no longer confined to the campus or the academic schedule. Technology is creating an open learning environment in which the student has evolved into an active learner and consumer of educational services, stimulating the growth of powerful market forces that could dramatically reshape the higher education enterprise.

Last year the U.S. National Academy of Science launched a project to better understand the implications of information technology for the future of the research university (Duderstadt and Wulf 2002). The premise was a simple one: the rapid evolution of digital technology will present many challenges and opportunities to higher education in general and the research university in particular, yet there is a sense that many of the most significant issues are neither well recognized nor understood either by leaders of our universities or those who support and depend on their activities.

Three primary conclusions were reached during the early phase of this study, which I chaired. First, we believe the extraordinary evolutionary pace of information technology will not only continue for the foreseeable future, but could well accelerate on a superexponential slope. Digital technology is characterized by an exponential pace of evolution, in which characteristics such computing speed, memory, and network transmission speeds for a given price increase by a factor of 100 to 1000 every decade. For planning purposes, one can assume that by the end of the decade we will have available effectively infinite bandwidth and infinite processing power (at least compared with current capabilities). The number of people linked together by digital technology will grow from millions to billions. We will evolve from 'e-commerce' and 'e-government' and 'e-learning' to 'e-everything,' since digital devices will increasingly become our primary interfaces, not only with our environment but with other people, groups, and social institutions.

Our second conclusion is that the impact of information technology on the university will likely be *profound, rapid, and discontinuous* – just as it has been and will continue to be for the economy, our society, and our social institutions (e.g., corporations, governments, and learning institutions). This is a disruptive technology (Christensen 1997) that will affect all of the activities of the university (teaching, research, and outreach), its organization (academic structure, faculty culture, financing, and management), and the broader higher education enterprise. However, at least for the near term – meaning a decade or less – we believe the university will continue to exist in pretty much its present form. Nevertheless, meeting the challenge of emerging competitors in the marketplace will demand significant changes in how we teach, how we conduct scholarship, and how our institutions are financed.

Universities must anticipate these forces. They must develop appropriate strategies and make adequate investments if they are to prosper during this period. Hence, our third conclusion: Universities should begin the development of their strategies for technology-driven change with a firm understanding of those key values, missions, and roles that should be protected and preserved during a time of transformation. Procrastination and inaction are the most dangerous courses for universities during a time of rapid technological change.

Global Sustainability

Global sustainability seems a particularly appropriate topic in the wake of the United Nations Global Summit on Sustainable Development in Johannesburg. As a scientist, I am convinced that there is compelling evidence that the growing population and invasive activities of humankind are now altering the fragile balance of our planet. The concerns are both multiplying in number and intensifying in severity including the following: the destruction of forests, wetlands, and other natural habitats by human activities leading to the extinction of millions of biological species and the loss of biodiversity; the build-up of greenhouse gases such as carbon dioxide and their possible impact on global climates; the pollution of our air, water, and land.

It could well be that coming to grips with the impact of our species on our planet, learning to live in a sustainable fashion on Spaceship Earth, will become the greatest challenge of all to our generation. We must find new ways to provide for a human society that at present has outstripped the limits of global sustainability. This will be particularly difficult for the United States, a nation that has difficulty in looking more than a generation ahead, encumbered by a political process that generally functions on an election-by-election basis, as the current debate over global change makes all too apparent. With just 4.5 per cent of the world's people, the United States controls 25 per cent of the world's wealth and produces 25 to 30 per cent of the World's pollution. It is remarkable that the richest nation on earth is the lowest per capita donor of international development assistance of any industrialized country.

Ironically, the tragic events of 11 September 2001 might be viewed as a wake-up call, if we view these terrorist attacks not simply as a brief and brutal criminal attack but rather the consequence of more fundamental causes. As the noted biologist Peter Raven put it in a recent address (2002, 954–8):

> The United States is a small part of a very large, poor, and rapidly changing world, and we, along with everyone else, must do a better job. Sustainability science has a good deal to say about how we can logically approach the challenges that await us, but the social dimensions of our relationships are also

of fundamental importance. Globalization appears to have become an irresistible force, but we must make it participatory and humane to alleviate the suffering of the world's poorest people and the effective disenfranchisement of many of its nations. As many have stated in the context of the current world situation, the best defense against terrorism is an educated people. Education, which promises to each individual the opportunity to express their individual talents fully, is fundamental to building a peaceful world.

There are thirty million people in the world today who are fully qualified to enter a university, but for whom no university place is available. Within a decade there will be 100 million university-ready people. Yet, as Sir John Daniel (1996), former head of the British Open University, has pointed out in most of the world higher education is mired in a crisis of access, cost, and flexibility. Unless we can address and solve this crisis, billions of people in coming generations will be denied the education so necessary to compete in, and survive in, an age of knowledge.

We must realize that the wealthy nations of the world have a particularly important role to play to assist developing nations in building the educational systems necessary if they are to meet their exploding needs. The university models characterizing most developed nations seem ill-suited to guiding us out of this global education crisis. Our colleges and universities continue to be focused on high-cost, low-technology, residential education and on the outmoded idea that quality in education is linked to exclusivity of access and extravagance of resources. Our current concept of the campus-based university could well deny higher education to nearly all of the billions of young people who will require it in the decades ahead.

Transforming the University to Serve a Global Knowledge Society

These social, economic, technological, and market forces are far more powerful than many within the higher education establishment realize. They are driving change at an unprecedented pace, perhaps even beyond the capacity of our colleges and universities to adapt. Our current paradigms for higher education, the nature of our academic programs, the organization of our colleges and universities, and the way that we finance, conduct, and distribute the services of higher education may not be able to adapt to the demands and realities of our times.

So how might one approach the challenge of transforming the university to serve the world of the twenty-first Century? Typically, discussions of change in higher education begin with bread-and-butter issues such as the financing of higher education, technology transfer, or expanding the university's broad array of services to society. From my own experience as a battle-scared veteran of leading change in one of our nation's largest public universities, let me suggest a somewhat different set of issues.

Values

It is important for any effort aimed at institutional transformation to always begin with the basics, to launch a careful reconsideration of the key roles and values of the university that should be protected and preserved during a period of change. For example, how would an institution prioritize among roles such as educating the young (undergraduate education), preserving and transmitting our culture (libraries, visual and performing arts), basic research and scholarship, and serving as a responsible critic of society? What are the most important values to protect? Clearly, academic freedom, an openness to new ideas, a commitment to rigorous study, and an aspiration to the achievement of excellence would be on the list for most institutions. But what about values and practices such as shared governance and tenure? Should these be preserved? At what expense?

Diversity

Diversity will become an increasingly important theme in higher education, driven by the dramatic changes occurring in the populations served by our universities, and affecting all of the characteristics of our institutions: their academic programs, their broader roles in our society, and their aspirations for excellence. In many developed nations, demographic change is first thought of in terms of the ageing of our populations. We are already feeling the consequences, as our national priorities increasingly focus on the concerns of the elderly (e.g., health care) rather than the needs of the young (e.g., education).

On a global basis, however, half of the world's population is under the age of twenty, with over two billion teenagers on planet Earth, most living in Asia, Africa, and Latin America. Their demand for education will be staggering. To sustain even current participation rates for higher education would require (as already mentioned elsewhere in this volume) creating a major new university every week to serve this growing population of young people in parts of the world with severely limited resources and little experience in higher education (Daniel 1996).

An equally profound demographic phenomenon is the increasing diversity of many of our nations with respect to race, ethnicity, and nationality. Moreover, women have already become the predominant gender in many of our nations, and they are rapidly assuming leadership roles in both the public and private sector. The full participation of currently underrepresented minorities and women is crucial to our commitment to equity and social justice, as well as to the future strength and prosperity of our societies. We cannot afford to waste the human talent, the cultural and social richness represented by those currently underrepresented in our society. Yet, the challenge of increasing diversity is complicated by social and economic factors.

As both a leader of society at large and a reflection of that society, the university has a unique responsibility to develop effective models of multicultural, pluralistic communities. We should strive to achieve new levels of understanding, tolerance, and mutual fulfilment for peoples of diverse racial and cultural backgrounds both on our campuses and beyond. Universities need to shift their attention from simple access to educational opportunity for underserved minority populations to success in achieving educational objectives. It has also become increasingly clear that they must do so within a political context that will require new policies and practices.

Subsidiarity and Autonomy

The governance of higher education varies greatly, shaped as it is by traditions and culture. Still, there are several general issues that need to be put on the table. Foremost among these are questions relating to whether our citizens and their governments view the university as a public good benefiting everyone. Or do they, instead, view education as an individual benefit, benefiting the individuals, the students, that receive it? Do governments view universities as a public investment for the future, or simply another expenditure, such as spending money on roads or health care? Is the university a government agency or is it a social institution? In all of our societies, government is under increasing pressure to demand accountability, but how they demand accountability, while perhaps appropriate for the Ministry of Transportation, may not work for universities.

Although many of the policies and practices characterizing the governance of higher education in the United States are unique to American culture, one practice with broader relevance arises from the belief that universities must have the capacity to control their own destiny, particularly during times of change. By this I mean not simply granting the faculty traditional perquisites such as academic freedom, but allowing universities more control over all aspects of their operations, including academic programs, budgets, student selection, and faculty hiring. Luc Weber, former rector of the University of Geneva, applies the economic term 'subsidiarity' to describe this, in the sense that it involves pushing authority and decision making down to the lowest possible level (Weber 2001). Centralization is a very awkward approach to higher education during a time of change.

In Michigan, this principle is built into our state constitution, which defines the autonomy of the University of Michigan, vested in our governing board, as firmly founded as that characterizing the legislature, governor, and judiciary (Shaw 1941). The university is, in effect, a 'coordinate branch of state government,' with full powers over its designated field of state endeavour, higher education. Of course, autonomy is never absolute and must occasionally be defended through judicial tests in what amounts to a growing record of state policies, legislation, and judicial decisions. It has been necessary on occasion to resist attempts by state government to intrude on our independence through judicial challenge, by occasionally filing suit against our state government, ever so politely but firmly, to protect our constitutional autonomy.

Alliances

The same market forces that drive our colleges and universities to focus on core competencies, where they can be competitive, also provide strong incentives to build alliances to address the broader, more diverse needs of society. Many of our research universities are under great pressure to expand enrolments to address the expanding populations of college-age students or growing educational needs of adults, possibly at the expense of their research and service missions. It might be far more constructive for these institutions to form close alliances with regional colleges and universities to meet these growing demands for educational opportunity with research university faculty developing curriculum and pedagogy, while other institutions provide the actual instruction.

International alliances will become increasingly important, whether through student and faculty exchanges programs such as the Erasmus-Socrates programs and agreements such as the Bologna Declaration or virtual constructs such as the collaborations made possible by advances in information technology. More broadly, alliances should be explored not only among institutions of higher education but also between higher education and the private sector (e.g., information technology and tele-communications companies). Differentiation among institutions should be encouraged, relying upon market forces rather than regulations to discourage duplication.

Experimentation

Many of the forces driving change in higher education are disruptive in nature, leading to quite unpredictable futures. Planning in the face of such uncertainty requires a more experimental approach to the trans-forming university. A personal example may be useful here. During the 1990s we led an effort at the University of Michigan to transform the insti-tution, to re-invent it so that it better served a rapidly changing world. We began with all of the usual steps, restructuring our financing, using total quality improvement methods to improve productivity and accountabil-ity, focusing our limited resources on fewer programs selected on the basis of quality and centrality, and so on. Yet with each step in the trans-formation we took, with every project we launched, with each objective we achieved, we became increasingly uneasy. We sensed that forces driv-ing change in our society and its institutions were far stronger and more profound than we had first thought. Change was occurring far more rap-idly than we had anticipated. The future was becoming less certain, as the range of possibilities expanded to include more radical options.

We came to the conclusion that in a world of such rapid and profound change, as the future became less certain, the most effective near-term strategy was to explore possible futures of the university through experi-mentation and discovery. That is, rather than continue to contemplate possibilities for the future through abstract study and debate, it seemed a more productive course to build several prototypes of future learning institutions as working experiments. In this way, we could actively explore possible paths to the future. Several examples illustrate this approach:

- During the 1990s we explored the possible future of becoming a 'pri-vately supported but publicly chartered university' by completely restructuring our financing, raising over $1.4 billion in a major fundraising campaign, increasing tuition levels (accompanied by a major expansion in need-based student financial aid), dramatically increasing research grants won by our faculty (over $650 million per year), and increasing our endowment ten-fold (to over $3 billion). Ironically, the more public (state) support declined as a component of our revenue base (dropping to less than 10 per cent by the late 1990s), the higher our Wall Street credit rating became, and finally we achieved the highest (AAA) rating, the first for a public university.

- Through a major strategic effort known as the Michigan Mandate, we altered very significantly the racial diversity of our students and faculty, doubling the population of minority students and faculty (to 25 per cent and 12 per cent, respectively), thereby providing a laboratory for exploring the themes of the 'diverse university.'
- We established campuses in Europe, Asia, and Latin America, linking them with robust information technology, to understand better the implications of becoming a 'world university.'
- We played leadership roles first in the building and management of the Internet (with IBM and MCI as partners), and more recently Internet2, to explore the 'cyberspace university' theme.

Of course, not all of our experiments were successful. Some crashed in flames, in some cases spectacularly! Even in these these cases, however, we learned something, if only our own ineffectiveness in dealing with cosmic forces such as college sports. All of these efforts were driven by the grassroots interests, abilities, and enthusiasm of the faculty and students. Such an exploratory approach was disconcerting to some and frustrating to others. Fortunately, however, there were many who viewed this phase as an exciting adventure. All of these initiatives were important in understanding better the possible futures facing our university and all have had influence on the evolution of our university.

Turning Threats into Opportunities

Our experience suggests the importance of attempting to approach issues and decisions concerning university transformation as opportunities rather than threats. The status quo is no longer an option. But once we accept that change is inevitable, we can use it as a strategic opportunity to control our destiny, while preserving the most important of our values and our traditions. Creative, visionary leaders can tap the energy created by threats such as the emerging for-profit marketplace and technology to

engage their campuses and to lead their institutions in new directions
that will reinforce and enhance their most important roles and values.

The Questions before Us

As an educator, it seems appropriate for me to leave the reader with a few
questions. First, how should we respond to the diverse educational and
intellectual needs of a knowledge-driven, global economy, as human capital becomes more important than physical and financial capital?
Although the educational needs of the young will continue to be a priority, we will also be challenged to address the sophisticated learning needs
of adults in the workplace while providing broader lifetime learning
opportunities for all of our populations.

Is higher education a public good, requiring public investment? Or is
it a private good, to be funded primarily by the commercial marketplace? The benefits of the university clearly flow to society as a whole,
but it is also the case that our public leaders have, instead, stressed the
benefits of education to the individual student. The issues of access and
diversity have largely disappeared from the broader debate about the
purpose of the university. How do we balance the roles of market forces
and public purpose in determining the future of higher education? Can
we control market forces through public policy and public investment
so that the most valuable traditions and values of the university are preserved? Or will the competitive and commercial pressures of the marketplace sweep over our institutions, leaving behind a higher education
enterprise characterized by mediocrity?

What should be the role of the research university within the broader
context of the changes likely to occur in the higher education enterprise? Should it be a leader in change? Or should it simply strive to protect the important traditions and values of the academy during this time
of change?

Finally, perhaps the most important question of all: Are we facing in
the years ahead a period of evolution, of revolution, or of the possible
extinction of the university as we know it today?

These are some of the issues that should frame the debate about the
future of the university in the twenty-first century. As social institutions,
universities reflect the values, needs, and character of the societies they
serve. These issues of access and opportunity, equality and justice, private
economic benefits and public purpose, freedom and accountability, all
are part of a broader public debate about the future of our societies and

our world. They provide the context for any consideration of the future of the university in a knowledge-driven global economy.

Conclusion

Let me conclude by providing my own answer to the last question. Our institutions, after all, are one of our civilization's most enduring legacies. Clearly, in an age of knowledge, higher education will flourish in the decades ahead. In a knowledge-intensive society the need for advanced education and knowledge will become ever more pressing, both for individuals and for our societies more broadly. Yet, it is also likely that the university as we know it today, or rather the current constellation of diverse institutions that comprise the higher education enterprise, will change in profound ways to serve a changing world. Of course, this is just what the university has done so many times in the past.

We have entered a period of significant change in higher education as our universities attempt to respond to the challenges, opportunities, and responsibilities before them (Glion Declaration 1998). Much of this change will be driven by market forces – by a limited resource base, changing societal needs, new technologies, and new competitors. But we also must remember that higher education has a public purpose and a public obligation (Zemsky and Wegner 1998). It is possible to shape and form the markets that will, in turn, reshape our institutions with appropriate civic purpose.

From this perspective, it is important to understand that the most critical challenge facing most institutions will be to develop the capacity for change. As noted earlier, universities must seek to remove the constraints that prevent them from responding to the needs of a rapidly changing society. They should strive to challenge, excite, and embolden all members of their academic communities to embark on what should be a great adventure for higher education. Only a concerted effort to understand the important traditions of the past, the challenges of the present, and the possibilities for the future can enable institutions to thrive during a time of such change.

REFERENCES
Bloch, Eric. (1988). National Science Foundation, Testimony to U.S. Congress.
Christensen, Clayton M. (1997). *The Innovator's Dilemma*. Cambridge: Harvard Business School Press.

Daniel, John S. (1996). *Mega-Universities and Knowledge Media.* London: Kogan Page.

Dolence, Michael G., and Donald M. Norris. (1997). *Transforming Higher Education: A Vision for Learning in the 21st Century.* Ann Arbor: Society for College and University Planning.

Drucker, Peter F. (1993). *Post-Capitalist Society.* New York: Harper Collins.

– (1994). The Age of Social Transformation. *Atlantic Monthly* 274(53–6): 53–80.

– (1997). Interview. *Forbes,* no, 159: 122–128.

Duderstadt, James J., (2000). *A University for the 21st Century.* Ann Arbor: University of Michigan Press.

Duderstadt, James J., and William Wulf, eds. (2002). *Preparing for the Revolution: The Impact of Information Technology on the Future of the Research University.* Washington, DC: National Academy Press.

Glion Declaration: The University at the Millennium (1998). *The Presidency.* (Washington, DC: American Council on Education, Fall): 27–31.

Kurzweil, Ray (1999). *The Age of Spiritual Machines: When Computers Exceed Human Intelligence.* New York: Viking.

Langenberg, D.N. (1995). Taking Control of Change: Reinventing the Public University for the 21st Century. In Kumar Patel, ed. *Reinventing the Research University: Proceedings of a Symposium Held at UCLA, 1994.* Los Angeles: University of California at Los Angles, pp. 89–98.

National Governors Association (2001). Policy Position H-R 44, Postseconary Education Policy (http://www.nga.org).

Osterbrock, Donald E., and Peter H. Raven, (1992). *Origins and Extinctions.* New Haven: Yale University Press.

Perelman, Lewis (1997). Barnstorming with Lewis Perelman. *Educom Review* 32(2): 18–36.

Peterson, Marvin. W., and David D. Dill. (1997). Understanding the Competitive Environment of the Postsecondary Knowledge Industry. In Marvin W. Peterson, David D. Dill, and Lisa A. Mets, eds. *Planning and Management for a Changing Environment.* San Francisco: Jossey-Bass, pp. 3–29.

Raven, Peter H. (2002). Science, Sustainability, and the Human Prospect. *Science,* no. 297: 954–8.

Shaw, Wilfred B., ed. (1941). *The University of Michigan: An Encyclopedic Survey.* Ann Arbor: University of Michigan Press.

Weber, Luc E. (2001). Critical University Decisions and Their Appropriate Makers: Some Lessons from the Economic Theory of Federalism. In Werner Z. Hirsch, and Luc E. Weber, eds. *Governance in Higher Education: The University in a State of Flux.* London: Economica, pp. 79–93.

Zemsky, Robert (1997). 'Rumbling, *Policy Perspectives.*' The Pew Higher Education Roundtable, sponsored by the Pew Charitable Trusts, Philadelphia, Institute for Research on Higher Education.

Zemsky, Robert, and Gregory Wegner. (1998). A Very Public Agenda. *Policy Perspectives* 8(2): 1–11.

Strengthening Nations, Regions, and Cities: Higher Education and Society

CHAPTER 6

Democratizing Knowledge:
Higher Education and Good Governance

Maureen O'Neil

Higher education can generate and disseminate knowledge deemed to be essential for development. However, since educational institutions generally reflect their cultural and political surroundings, in countries where civil and political rights are denied and where 'disciplines at risk' are suppressed, higher education cannot thrive, and development falters. To promote higher education, and to democratize ownership of knowledge throughout communities, the promotion of good governance for democratic and sustainable development is required.

This is the ground that the International Development Research Centre (IDRC) has been working since its creation by Parliament in 1970. The Centre's support of development research has always been rooted in its founding principle that knowledge can free people in their communities to shape their own futures, and fulfil their own lives. For more than thirty years, IDRC has counted institutions of higher education among its most important partners – in Canada and throughout the developing world.

IDRC seeks to create linkages among institutions of higher education in the industrial, transitional, and developing countries. To that end, a necessary prior condition is securing the connection between higher education in any society and the exercise of civil and political rights in that society.

There is a close and inescapable relationship between the quality of higher learning and scholarship, on the one hand, and the quality of effective and democratic governance, on the other. Any successful promotion of development must recognize the intimate interaction between higher education and open, responsible government. Just as it is very hard to imagine sustainable and democratic development without promoting higher education, it is quite futile to promote higher education in a society where civil and political rights are systematically suppressed and denied.

There is a tendency to measure the value of higher education in instrumental terms: correlating numbers of graduate engineers with GDP performance, or investments in medical education with numbers of physicians produced. What should be of equal concern are the more intrinsic benefits of higher education, as both a private and a public good.

Experience shows that countries that thrive best in the global economy are those that are truly open. Openness means more than open trade, open investment, or open borders. It also refers to open societies, ones that invite new ideas, show a high tolerance for dissent and criticism, and freely engage in the rethinking and reworking of their own governance. In short, successful societies respect and protect the full exercise of civil and political rights. The exercise of these rights and freedoms not only *serves* human development; it is, intrinsically, an *essential element* of human development.

Formulating and testing new ideas, contributing criticism, and advancing better methods and better values for governance – these are activities that ought to find a natural space in any society's institutions of higher education.

All of the disciplines that bear on the procedures and values of good governance are disciplines at risk in many developing countries. These are not just the obviously contentious disciplines of political science or economics, or sociology or public health, that often directly engage in challenging government or contributing ideas to policy development. Disciplines at risk also include the humanities, history, philosophy, and the arts, disciplines that harbour the kind of vigorous and creative thought that alarms the autocratic, and threatens the corrupt. These are all disciplines at risk in unfree societies, and their practitioners often place themselves personally at risk in such countries.

It must be recognized that, in many developing countries, most of these disciplines are impoverished and unpopulated, even in otherwise robust institutions. These are disciplines deprived of resources, and often suppressed, not just because those countries are poor. Rather, they are deliberately kept weak precisely because they represent a threat to those who exercise the power of the state.

Most would agree that higher education ought to constitute a powerful engine of economic, social, and human development. What also needs to be acknowledged is that universities and colleges are generally only open, inventive, and free within cultures and political systems that are open, inventive, and free. Universities, by and large, resemble and reflect the cultures in which they operate. A determined questioning of convention and authority is not the natural or effortless role of an institution in a society that neither permits nor rewards questioning of convention or authority.

In many officially Islamic social and political systems, for example, we are rarely likely to observe a lively and cosmopolitan university program in political philosophy, or a graduate seminar in contested theories of gender and power. It is important to recognize the exceptions to this. In Indonesia, the largest Muslim community in the world, we see an enduring (if embattled) tradition of tolerance, moderation, and criticism in Muslim intellectual discourse. But even in more secular countries, the disciplines at risk are commonly confined by taboos enforced by the state. For example, in Singapore, where there is an otherwise good university, scholars understand they are not allowed to publish any commentary that openly addresses questions of racism (Altbach 2001). Scholars in Malaysia face a panoply of prohibitions, where entire subjects are banned from deep public analysis.[1]

Free thought and free expression benefit individuals and societies and build stronger and more prosperous democracies. However, in too many developing states, free thought and free expression – the essentials of practising disciplines at risk – are not encouraged as useful or virtuous. Theocrats and autocrats condemn these values as disruptive and wrong. Plutocrats and kleptocrats suppress them as threats. These observations lead to three prescriptive conclusions.

First, higher education as a category must be disaggregated if we are to understand and manage the linkages between higher education and development. Engineering and similarly 'apolitical' schools might well thrive in a closed society; they might be tolerated, or even encouraged. But universities as centres of moral, social, and political inquiry and argument require around them a social and political environment where inquiry and argument enjoy at least some measure of esteem and protection. These open societies are the ones most likely to prosper in the global economy, and to fulfil the aspirations of their people. So it is the openness we should be promoting as part of any strategy of education or development.

Second, the connections between higher education and development need to be seen in the light of a simple but difficult question: Who owns knowledge? Ownership of knowledge goes to such fiercely contested issues as protection of intellectual property rights and the exploitation of indigenous knowledge. Questions of knowledge ownership, however, reach far beyond these familiar and important stakeholder rivalries. In the end, true development occurs when knowledge is owned – and operated – by communities, and by the women and men who form those communities. Promoting networks for research and learning in the South does not only refer to research and learning for Southern researchers and scholars, but also the advancement of knowledge for people, in their own communities. Amartya Sen (2001), the Nobel Prize–winning economist, defines development as freedom. At the core of any meaningful freedom must be the acquisition and application of knowledge – an expanded understanding of choices, of problems, and their possible solutions. This democratization of knowledge is a critical enabling link between higher education and sustainable development.

Third, productive and equitable development requires an integration of higher education strategies with development strategies. Higher education cannot be an afterthought to the work of development. It needs to be included as forethought, a necessity in any development policy intended to be both sustainable and democratic. One image serves to ilustrate this. Imagine that every institution of higher education in Canada were suddenly and completely closed; no more faculties, no more students, anywhere in the country. What harm would this bring, instantly and in the long run, to the Canadian economy? What damage would it cause to families throughout our society? What violence would it inject into social cleavages of class, ethnicity, generation, and region? Amid the frustration and despair of this calamity, what would be left of our country? The bleak catastrophe in that image quite accurately describes today's reality in dozens of poor countries lacking even the rudiments of accessible higher education. Again, the conclusion is that higher education – open, critical, innovative – is not a luxury reserved for the rich. It is a necessity, especially for the poor.

Those of us labouring at the intersection of higher education and development will have to respond to these two imperatives, both at once: strengthening linkages among institutions, across and between North and South, and strengthening the institutions and practices of democratic governance – the attributes of an open society that make genuine higher education possible.

On the first, recent scholarship and practice here at the University of Toronto has shed light on how institutional networks come into being and what does and does not work (Stein et al. 2001). Strategic international partnerships have great potential to share knowledge and create knowledge across and between North and South. Canadian universities, compelled to reinvent the ways they raise their own funds to supplement fees and government grants, for example, are well placed to transfer these fund-raising innovations to campuses in developing countries.

As to the second imperative, strengthening the institutions and practices of democracy, nobody has a stronger interest in the success of that enterprise than people in higher education. No society will prosper in freedom without vigorous institutions of higher education. At the same time, no institutions of higher education will thrive where ordinary civil and political rights are suppressed.

It is this interaction of education and development that shapes our collective future as global citizens.

NOTE

1 For example, consider the restrictions placed on the use of Singapore's Speaker's Corner: 'Speakers must not speak on any matter which relates directly or indirectly to any religious beliefs or religion. Speakers must also not speak on any matter that may cause feelings of enmity, hatred, ill will or hostility between the different racial or religious groups in Singapore.' http://www.spinet.gov.sg/speaker/faq.htm

   The Malaysian University Act explicitly forbids students from participating in opposition politics: 'Limited academic freedom exists in Malaysia and Singapore. These countries exemplify a pattern of restrictions that is not unique but is not much discussed. The universities are in general of excellent quality and well supported by government. In many fields, teaching and research face few restrictions. However, in areas considered sensitive by government authorities, academic freedom is severely curtailed, especially in the social sciences.' (Altbach 2001).

REFERENCES

Altbach, P.G. (2001). Academic Freedom: International Warning Signs. *International Higher Education*, Summer. http://www.bc.edu/bc_org/avp/soe/cihe/newsletter/News24/text001.htm

Sen, A.K. (2001). *Development as Freedom*. New York: Knopf.

Stein, J.G., R. Stren, and J. Fitzgibbon. (2001). *Networks of Knowledge: Collaborative Innovation in International Learning*. Toronto: University of Toronto Press.

CHAPTER 7

Reflections on the Difficulty of Balancing the University's Economic and Non-economic Objectives in Periods When Its Economic Role Is Highly Valued

Michael L. Skolnik

During the past few years there has been an outpouring of statements by politicians, business leaders, and the media heralding the arrival of the knowledge economy, an era 'in which the application of knowledge replaces capital, raw material, and labour as the main means of production' (University of Toronto 2002). Given the central role of higher education in the production, dissemination, and conservation of knowledge, implicit in the idea of the knowledge economy is the belief that a nation's economic well-being depends critically upon the state of its higher education.

Insofar as this perception is valid, one should expect the present decade to be a time of intense interest in the contribution of higher education to national economies, and certainly the symposium that gave rise to this book is an indicator of such interest. Having studied this relationship for my entire professional life, I would say that not since the 1960s has there been such strong and widespread belief in the importance of education to national economic well being as is the case today. The 1960s was the decade in which the phrase 'human capital' was first popularized. It was then that economists identified education as the previously unknown factor which accounted for much of the substantial portion of economic growth that could not be explained by increases in the more traditional factors of production: labour, capital, and natural resources.

The plethora of studies showing the large contribution that education made to economic growth provided intellectual support for the massive increase in public spending on higher education that occurred in the 1960s, and also for the way that newly formed systems of higher education were shaped during that decade. The next decade, however, gave many observers cause to wonder if the relationship between higher education and economic growth really was as simple as many of the 1960s documents suggested. Newly found concern about the possibility of over-education was associated with a questioning of whether the economic case for expansion of higher education had been oversold in the previous decade.

If we are now to witness a similar period of unbridled enthusiasm over the contribution of higher education to economic growth, it is of interest to look back to the last time something similar occurred in public discourse and compare the two periods. Although – or perhaps because – the differences in the social and economic context of higher education between these two periods are so great, it is to be hoped that such a comparison will provide some useful perspectives on the changing role of higher education.

In embarking upon any comparative examination, it is important to have a particular focus in mind. In my comparison of two periods which are striking for their preoccupation with the contribution of higher education to economic growth, there are two issues which I will concentrate on. These are the mission of the university, or more specifically the balance between the economic and non-economic objectives of the university and the structure of higher education, in particular the relationship between the university and non-university sectors of post-secondary education. I shall discuss each issue in turn, after first outlining the broad patterns and context of the 1960s situation and how the present situation compares with it.

There are many commonalities among industrialized countries in regard to the trends and issues discussed in this chapter. Accordingly, literature from several jurisdictions is cited. However, each jurisdiction has its own unequal circumstances and experiences too. This chapter focuses primarily upon the Canadian experience, and more specifically that of Ontario.

The Idea of Education and the Economy – Then and Now

By far the most important factor of production is the human factor ... We recommend that the advancement of education at all levels be given a very high place in public policy, and that investment in education be accorded the highest rank in the scale of priorities.

Economic Council of Canada,
Second Annual Review, 1965

The powerhouses of the new global economy are innovation and ideas, creativity, skills and knowledge. These are now the tools for success and prosperity as much as natural resources and physical labour power were in the past century.

David Blunkett, Secretary of State for Education and Employment,
United Kingdom, 2000.

Although the concept of human capital was not new, the 1960s was when it really became prominent in discussions of economic policy. This was the decade when the study of economic aspects of education first became an important sub-field within the discipline of economics, and economics journals were filled with reports of studies – many of them commissioned by governments – of the economic benefits of spending on education.

The now-defunct Economic Council of Canada was established in the mid-1960s to advise the Government of Canada on economic policy. In just its second annual review the main emphasis in its economic policy recommendations was education. Among the research that the council drew upon to support this recommendation was a study which the council had commissioned entitled, *The Contribution of Education to Economic Growth* by Gordon W. Bertram (1966[1]). In this study, Bertram was building upon the work of scholars in the United States who had tried to quantify the contribution of education to economic growth, particularly Edward F. Denison's *The Sources of Economic Growth in the United States and the Alternatives before Us* (1962). Denison had concluded that over the period 1929–57 education had been responsible for 23 per cent of the growth in U.S. national income. The corresponding figure which Bertram estimated for the same period for Canada was 11.4 per cent (Bertram 1966, 56).

One of the reasons that Bertram found for the difference in the contribution of education to economic growth in the two countries was that educational levels were considerably lower in Canada than in the United States. In 1961, median years of schooling were 9.53 in Canada compared with 11.26 in the United States, a difference of about 18 per cent (ibid., 82). Moreover, in 1960 the participation rate in post-secondary education in Canada was about half the rate in the United States (Ontario Ministry of Colleges and Universities 1981, Table 3.1). Of the difference in income per capita between Canada and the United States, which was about 25 per cent in the early 1960s, Bertram estimated that about a third was the result of differences in educational levels. Bertram concluded that 'increasing efforts in the area of education are a prerequisite[2] not only for the maintenance or acceleration of productivity growth in Canada, but also for the narrowing of the existing differences in the absolute levels of productivity, and therefore the living standard, between Canada and the United States' (ibid., 62).

As if in response to the exhortations of Bertram and the Economic Council of Canada, public spending on higher education soared in the second half of the 1960s. In Ontario, it increased from Can. $76 million in 1965 to Can. $360 million in 1969, and from under 1 per cent of the provincial budget to 11 per cent (Axelrod 1982, 141). Not only were many new universities established during the 1960s, but whole new systems of community colleges were created across Canada.

As the unprecedented increase in spending on higher education occurred in parallel with, or even more conveniently for this argument, just following, the onset of vigorous advocacy of educational expansion for economic reasons, it is natural to conclude that the latter was the principal motivation for the former. There is other evidence consistent with this view, and I believe this to be the consensus among those who have considered the question. However, this is not the only possible explanation for the educational expansion. There was, after all, something called the postwar baby boom, and by the late 1960s, an explosion in the population of individuals of the traditional age for post-secondary education. In addition to responding to burgeoning social demand for places in higher education in the aggregate, there was an increasing consciousness that many segments of society had been underrepresented among university students. The movement to correct this state of affairs, part of what has been called the democratization[3] of higher education, however, probably did not get fully under way until the end of that decade.

In what has been probably the most in-depth examination of this question in Ontario, Axelrod (1982) attributes the primary motivation for the expansion to economic considerations and gives democratization a secondary role. He adds, however, that 'in a period when all investment in higher education was viewed as inevitably profitable, it was unnecessary for official spokesmen to distinguish between the democratic and economic benefits of post-secondary education' (ibid., 28).

Possibly the best indication of the strength of economic motivation in the expansion of post-secondary education in Ontario in the 1960s was to be found in the reshaping of post-secondary technical and vocational education. In 1963, postsecondary education in Ontario consisted of fifteen universities; seven institutes of technology, only one of which had an enrolment much in excess of 500 students; eleven teachers' colleges; and a college of art (Committee of Presidents 1963, 10–15). The greatest expansionary[4] change to this structure initiated during the 1960s was the establishment of a system of twenty-two colleges of applied arts and technology (CAATs). In introducing the legislation to establish these colleges, Minister of Education William G. Davis underscored the economic rationale for the initiative:

> Our true wealth resides in an educated citizenry; our shrewdest and most profitable investment rests in the education of our people. A general phenomenon of our day that brainworkers – ('knowledge workers,' as they are more frequently labeled, to contrast them with 'manual workers'), and these, in the future of an ever-higher calibre – are the prime economic need for societies in advanced states of industrialism. (1966, xx)

Unlike community colleges in the United States and some other Canadian provinces, the junior college, or transfer, function was not part of the mandate of the CAATs. Their role was to provide trained workers for industry. The decision by those who designed the new college system that the colleges would be almost exclusively employment-training institutions, though not taken lightly, became the most second-guessed decision in the history of post-secondary education in Ontario. This decision took to the extreme a trend which was already well under way in the United States. During the 1960s, community colleges in the United States were in the process of being transformed from what were predominantly university transfer institutions into what were becoming predominantly employment-training institutions. This transformation reflected a strong re-orientation of postsecondary education towards serving society's economic goals.[5]

Strongly manifested though it was during the mid- to late 1960s, the unbridled enthusiasm about the economic benefits of public expenditure on post-secondary education did not last very long. By the early 1970s, reports of graduate unemployment or, the new phenomenon, underemployment, became more frequent, and studies of the social rate of return to investment in post-secondary education began to show substantially lower returns. The consequence was that, as Axelrod (1982, 41) expressed it, 'in a shift as dramatic as that which had inspired the rapid expansion of the system, the public attitude toward higher education became suddenly critical.' The large public expenditures on post-secondary education that so recently had seemed like such a good investment now began to seem like a crushing weight.

The exact timing and magnitude of the turnaround in public largesse varied from province to province, and state to state. That the bubble had burst in at least parts of the United States by early in the 1970s was indicated by the title of an essay in a 1972 publication by the American Council on Education: 'More for Less: Higher Education's New Priority' (Smith 1972). Early indications of similar problems closer to home came in a 1975 review by the Council of Ontario Universities, and a few years later in a discussion paper by the Ontario Council on University Affairs (OCUA). That study had the provocative title, *System on the Brink* (OCUA, 1979). There have been ups and downs in public funding since the 1970s, but in few places, and certainly not Ontario, have higher education institutions felt as well off at any time since as they did in the late 1960s.[6]

As to the question of whether their perceived centrality to the knowledge economy will mean that higher education institutions can look forward in the present decade to being treated anything like they were in the 1960s, some important differences in the contexts of higher education in the two periods suggest otherwise. The world has changed over the past four decades in ways too numerous to catalogue in this chapter, but among more recent developments two that have particular implications for higher education are globalization and privatization.

Globalization has meant that higher education is now seen by government, and increasingly sees itself, as 'an actor in a global environment' (Levin 2001, 39). In this global environment, enterprises compete worldwide for customers largely through product innovation, rapid response to demand, and cost reduction. The global environment impinges upon higher education in two important ways. One is that higher education is increasingly looked upon by government as a major national resource to assist the nation's business enterprises to compete more successfully in the global marketplace. The other is that the provision of higher education is itself viewed as an industry subject to global forces of competition, and colleges and universities are under similar pressures for innovation, rapid response to customer demand, and cost cutting in order to survive.

Perhaps there is no logical necessity for governmental response to the pressures of globalization on higher education to include privatization. Nevertheless, in most Western nations, Canada included, privatization in higher education has been proceeding apace with globalization. In part this has been a reflection of more general societal trends: perceptions of public resistance to ever increasing levels of taxation combined with seemingly unanswerable questions about the relative efficiency of public and private enterprises. In part, also, it has reflected concerns particular to higher education, such as in a society already blessed with

mass higher education, how much of the incremental benefits of producing another graduate accrue mainly to that graduate and how much
the society as a whole benefits. One manifestation of privatization has
been increasing reliance upon private sources of funding for what are
generally thought of as public post-secondary education institutions. For
example, in Ontario the proportion of university operating revenue that
came from the government operating grant declined from 79.7 per cent
in 1970–1 to 54.8 per cent in 1998–9 (Ontario 1981, Table 5.2.1; Council
of Ontario Universities 2001, 18). An element of the increased private
component of university funding that has received a lot of attention of
late is that of contracts and grants from business corporations which can
be spent only in specific ways consonant with the interests of the donors,
and which usually carry with them various types of non-financial restrictions as well. The increased dependence of universities on funding from
business has given rise to concerns about undue influence that corporations may have on such things as setting the universities' research
agenda, reporting of findings, and even hiring of faculty.

Corresponding to the decline in the relative importance of provincial
operating grants, there has been a substantial increase in the relative
importance of student fees, from around 15 per cent of operating funding in the late 1960s to about 40 per cent and rising at the beginning of
the present century. In theory this should make universities more
responsive to the preferences of students, but it is difficult to find evidence that this has actually happened. We also lack systematic evidence
about how the goals and motivations of Canadian students may have
changed over the past several decades. Such data are available for the
United States through the national surveys of freshmen students that
Alexander Astin and his colleagues at the Higher Education Research
Institute at the University of California at Los Angeles have been conducting for over thirty years. These surveys showed that, in the late
1960s, 'developing a meaningful philosophy of life' was the top value,
being rated as essential or very important by over 80 per cent of freshmen. Another value, 'being well off financially,' was fifth or sixth on the
list, endorsed by less than 45 per cent. By the mid- 1990s the tables had
turned in regard to ratings of these two values. Being financially well-off
was then the top value, getting a rating of nearly 75 per cent, and developing a meaningful philosophy of life had dropped to sixth, at just over
40 per cent (Astin et al., 1997, 12–13). Insofar as a similar trend in the
values of students may have occurred in Canadian universities over a
period in which universities have become far more dependent upon stu-

dent fees, this could constitute a significant change in the context in which universities operate.[7]

Yet another manifestation of privatization is the anticipation of an increased appearance of private degree-granting institutions, as was made possible in Ontario recently by enactment of the Postsecondary Education Choice and Excellence Act, 2000. There is reason to expect that most of the private organizations that will seek to take advantage of this new opportunity will be those which emphasize preparation for jobs rather than liberal arts. Insofar as this perception of the orientation of new private degree-granting institutions in Ontario is valid, the implications for the province's publicly assisted universities are difficult to predict. On the one hand, the emergence of new private institutions with a strong vocational orientation might free the public institutions from having to address this demand and allow them to retain their traditional emphasis on the liberal arts. On the other hand, the public institutions might find that they have to adopt a stronger vocational orientation to keep their market share in face of the new competition.

The possibly increased presence of a private degree-granting sector is one of several differences between the 1960s and the twenty-first century which may have implications for the way that higher education is able to balance its service to instrumental, economic goals of individuals and society with its fidelity to its other goals. I turn now to the issues relevant to that balance.

The Dualistic Nature of Higher Education

> ... the intellectual, spiritual, social, moral, and physical development of its members and the betterment of society.
>
> from the statement of objects and purposes of the university,
> York University Act, 1965

> ... to provide undergraduate and postgraduate programs with a primary focus on those programs that are innovative and responsive to the individual needs of students and to the market driven needs of employers;
>
> from the statement of the objects of the university,
> University of Ontario Institute of Technology Act, 2002

The idea that higher education has two quite different types of objectives is both of longstanding duration and varied forms of expression. The Royal Commission on the University of Toronto observed in 1906 that 'The two distinct objects of university education are mental culture and practical utility' (cited in Axelrod 1982, 11). In a book on the philosophy of higher education, Brubacher asserted that the mission of the university can be divided into two broad categories: knowledge for its own sake and knowledge for practical ends (Brubacher 1982). The basis of several systems of classification of university types is whether the objectives of the institution are predominantly idealistic or utilitarian (Janne 1970; Borrero 1993; Kybartas, 1996).

The notion that some kind of dualism lies at the heart of higher education is widespread, but it is not an easy matter to explicate precisely the nature of the relevant distinction. The common juxtaposition of practical with whatever the opposite of practical is does not seem to do the trick for a number of reasons. For one thing, there is at least some truth in the old saw that nothing is more practical than a good theory. The classical liberal arts curriculum was often considered to be at the opposite end of the continuum from a practical education, insofar as it might have been successful in inculcating morality, taste, character, and judgment. What is not practical about those things?[8]

Another way of partitioning the different types of objectives of higher education is between vocational and avocational. This distinction recognizes that, from its earliest days, one of the major expectations for higher education was that it would prepare people for work, but that is not all that it would do. It was not just youths in the 'me generation' of the 1990s who came to university in search of a good job. As historian of higher education Harold Perkin noted, what stimulated the growth of the earliest universities was the increasing demand 'for trained elites to serve the bureaucracies of church and state and the emerging professions of clergy, law, and medicine' (Perkin 1991, 171).

Apart from the fact that 'avocational' seems a very understated term for the objectives of higher education that do not have to do with graduates getting jobs, there are two problems with this way of partitioning the objectives of higher education. One is that it does not seem to relate to the research function, which, itself, includes more and less instrumental orientations. The other is that it reflects a compartmentalization of human beings into their vocational selves and their other selves. As particularly those of us who teach in a professional school appreciate, what people do in their jobs both derives from, and infuses, their total being. There is really no boundary between the professional and the personal. Thus, educational experiences which on the surface have nothing to do with an individual's intended field of employment may contribute a lot to their effectiveness in their line of work, and courses designed to be occupationally related may have a major impact on the broader development of the person as a human being. Of course, the more narrowly focused occupationally related courses are, the less likely they are to have the latter effect. So, the vocational-avocational distinction is probably useful in helping to depict the dualistic nature of higher education, but only in a fairly rough manner. And, because it can cover both the vocational-avocational distinction and the distinction between research which is undertaken with and without commercial applications in mind, the distinction between economic and non-economic objectives is a more inclusive, although equally rough, way of referring to a fundamental dichotomy of purpose in higher education.

However clumsily and imperfectly I have captured the dualistic nature of higher education, I hope that it provides at least a framework for discussing one of the most frequently heard observations about recent changes in higher education. For example, in surveying the literature on the impact of globalization, Levin notes that 'as a consequence of globalization, higher education may have accumulated more vocational objectives than those traditionally associated with a liberal education – that is, economic ends as opposed to democratic[9] ones' (2001, 39). Fisher and Rubenson (1998, 95) maintain that Canadian universities have become more commercial and entrepreneurial, while their 'civilizing mission' is becoming less central to the universities. Also consistent with this perception are the data from the United States that I cited earlier, which show a significant shift in values of freshmen from developing a meaningful philosophy of life to being financially well-off.

The relative prominence of the economic and non-economic orientations which characterize the dualistic nature of higher education have shifted frequently from time to time and varied from place to place. There have almost always been some commentators who decried the dominance of the economic ethos even when few of their peers seemed to. For example, there was Veblen's (1918) acerbic depiction of the business-dominated American university in the early twentieth century. Axelrod concluded that by the 1970s higher education in Canada already 'was a simple (if inefficient) economic and technocratic commodity in the service of business and government' (1982, 219). My own observation and reading suggests that such perceptions were in a minority before the 1990s. However, at the beginning of the twenty-first century, as higher education is about to be swept along on the tide of the knowledge economy, similar cries of concern seem to be approaching a consensus about the state of the academy.

As Clark Kerr noted, the university has weathered the most severe storms in its history and is one of just a few societal institutions to have existed a millennium or more in recognizable form. It may well be that the pendulum will inevitably swing back towards the university's civilizing mission.

The contextual differences that I noted earlier between the 1960s and the 2000s suggest that similar movements to harness higher education to the yoke of economic growth will likely have different implications for the balance between its economic and non-economic objectives today than was the case thirty-five years ago. In the 1960s both our society as a whole and the universities still perceived themselves as relatively affluent, and thus capable of addressing more than one major challenge at a time. In 2004, universities have a vastly larger infrastructure to maintain than in the 1960s, and they have already suffered several decades of what they perceive as inadequate funding. As well, they are under stronger competitive pressure to deliver economic returns. For example, as Professor Polanyi (2002) has observed critically, the normal peer assessment of research proposals in Canada must now include comment on the economic returns of the proposed research. In these circumstances, there is an understandable lack of confidence within the university that it can play the part expected of it in the knowledge economy and at the same time pursue its non-economic objectives with the vigour that they deserve. As such, we run the great risk, as Alison Wolf (2002, 254) has expressed it, that '[o]ur preoccupation with education as an engine of economic growth has ... narrowed – dismally and progressively – our vision of education.'

It is interesting to note that in cases where its role as an engine of economic growth is not involved the university tends to have an easier time resisting the influence of external parties bearing money. Recently McGill University 'rebuffed a hefty sum' from a would-be donor who wanted the university to create a chair in the philosophy department for the study of Ayn Rand's philosophy of objectivism (Dubinsky 2002). McGill's principal Bernard Shapiro maintained that the offer of a donation should be turned down because the proposed area of study was too narrow to be pursued in perpetuity. Could the same be said about many of the job-specific areas in which universities have created programs, such as wood processing or commercial of aviation management?[10]

I would like to conclude this section by focusing attention on a comparison of the key phrases from the statutes of two Ontario universities, one created in the 1960s and one in 2002. Excerpts from the charters of the two institutions pertaining to their stipulated goals appear at the beginning of this section. York University was chartered in 1965, just on the eve of the first period of preoccupation with the economic role of higher education with which this paper is concerned. I have always found this statement of objectives remarkable for its breadth and inspirational tone. The University of Ontario Institute of Technology (UOIT) was chartered in June 2002, and this statement of one of its objectives underscores the role of higher education in the knowledge economy of the early twenty-first century. It would be difficult to paint the polarity that I have been describing in more vivid terms. Some may criticize my sampling, but insofar as it is at all reflective of the changed tenor of the times, it should cause us to ask how as a society we can gain what is prized in 2002 without jeopardizing the values that were formulated in such an inspiring way in 1965.[11] There is nothing wrong with having a post-secondary institution with a mission like that of the UOIT; in fact, it may be a good idea to have one or a few such institutions. However, a question that is fundamental to this chapter is whether the entire university sector should be expected to move substantially in the direction indicated by the UOIT mission statement, as compared, for example with the direction of the York University mission statement. This question, in turn, raises questions about the desired structure of post-secondary education. I turn now to one of the major issues in the structure of post-secondary education.

The Binary Structure of Postsecondary Education

Practical importance is not a sufficient title to academic recognition: if that is the best that can be said, it is an excellent reason for exclusion.

Abraham Flexner, 1930

Besides being the time of the earlier significant recognition of the economic contributions of higher education, the 1960s were also the time when the binary structure of higher education which is so common in North America and other industrialized regions was established. The essence of the binary structure is that higher education is partitioned into two main sectors which have quite different mandates. One is the university sector, which is responsible for the range of functions and programs, which have both economic and non-economic objectives, that are connoted by the term 'university.' The non-university post-secondary sector has been shaped differently in different jurisdictions. In Ontario, it consists of the Colleges of Applied Arts and Technology

(CAATs), and, as noted previously, their mandate has been primarily that of preparing people for employment. In this respect, the Ontario colleges were more like non-university post-secondary institutions in Europe than like community colleges in the United States.

Because the CAATs were also given some responsibility for general education and adult education of a non-vocational nature, it would not be accurate to say that historically the logic of Ontario's binary structure was that one sector would concentrate exclusively on delivering the economic goods, while the other would wrestle with balancing economic and non-economic objectives. On the other hand, given that the CAATs' job preparation function greatly overshadowed its other functions, this perception would not be too far from the truth.[12] Even in the United States, where originally community colleges had a broader role than job preparation, the difference between the community college and university sectors has been described as 'realistic & practical emphases ... vs. learning for its own sake' (Susskind 1996, 5).

The concept in the 1960s of the relationship between education and work, which was the foundation of the binary structures established during that decade, was static and simplistic. It was assumed that the population was divided into two categories, those who were capable of the kind of quantitative and verbal reasoning characteristic of university studies and those who weren't (Committee of Presidents 1963, 30). And it was assumed that jobs could be divided into analogous categories. Thus, one segment of the population would attend university to be educated for higher level jobs, and the other segment would attend community colleges to prepare for jobs in the middle of the occupational hierarchy, between unskilled jobs and the jobs for which universities provided preparation. While the university sector had a hierarchy of academic credentials which university students could ascend, Ontario community colleges were intended to provide a terminal education.

By the 1990s it was apparent that the 1960s concept of the relationship between education and work was becoming outmoded. One reason for this was that the middle-level jobs which were the community colleges' bread and butter were increasingly requiring more complex and sophisticated knowledge and skills equivalent or similar to those of university graduates. Moreover, large numbers of graduates of community college programs were demonstrating that when given the opportunity they could succeed in university programs – although from the perspective of faculty and administrators in the colleges such opportunities were not sufficiently available. In addition, developments in technology and the organization of work were changing the way that jobs were configured, and correspondingly, it was becoming increasingly necessary for workers to change, adapt, and grow throughout their working lives. Thus, it seemed that one of the most important things for any type of post-secondary education to do was to produce graduates who had foundations which enabled them subsequently to continue to learn and adapt. It also became apparent that 'terminal education' was a contradiction in terms. Any program of study which arouses students' curiosity, engages them in reflection on the relationship of their field of work to their sense of self, provides them an experience of the joy of learning, and gives them even a hint of the vast stores of knowledge which might be relevant to their lives and of which they are presently ignorant, is likely to foster some desire for further learning.

In the context of the above-noted changes in the relationship between education and work, related developments have begun to undermine the stability of the binary structure of post-secondary education. Community colleges developed such expertise in applied fields of study that were not offered by universities that college programs in these areas have become attractive to university graduates. Indeed, offering post-graduate programs for university graduates has been a major channel of growth for colleges in recent years. Moreover, the expertise that colleges have attained in such areas has resulted in the colleges obtaining contracts and grants, including from the national granting councils, for applied research. One Toronto area college now has about Can. $20 million of externally funded research activity. Further, the expertise that community colleges have to offer programs in numerous applied fields not offered by universities has now been recognized by governments in Ontario, Alberta, and several American states in allowing colleges to offer applied baccalaureate degrees. The kinds of developments which I have just been describing are not unique to North America. Wolf (2002, 88) has noted that in all member states of the European Union there have been movements to bring more of an academic character into the nations' vocational education tracks.

In parallel with community colleges taking on more of the trappings of the university – more complex and sophisticated content in their occupational programs, expansion of liberal arts and research, and offering whole or substantial parts of degree programs – the trend towards greater vocationalism and utilitarianism in the universities has, as some commentators have noted, resulted in a blurring of the boundary between the two sectors (Fisher and Rubenson 1998, 94–5). Fisher and Rubenson describe the increasing vocational emphases in the universities in British Columbia, for example, the new undergraduate programs at the University of British Columbia in occupational hygiene and advanced wood processing which were tailored to the needs of industry (ibid., 90).

It would be equally erroneous to overstate the extent to which community colleges and universities in Canada, and particularly in Ontario, have begun to converge, as it would be to fail to notice this trend. For example, community college leaders who have advocated strengthening the academic character of their institutions have insisted that this is to enhance rather than abandon the fundamental vocational orientation of their institutions.[13] Nevertheless, the apparent blurring of the boundaries in the once clear binary structures raises questions from a public policy perspective as to how universities, colleges, and government should respond to this trend. I offer a perspective on this issue in the concluding section of the paper.

Conclusion

The major thesis of this chapter is that not since the 1960s has there been such strong and unqualified belief on the part of governments and the public in the vital importance of higher education to national economic well-being. However, in contrast to the situation in the 1960s, today the capacity of the universities to respond to these economic challenges and at the same time maintain a healthy balance between the economic and non-economic aspects of their nature is greatly jeopardized.

One of the factors that made it possible for the universities to maintain their balance was the binary structure of higher education which in Canada was established in the 1960s. Within this structure, a large amount of the demand for utilitarian service to provincial and national economic goals was met by the community college sector, leaving the universities some room to perform as, to use Axelrod's wonderful phrase, 'islands of culture and critical thought in a materialistic society' (Axelrod 1982, 6).

Within the past decade, there has been enough blurring of the boundaries in the original binary structure in Canada as to raise questions about its current viability, and in fact, in some countries, the binary structures that were created in the 1960s have disintegrated. The two trends which have most contributed to the weakening of the binary structure are the increased skill levels required of graduates and the correspondingly increased sophistication in content of subject matter in the community college sector; and the increased emphasis in the university sector on training and research that responds to the market and offers the prospect of relatively quick economic returns.

The most common response to the blurring of the sectoral boundaries, especially from university leaders, has been to regret that this is happening and to place the blame for it on academic drift in 'the other sector' resulting from the aggrandizing aspirations of community college leaders. Such a diagnosis is erroneous for two reasons. First, it fails to appreciate that community colleges are one of the most socially responsive institutions ever devised. Their evolution into what have been called 'higher end' programs has been primarily in response to changes in the level of knowledge and skill required in the segment of the workforce to which their programs have traditionally been targeted. It is naive to assume that the profile of activities of the community college which was established in the 1060s should be fixed for all time. Second, this diagnosis ignores the way that universities have contributed to the blurring of the boundary by engaging in economically oriented activities of a highly specific, applied nature which respond to market forces and attempt to produce short-term economic returns.

Abraham Flexner argued that just because an educational activity was worth doing it did not follow that the university should be the institution to do it. He maintained that universities should concentrate on doing 'supremely well what they almost alone can do' (Flexner 1930, p. 27). If universities have to resort to legal and political strategies in order to bar other institutions from engaging in some activities, one has to wonder if these activities are really where the universities should be putting their scarce resources. At a time when the university is in grave danger of ceasing to be much more than a quasi-government agency to promote economic growth, the idea that community colleges – and perhaps some new special-mission institutions of degree-granting status – could relieve the mainstream university of some of the responsibility for high-level academic work of an applied nature should be good news. The more that institutions that were established for the express purpose of contributing to economic growth can be enabled to do so in a deeper and wider manner, the more can institutions which have other substantial reasons for being fulfil their promise.

Thus, a university which was concerned about maintaining a healthy balance between serving its economic and non-economic objectives would not only welcome, but encourage and support the movement of community colleges and special mission post-secondary institutions into sophisticated areas of applied knowledge that respond to market-driven needs of business and government. It would recognize that even though it has a role to play with respect to society's economic aspirations, it alone has vital roles in the advancement and conservation of knowledge, the search for truth, and what Flexner called 'the ceaseless struggle to see things in relation,' which can easily be jeopardized if it makes service to economic growth its primary allegiance. Of course, the temptations towards the latter are great in an era like the first decade of the twenty-first century, as they were in previous times that celebrated the contribution of higher education to economic growth. That is why it is important to keep the following conclusion of Alison Wolf (2002, 254) in mind: 'The contribution of education to economic life ... is only one aspect of education, not the entirety, and it does not deserve the overwhelming emphasis which it now enjoys ... Our recent forebears, living in significantly poorer times, were occupied above all with the cultural, moral, and intellectual purposes of education. We impoverish ourselves by our indifference to these.'

NOTES

1 Although the Council's Second Annual Review was dated December 1965, and Bertram's study was not published until June 1966, the review makes clear that the latter was input into the former.

2 A prerequisite perhaps, but not a sufficient condition. Canada has closed the gap in post-secondary participation rates and has even surpassed the United States in the percentage of the working age population with post-secondary credentials (Statistics Canada 2003), but per capita GDP was still 21 per cent less in Canada than in the United States in 2000 (OECD 2002). This is another example showing why advocates of spending on education in the name of economic growth should be more cautious in their claims.

3 The other major element of democratization pertained to giving faculty and students a greater voice in the running of institutions.

4 A major reform of teacher education was about to take place at this time, but it involved concentration rather than an increase in the number of sites offering teacher education.

5 Brint and Karabel (1989) argue that the transformation was motivated not so much by national economic goals as by the self-interest of the institutions. It would appear, however, that the two coincided.

6 Howard Bowen (1980) maintained that 1969–70 was the most appropriate

base year to use in estimating how much the funding of higher education in the United States had deteriorated. For many years, the Council of Ontario Universities used 1977–8 as the base year in estimating the magnitude of underfunding of universities in Ontario (Skolnik, 1986).

7 Examination of how the distribution of enrolment by field of study has changed over time could provide some useful evidence of changes in student values. However, changes in the way that such data are tabulated make broad comparisons over time difficult. For example, in earlier years, commerce was grouped with career programs like journalism and social work. Now, it is grouped under social sciences, as is social work (and law). At the individual discipline level, we can observe that the percentage of full-time undergraduate students choosing commerce as their field of study increased from 3.6 in 1969–70 to 10.3 in 1999–2000 (derived from Ontario 1981, Table 1.4.1; Council of Ontario Universities 2001, Table 3.1.4a).

8 Some would argue, however, that the concept of liberal education is not associated with such outcomes; rather, that it refers only to the development of the mind through the study of knowledge and ideas which are deemed to be of intrinsic merit as the objects of study 'independent of the demands of any particular trade or profession' (Partington 1987, 14).

9 Levin's use of the term 'democratic' opposite 'vocational' or 'economic' is symptomatic of the difficulty that many commentators have in finding appropriate pairs of words to describe the dual nature of higher education. There is nothing inherently undemocratic about vocational education. What could be undemocratic is the process through which students get allocated to programs that are more vocationally as opposed to academically oriented. The economic or non-economic benefits of education could be distributed more or less democratically.

10 Of course, such job specific program areas are not, at least obviously, as politically incorrect as Ayn Rand is in Canada today. In the newspaper story about McGill's rejection of this donation, it was noted that an unnamed professor had written to the dean of arts comparing having an Ayn Rand Chair with having an Adolf Hitler Chair. Apparently the professor had not read Rand's writings. Rand's extreme individualism is the antithesis of Hitler's collectivist ideology, which made the individual totally subservient to the German nation.

11 It should be emphasized that the passages quoted are, for brevity, excerpts from the respective statements of the objectives of each institution. The difference in tone between the two statutes is apparent in the full statutes.

12 The assignment to Ontario CAATs of responsibility for educational objectives of a non-economic nature was never as clear or consistent as was the

case for colleges in several other provinces, as a survey by Dennison and Levin (1988) demonstrated.

13 The community college literature is also replete with warnings of the adverse consequences that would follow should there be a mass transformation of non-university post-secondary institutions into universities, as happened when the former polytechnics in the United Kingdom were made overnight into universities (Ward 2002).

REFERENCES

Axelrod, Paul. (1982). *Scholars and Dollars: Politics, Economics, and the Universities of Ontario, 1945–1980.* Toronto: University of Toronto Press, 1982.

Astin, Alexander W., Sarah H. Parrott, William S. Korn, and Linda J. Sax. (1997). *The American Freshman: Thirty Year Trends.* Los Angeles: Higher Education Research Institute, UCLA.

Bertram, Gordon W. (1966). *The Contribution of Education to Economic Growth.* Ottawa: Economic Council of Canada. Staff Study No. 12.

Borrero, Alfonso Cabal. (1993). *The University as an Institution Today.* Ottawa and Paris: IRDC and UNESCO.

Bowen, Howard R. (1980). *The Costs of Higher Education.* San Francisco: Jossey-Bass.

Brint, Steven, and Jerome Karabel. (1989). *The Diverted Dream: Community Colleges and the Promise of Educational Opportunity in America, 1900–1985.* New York: Oxford University Press.

Brubacher, John S. (1982). *On the Philosophy of Higher Education.* San Francisco: Jossey-Bass.

Committee of Presidents of Provincially Assisted Universities and Colleges of Ontario. (1963). *The Structure of Postsecondary Education in Ontario.* Toronto: University of Toronto Press.

Council of Ontario Universities. (1975). *New Structure, New Environment. Review 1972-73 to 1974-75.* Toronto: author.

Council of Ontario Universities. (2001). *Ontario Universities 2000: Resource Document.* Toronto: author.

Davis, Hon. William G. (1966). 'Statement by the Minister in the Legislature, 21 May 1965.' In *Colleges of Applied Arts and Technology: Basic Documents.* Toronto: Ontario Department of Education, June, pp. 5–16.

Denison, Edward F. (1962). *The Sources of Economic Growth in the United States and the Alternatives before Us.* New York: Committee in Economic Development.

Dennison, John, and John Levin. (1988). Goals of Community Colleges in Canada. *Canadian Journal of Higher Education* 18 (1): 49–64.

Dubinsky, Zach. (2002). McGill Shrugged. *Montreal Gazette* 27 July pp. A1, A7.

Economic Council of Canada. (1965). *Second Annual Review. Towards Sustained and Balanced Economic Growth.* Ottawa: Queen's Printer.

Fisher, Donald, and Kjell Rubenson. (1998). The Changing Political Economy: The Private and Public Lives of Canadian Universities. In J. Currie and J. Newsom, eds. *Universities and Globalization: Critical Perspectives.* London: Sage pp. 77–98.

Flexner, Abraham. (1930). *Universities: American, English, German.* New York: Oxford University Press.

Janne, Henri. (1970). *The University and the Needs of Contemporary Society.* Paris: International Association of Universities.

Kerr, Clark. (1982). *The Uses of the University,* 3rd ed. Cambridge: Harvard University Press.

Kybartas, Raymond P. (1996). Conceptions of the University: Towards a Classification System Based upon Ideal Types. Doctoral thesis, University of Toronto.

Levin, John S. (2001). *Globalizing the Community College.* New York: Palgrave.

Ontario Council on University Affairs. (1979). *System on the Brink: A Financial Analysis of the Ontario University System 1979.* Toronto: author.

Ontario Ministry of Colleges and Universities. (1981). *Preliminary Report of the Committee on the Future Role of Universities in Ontario: Background Data.* Toronto: author.

Organization for Economic Cooperation and Development (OECD). (2002). *National Accounts of OECD countries, Main aggregates, vol. 1,* updated July. Paris: author.

Partington, Geoffrey. (1987). The Disorientation of Western Education. *Encounter* 68 (1): 5–15.

Perkin, Harold. (1991). History of Universities. In Philip G. Altbach, ed. *International Higher Education: An Encyclopedia,* vol. 1. New York: Garland, pp. 169–204.

Polanyi, John C. 2002. Fostering Better Science. *Toronto Star,* 30 Sept., A21.

Royal Commission on the University of Toronto (Joseph Flavelle, Chairman). (1906). Toronto: Legislative Assembly of Ontario.

Skolnik, Michael L. If the Cut Is So Deep, Where Is the Blood? Problems in Research on the Effects of Financial Restraint. (1986). *Review of Higher Education* 9(4). 435–55.

Smith, Virginia B. (1972). More for Less: Higher Education's New Priority. In Logan Wilson with Olive Mills, ed. *Universal Higher Education: Costs, Benefits, Options.* Washington, DC: American Council on Education.

Statistics Canada. (2003). *Education in Canada: Raising the Standard.* 2001 Census analysis series. Ottawa: author.

Susskind, Tamara Y. (1996). Opportunities and Challenges: Bridging the Two-Year Four-Year Gap. Presented at a Symposium on Articulation sponsored by Oakland Community College, Auburn Hills, Michigan, 4–8, Aug. ERIC Document ED399990.

University of Ontario Institute of Technology Act. 2002. S.O. 2002. c. 8 Sched. O.

University of Toronto. 2002. Symposium Summary: Creating Knowledge, Strengthening Nations: The Changing Role of Higher Education. Toronto: University of Toronto, International Programs Development Office, 23 July.

Veblen, Thorstein.(1918). *The Higher Learning in America.* New York: Huebsch.

Ward, Cynthia V.L. (2002). A Lesson from the British Polytechnics for American Community Colleges. *Community College Review* 29(2): 1–17.

Wolf, Alison. (2002). *Does Education Matter: Myths about Education and Economic Growth.* London: Penguin.

York University Act 1965, S.O. 1965, Ch. 143.

CHAPTER 8

The Contribution of Higher Education to Reconstructing South African Society: Opportunities, Constraints, and Cautionary Tales

George Subotzky

The changing role of higher education in creating knowledge and strengthening nations raises particular challenges for developing countries. In the contemporary context, strengthening developing countries entails a 'dual development imperative': On the one hand, the basic needs of the majority poor must be addressed, by providing adequate social services and through the substantive redistribution of opportunity and wealth. On the other, it is necessary to engage as effectively as possible in both the new knowledge society and the highly competitive global economy. These two goals are in tension, governed as they are by opposing redistributive and global discourses and practices. The case of South Africa is particularly informative in addressing these contradictory demands.

With the political victory over apartheid, expectations were high for a fundamental transformation of society that would reduce the embedded inequalities that sharply divided the social structure of South Africa. The large-scale reconstruction of the higher education system was identified as an immediate policy goal, as a precondition enabling the role of higher education in building the new society. Then higher education could contribute towards national development and other priorities of the new democracy. The policy framework for progressive transformation was impressive. However, for numerous reasons, progress towards the dual development imperative and higher education policy goals has been very uneven. Current conditions in South African society and its higher education system can be characterized as ambiguous. They reflect a combination of tenacious continuities with the apartheid past and some remarkable, if mainly unanticipated changes. Examining the reasons for this and identifying the constraints facing higher education in contributing effectively towards national development may hold lessons for other developing countries.

Two inter-related themes are woven throughout this account of recent South African higher education policy and the cautionary tales we can derive from it. First, concerns for equity and redistribution have been largely displaced. Advancing the public good through pursuing redress, equity, and redistributive justice, in higher education as well as in other areas of public policy, is increasingly constrained by the hegemony of 'global' market-oriented, neo-liberalism. The dominance of the single market model and its higher education equivalent – the entrepreneurial university, which has become the benchmark of innovation and relevance – ignores the pursuit of equity and redress or, worse, discredits it as outmoded idealism. Second, there is a gap between transformative purpose and actual outcomes. Despite the best of progressive intentions, certain developments in South African higher education have been unanticipated; they were driven by factors other than policy, and, in some cases, they have been counterproductive. These two strands are linked. Together, they obstruct the advancement of transformative development goals, which are priorities in developing countries particularly.

The chapter begins by outlining South Africa's current political economy as context for the first theme. Among the purposes of higher education is the furtherance of national development. The second theme is examined through a focus on various instances of recent higher education policy and planning in South Africa. However, the two themes are conjoined: The disjunctive gap between anticipated progressive policy intentions and actual outcomes hinders the effective contribution of higher education to national development. Certainly, that has been the case in post-apartheid South Africa.

Current Political Economic Tensions in South Africa

The tenor of the anti-apartheid struggle was leftist. South Africa had a relatively advanced infrastructure, resources, and capacity, as well as a rich, progressive policy environment. Thus, expectations were high that substantive progress towards redistributive transformation would be made by the new African National Congress (ANC) government. Many South Africans, and others, hoped and expected the new leadership to vigorously pursue a 'third way': The implicit assumption was that the new administration was going to transformatively reduce poverty and inequities, while positioning the nation advantageously in the global arena. Indeed, the new South Africa represented for many the potential for an exemplary case. Not only would it provide a badly needed African success story but also an alternative to the vagaries and hidden interests of trickle-down economics which, all evidence suggests, exacerbate socio-economic stratification.

The transformative ideals of post-apartheid South African society are essentially two-fold: to establish the organs and structures of democratic constitutional government and to pursue social justice through reconstructing the racially divided social order and redistributing wealth and opportunity. The first was admirably, even miraculously, attained shortly after the first democratic elections, which were held in 1994. The progressive character of the new constitution, the new public policy framework, the human rights and other regulatory commissions, and public protector bodies have all attracted international admiration. In addition, some measure of redistribution has occurred through the equalization of race-based disparities in per capita expenditure on health care, education, and social services.

The second ideal remains seriously frustrated, however. Paradoxically, under a progressive ANC government, South Africa's sharply divided social order – along the lines of race, class, gender, and locality – remains largely intact. Indeed, it has become more stratified, despite the partial deracialization of the middle class.

The unanticipated moderateness of the ANC's post-1994 macroeconomic policies stands in marked contrast to the explicit left-leaning ideology that shaped its identity and purpose as a liberation movement. The ANC government, in effect, instituted a self-imposed structural adjustment program which involved the voluntarily adoption of neo-liberal economic orthodoxies. The intention was to create conditions conducive to attracting fixed foreign investment. Thus, a range of conservative macroeconomic measures were implemented that earlier would have been unthinkable as part of ANC policy. Although it remained symbolically committed to alleviating poverty generating employment, and promoting redistribution, the government's actual orientation clearly has been towards compliance with the global discourse and its monetarist precepts. Yet, despite constantly striving to be a 'well-behaved' economy, and with all its economic fundamentals in place in the eyes of international investors and the Breton Woods institutions, the expected benefits have not materialized. Instead of attracting substantial fixed foreign investment, South Africa has been automatically associated with other troubled emerging economies. It has been subjected to successive waves of short-term speculative investments, accompanied by manipulations and fluctuations of the currency exchange rate which have created enormous turmoil in local markets. The anticipated kick-start to economic growth and subsequent redistribution of wealth and opportunity has not transpired. Rising inflation drove up basic food costs which had an enormous effect on the poor in particular although inflation has shown a recent downward trend. Unemployment growth is unabated, and social services, housing, and land redistribution remain grossly inadequate for the majority of the population. These conditions have generated high crime rates and expanded informal economic activities. They have also intensified the HIV/AIDS crisis, so that South Africa now has the world's worst prevalence rate for HIV/AIDS. Despite government claims to the contrary, key socio-economic indicators show that during eight years of new government policy, poverty and social stratification has been exacerbated, rather than reduced (Terreblanche 2003).

This scenario prompts obvious questions: What shaped the choices made by the choices ANC government? Is compliance with the global discourse inevitable – according to the 'TINA' (there is no alternative) position – or are there meaningful options available? Two broad views on this may be distilled.

The prevailing view of the government of South Africa, as well as of some analysts, is that acceptance of the realities and constraints of a developing country within the global order[1] – and in particular such a country's limited potential for redistributive intervention – represents policy maturity. Correspondingly, advocating such alternatives is, in this view, dismissed as a naive, anachronistic, nostalgic remnant of left rhetoric that is characterized as high on critique but low on alternatives. This discursive position derives from the coincidence of South Africa's political transition during the 1990s with the intensification of globalization, the triumphalist ascendancy of neo-liberalism, the demise of the Soviet bloc, and the emergence of universal hostility to and scepticism of the left. Dominant market discourses and practices have closed down the discursive space for interventionist redistribution. This is the context that shaped South Africa's recent formulation of macroeconomic and social policy. The new government appears convinced that the only effective development path is the eventual redistribution through international investor-led growth – even though its current growth, employment, and redistribution strategy has largely not achieved its targets. Furthermore, it has elicited severe criticism from, among others, the ANC's tri-partite alliance partners, the South African Communist Party and the leftist Congress of South African Trade Unions. Apparently the government fears ostracizing itself from global networks and foreign investors if it contravenes the dictates of neo-liberal economic orthodoxy. Terreblanche (2003) traces the roots of this position to the key shift in the balance of forces in South Africa which occurred during the period of negotiations prior to the 1994 elections. Global market-driven discourse, strongly advocated by the corporate sector, over took the redistributive concerns of the ANC and its political allies. This shift laid the foundation for the neo-liberal monetarist and other measures that characterize South Africa's recent macro-economic policy.

Nevertheless, expectations persist that, given the progressive aspirations of the anti-apartheid struggle, South Africa – foremost perhaps among developing countries – holds great promise in finding meaningful ways of mediating the contradictory demands of the dual development imperative. In this view, the new government should exhibit strong political will in following the examples of some emerging economies, such as Brazil and Malaysia, which have in diverse ways countered the global market paradigm. In so doing, it should pursue the principle of *growth through redistribution* which underlay the government's 1994 reconstruction and development programe, rather than its current emphasis on the trickle-down principle of *redistribution through growth*. It must be acknowledged that the depth and persistence of structural inequalities will continue to frustrate fundamental socioeconomic change. However, the government's acceptance of the global discourse is, in this view, seen to renege on the social mandate with which it was elected in 1994. The ANC had promised that not only would democratic government be established, but the quality of life for the majority would also be substantially improved. The adoption of the global discourse by the ANC government thus represents, for many, a major shift from its previous progressive redistributive intentions; it has diverted it from substantively addressing immediate socioeconomic priorities.

In this view, the evidence is inescapable that the market-driven, trickle-down approach will never adequately meet the needs of the poor, both in the developed and developing worlds. Disparities in access to wealth and opportunity are growing dramatically globally. The chilling Castellian prospect of a burgeoning 'fourth world' population, lacking basic needs, opportunities, and services, and increasingly marginalized from engaging in, and benefiting from the knowledge-driven society seems to be materializing (see Castells, 2001). The growing corpus of anti-globalization critique is raising awareness that the contradictions of the current 'system' of unregulated markets – resulting in widening social stratification, global instability, and cumulative ecological effects – are simply not sustainable. Increasingly informed moral imperative, however, is not sufficient to prompt changes. Government interventions are necessary. Public works project and programs for the skills development of new are now being touted in South Africa, but these are not on a large enough scale to make a substantial difference. A coordinated, cross-sectoral program, driven by bold and sustained political will, is required to reduce poverty.

The current hegemony of the market-oriented global discourse and practices impedes the pursuit of one pole of the dual development imperative with which developing countries are faced: the basic needs of their societies must be addressed, and wealth and opportunity redistributed, through appropriate forms of government intervention. In this discursive context, the broader purpose of higher education tends to be constricted to serving market-oriented economic development. The following section elaborates on this.

Meeting Development Priorities through Addressing the Multiple Purposes of Higher Education: Avoiding a Single Market-Oriented Model

In current debates, the over-riding tendency is to interpret the contemporary role of higher education exclusively in terms of the needs of the market-driven globalized knowledge economy.[2] However, a single, globally oriented economic path will not adequately meet the dual development goals of developing countries, nor will the adoption of the dominant global orientation of higher education towards economic concerns contribute effectively to furthering the priorities of a developing country.

The current benchmark of institutional innovation is the 'entrepreneurial' university, of which Clark (1998) provides an influential and definitive account. Numerous policy analyses and institutional mission statements now aspire to this market-oriented model. They are reproducing common formulas to foster competitive innovation through partnerships between higher education and industry and incubator companies. They are commodifying knowledge and services, and promoting efficiency-driven managerial approaches. The homogeneity of these trends testifies both to the power of global higher education policy discourse and to national and institutional phobias of being left behind by contemporary developments.

For several reasons, however, it is neither possible nor desirable that all institutions of higher education aspire to this unified model of innovation. First, differentiated institutional types and functions are required in all systems to meet the needs of an increasingly diverse labour market and non-traditional student bodies. Second, the capacity to function as leading entrepreneurial institutions is neither unlimited nor easily reproduced; aspiring towards models by formulaically emulating trend-setters is almost invariably a futile exercise. Third, and most relevant for the purposes of this chapter, preoccupation with the market model diverts higher education institutions from performing their multiple public roles and purposes and thus from contributing towards the public good (Singh 2001; Jonathan 2001). Exclusively emphasizing market-oriented innovation runs the risk of narrowly and instrumentally limiting the purpose of higher education to serving economic needs, mainly of the private sector. Particularly in developing countries, higher education has a crucial public role to play in strengthening democracy, social justice, and human rights (Kassimir et al. 2002), in contributing to social development broadly conceived, and in constituting sites of independent critical inquiry and service. Poverty, social dislocation, and HIV/AIDS are decimating poor societies around the world. Higher education, with its knowledge and resources, must be applied to reduce these pressing socioeconomic problems with the same vigour with which entrepreneurial opportunities are pursued. Thus, the prevailing market orientation should be complemented through service learning (see Chapter 11 this volume) and related knowledge production (Subotzky 1999).

It is important to recognize that institutions of higher education simultaneously perform a range of sometimes contradictory functions, with different emphases in different contexts. Despite increasing pressure for them to function as a productive force in the new information economy, they should remain 'conflictual spaces' (Castells 2001; Singh 2001) in which ongoing competition among these various functions occurs. The overemphasis of the entrepreneurial university model, and the ensuing constriction of the broader purposes of higher education to market concerns, impede the ability of a developing country to address its range of basic socioeconomic development priorities.

Pursuit of the goals of equity, redress, and redistributive justice, and addressing basic needs is hampered in developing countries by prioritizing global market discourses. Likewise, following the single model of the entrepreneurial university will subvert the broader social purposes of higher education. With this background, we will now examine key aspects of policy on higher education in post-apartheid South Africa.

Higher Education Policy Development in South Africa: Challenges and Cautionary Tales

The system of higher education inherited from the apartheid era was generally highly fractured, skewed, inequitable, and inefficient – these are the conclusions of investigations reported by both the National Commission on Higher Education (NCHE, 1996) and the federal Department of Education (1997, 2001).[3] Under apartheid, it was neither directed towards, nor capable of meeting the development needs of the population as a whole. The impact of this legacy was devastating. Nothing short of a complete reconstruction of the higher education system would be adequate in pursuing equity and meeting the challenges of transformation and national development.

Following political negotiations and the 1994 election, a progressive framework was established for the fundamental and large-scale transformation of higher education. Building on the NCHE (1996) recommendations, this was formally set out in the DOE's *White Paper 3: A Programme for Higher Education Transformation* (1997) and the Higher Education Act of 1997. The white paper represented a carefully constructed discursive 'settlement.' On the one hand, it addressed concerns for transformation, equity, and redress which lie at the heart of the redistributive discourse. On the other, it also espoused the goals of effectiveness, efficiency, and the development of high-level skills central to the global discourse. As a result of its largely symbolic nature, the white paper enjoyed widespread acceptance among stakeholders in higher education, while avoiding the policy contestations which inevitably arise around the details of implementation. Some analysts (e.g., Jansen 2001) see a mischievous and diversionary political intention in developing symbolic policy. Others interpret this as a necessary step in mobilizing consensus, in making a decisive break with the past, and in achieving a settlement between national and global concerns (e.g., Cloete et al. 2002; Subotzky 2003). Four years later the *National Plan for Higher Education* (DOE 2001) provided the structural and operational steps to incrementally implement the goals of the white paper.

For a variety of reasons, implementation was delayed and partial. Change transpired, but not always in the intended way and certainly not always as a direct result of policy and planning. A range of selected issues are now examined to understand the dynamics of change and continuity that characterize the current system of higher education. Perhaps lessons may be drawn from the South African experience of policy formulation and implementation.

The Context of Equity and Redress

Given South Africa's history, equity and redress are particularly pointed issues. These goals had figured prominently and symbolically in all previous key policy documents. However, as time went on, various subtle discursive shifts in meaning and interpretation of equity and redress became evident (Barnes 2003; Subotzky 2001). In the early 1990s, based on analyses of the vast disparities structurally rooted in apartheid, it seemed that redress of past institutional inequalities would be a matter of automatic historical entitlement and would be provided by the new government in the form of reparations-like funding. A further assumption was that this would entail strict parity between black and white educational institutions in terms of teaching and research program offerings and infrastructure. This was based on the principle of simple equality, in terms of which any persistent form of differentiation represented the perpetuation of disadvantage. However, given limited resources and the need for different kinds of educational institutions to meet labour market requirements and to accommodate student diversity, the crucial distinction was drawn between disadvantage and differentiation (Badat et al., 1994). Not all institutions could or should aspire towards a single institutional model, inevitably, that of a top-rate research university. Redress became reinterpreted as the means to enable institutions to target specific apartheid-rooted deficits in order to establish newly defined niche areas of specialization within a nationally planned and coordinated differentiated landscape. Extensive debates highlighted the complex relationships between equity, efficiency, and excellence. Admittedly, under conditions of scarce resources, equity is in tension with efficiency, excellence, and development. However, pursuing equity by ensuring greater access and success of diverse staff and students potentially advances both efficiency and excellence (Subotzky 2001). Likewise, increased participation without assuring appropriate quality, and hence success, simply undermines the underlying purpose of equity.

Government, while strongly symbolically committed to redress and equity, came to reject the automatic assumptions of entitlement by historically disadvantaged institutions (HDIs) on the basis of historical allegiance and their claimed contributions to the anti-apartheid struggle (some of which have been somewhat exaggerated). As the discourse of market-related efficiency became more evident, the quality, efficiency, and effectiveness of programs in the HDIs were scrutinized more sharply and with less sympathy. In addition, cases of severe mismanagement which surfaced during the mid to late 1990s at several HDIs prompted a more sceptical approach, in which not all of the problems of HDIs could be attributed to apartheid. This emerging position was based on an implicit assumption of institutional agency and responsibility, associated with market values and discourse, which challenged the view that the HDIs were simply victims of structurally and historically determined discrimination.

In a further shift in meaning, the *National Plan for Higher Education* distinguished between institutional and social redress. The latter referred to financial aid measures for individual disadvantaged students, whether enrolled in advantaged or disadvantaged institutions. This was prompted by the tremendous increases in numbers of black students at advantaged institutions. In turn, this gave rise to suggestions that the apartheid categories of advantaged and disadvantaged institutions are now anachronistic. According to this ahistorical perspective, redress should be subsumed into the ongoing institutional developmental planning process as part of systemic transformation. This consolidated the view that HDIs should no longer take history as the root of their problems, and they should not use past disadvantage to hide inefficiencies. Individual and collective responsibility for shortcomings must, of course, be taken. This new emphasis on agency, however, seriously underestimates the embeddedness of historical disadvantage in current institutional cultures (Barnes 2003).

These discursive shifts, along with the growing emphasis on fiscal constraint, accountability, efficiency, and 'realism' in governance, which emerged during the late 1990s, served to displace equity and redress, if not symbolically (which government would deny) then certainly operationally. This trend has been identified in every analysis of current policy. Research by Cloete et al. (2002) revealed that the previous minister of education lobbied hard for a redress policy but was obstructed in this by the Treasury. This occurred precisely at the time (around 1996) when advocates of the global discourse and orientation were consolidating their position within the corridors of power. As a result, government's redress policy to date has assumed a distinctly ad hoc character (see Barnes 2003).[4] Recently, 'redress' has all but disappeared as a term. It has been largely subsumed into the merger process (see below) and an institutional development 'factor,' which forms a component of the proposed new funding framework, according to which HDIs will be compensated for limited aspects of disadvantage. However, the jury is still out on whether these measures will substantially address the range of current legitimate redress concerns (ibid.).

This experience exemplifies how concerns for equity and redress are

easily lost amidst the growing dominance of market-related global discourse. In a developing country, equity and development concerns are
closely linked. Without increased participation in both education and
the economy, national development goals will remain elusive.

The Challenges of Implementation and Unanticipated Change

After completing the 1997 white paper, the government was diverted
from immediately implementing its comprehensive policy goals by a
combination of factors. As a result, the period between the white paper
and the long-awaited release of the *National Plan on Higher Education* (in
2001) constituted, as the plan itself suggests, an 'implementation vacuum.' This gap highlights not only the challenges of implementation
but also the false assumptions surrounding 'grand' policy (explored in
the next section) and, in turn, the false assumptions about what constitutes an effective contribution towards national development.

The factors contributing towards the implementation vacuum and
inhibiting progress in achieving progressive policy goals include the following: (1) a number of unanticipated priorities and operational diver-
sions, such as regulating the burgeoning private higher education sector
and addressing the management and financial crises in some historically
disadvantaged universities; (2) the self-acknowledged lack of capacity in
the Department of Education; and (3) the nature of the white paper as
symbolic policy, which meant that detailed planning and operational
details still had to be elaborated before implementation. Virtually all
recent policy analyses seek to explain this gap. Motala and Pampallis
(2001), for example, link this directly to the broader political economic
conditions outlined above. Jansen and Sayed (2001) and Subotzky
(2003) emphasize the discursive shift from government's original progressive equity orientation to the global market-driven approach. Kraak
(2001) gives 'policy slippage' between the ANC's initial intentions and its
'selling out' to globalization forces as the explanation. In contrast,
Muller (2001) interprets the implementation gap as a period of 'policy
maturation' from naive assumptions about total transformation to an
understanding of the necessity of incremental change and the need for
what Cloete et al. (2002) call 'differentiated' policy (see below).

In the ensuing absence of both regulatory measures and incentives for
change, various unanticipated developments occurred. Most importantly, many Afrikaans universities and some 'technikons' (roughly, polytechnics) seized the opportunity of unregulated market conditions to

expand into new entrepreneurial frontiers in distance and telematic education, satellite campuses, and partnerships with private providers. The latter involved training large numbers of African teachers, which led to a dramatic rise in African enrolments in these institutions. However, the government regarded these developments, along with the rapid and unregulated proliferation of private providers, as the chaotic, unfettered action of the market, which directly threatened its plans for a coordinated transformation of the system. Concerned particularly about the quality and sustainability of these initiatives, it immediately instituted regulatory measures. Alongside this, an unanticipated decline in enrolments occurred after 1998, which jeopardized the sustainability of some HDIs and called into question overall systemic growth projections for the higher education system.

These institutional initiatives and changes, as Cloete et al. (2002) argue, were not the direct result of policy. Different interpretations of symbolic policy and of various opportunities and outcomes arose from the dynamic interplay among policy, market conditions, and institutional strategies. All of these were shaped by prevailing global trends. This highlights the multiple dynamics and drivers of change in higher education. Often change occurs in spite of, rather than because of plans and intentions. The implementation vacuum, together with the rapid changes arising from institutional initiatives, other unanticipated developments, and persistent structural impediments generated the uneasy combination of change and continuity that characterizes the current situation of higher education in South Africa. As we have seen, the new government was faced with multiple obstacles in formulating and implementing policy, managing change, and moving decisively towards enhancing national development.

Planning and the Dangers of Rationalist Assumptions

The 2001 *National Plan for Higher Education* represents a system-wide policy and planning framework aimed at steering change towards achieving national goals for higher education and national development priorities as part of post-apartheid socioeconomic reconstruction. Embedded in this planning framework are assumptions about the nature of systemic and institutional change, the nature of policy, and in particular, the extent to which policies and plans lead to anticipated outcomes. In this lies another important lesson from the South African experience.

Regarding change at the institutional level, the new worldwide emphasis on innovative entrepreneurialism in an increasingly competitive environment has generated the need for centralized institutional strategic planning, framed by an identifiable corporate identity. As was repeatedly stressed in the national plan, and by numerous commentators, institutional capacity to develop and implement strategic plans is critical to the success of the transformation process. Capacity aside, recent research suggests that even where abundant capacity is evident (as is generally the case in the United States), the effectiveness of management planning initiatives to achieve intended change cannot be assumed. Rhoades (2000) concludes that several key premises of current university strategic management thinking amount to little more than 'myths.' It is now commonly held that institutions of higher education are complex, loosely coupled organizations, comprising multiple centres of authority and interests which give rise to intricate dynamics of formal and informal decision-making and contestations. In addition, faculty members often have stronger cosmopolitan allegiances to their disciplinary networks than to their local institutions. It is often through these linkages that independent innovative initiatives arise in the substructures of departments and centres. These are not necessarily subversive of centralized managerial planning objectives; indeed, they can sometimes realize the institution's goals – but in spite of, and not because of them. Within these complex dynamics, intricate overt and covert strategies are utilized to facilitate decision-making and to effect or obstruct change. This is especially so given the growing concentrations of power in executive management and the increasing tensions between corporate and academic styles of management. For these reasons, it is often strategically counterproductive for the sectoral interests of particular agents to reveal such strategies as part of the culture of consciousness-raising disclosure associated with the current vogue of the 'learning organization.' This insight, in fact, suggests the notion of 'strategic organizational non-learning' as a way of describing these kinds of clandestine manoeuvres to achieve change (Breier and Subotzky 2003). Instead of the often assumed institution-wide model of coordinated change, based on a consensual singleness of purpose, a much more politicized model of institutional change emerges: one which acknowledges contestation, conflicting interests, and 'Machiavellian strategies' (ibid.). The lesson from this experience is that, in light of these complex linkages and dynamics of change, rationalist assumptions about the extent to which change is effected through central steerage and strategic planning must be tempered.

At the systemic level, similar assumptions about the efficacy of large-scale change initiatives relate to what Cloete et al. (2002) call 'big bang policy,' which carries the expectation of 'transformation at once.' Implicit in this is an assumption that a grand system-wide 'comprehensive policy' approach, driven by strong-willed centralized decision-making in the national interest, is necessary to override sectoral interests and regional variations. This is clearly manifest in the education minister's current approach to the mergers and in the tensions this has generated among stakeholders (described below).

Consensus was easily attained consultatively at the level of symbolic policy formulation. However, a different kind of change strategy, which Cloete at al. (2002) call 'differentiated' policy, is required in the subsequent phases which address details of implementation where contestation inevitably arises. Citing Finnish and Dutch examples of linking higher education and the economy and the implementation of merger policies, respectively, Cloete et al. argue that differentiated policy, based on the information-rich interaction between government, institutions, and society, will be more effective in facilitating change and implementing policy. This view draws from Carnoy's vision of a network state which is 'made of shared institutions, and enacted by bargaining and interactive iteration all along the chain of decision-making' (cited in Cloete et al. 2001, 485). This is a state 'whose efficiency is defined in terms of its capacity to create and sustain networks – global, regional, and local, and through these networks, to promote economic growth and develop new forms of social integration' (ibid.).

This differentiated policy approach might find suitable application in another key national development: the attempt to link planning of higher education and human resource development (HRD). Kraak (2003) assumes that to achieve national priorities, coordinated and integrated 'joined-up' cross-sectoral policy and planning is required. In light of now-discredited 'manpower' planning projections, it is commonly held that higher education outputs and labour market needs cannot be precisely matched. Pursuing the goal of coordinated planning runs the risk of adopting another assumption, which is that more complex planning frameworks and capacity will automatically achieve a closer match. However, the rapidly changing dynamics of the labour market create an indeterminacy that resists even the most complex planning approaches. Quantifying labour market needs cannot be an exact science. Nonetheless, it is possible to identify broad areas where there are shortages of skills, and through greater interaction with employers and other social partners, identify the optimum mix of knowledge and skills required in the workplace. An effective HRD strategy will strive progressively towards greater exactness in mapping shortages with a view to aligning the outputs of higher education more closely with the needs of the labour market. This kind of 'incremental fine-tuning' involves, as Schwartzman (2002) illustrates, careful monitoring of labour market trends, sophisticated information, and clarity of developmental objectives by all key participants – precisely the kind of network envisaged by Carnoy. However, this vision of a networked state, and its goal of iterative relations generating new forms of 'social integration,' may optimistically underestimate the depth of social divisions, conflictual interests, and asymmetrical capacities among developing country governments, institutions, and stakeholders, especially given the knowledge intensity of this approach. Evidence of this is the current rather combative relationship between the South African higher education ministry and other stakeholders in higher education. This is closing down, rather than opening up opportunities for participatory involvement in policy-making and will now be described.

Mergers: The Challenges of Integrated Planning and Consultation

The 2001 *National Plan for Higher Education* provides the detailed framework and operational steps to implement the goals of the 1996 white paper produced by the Department of Education. Among other things, it established targets for increased participation and rates of graduation, for reshaped enrolments by field of study, and for staff equity. The plan also provided for the restructuring of the institutional landscape through mergers, but without reducing the number of institutional sites and capacity for expanded participation. The department argued that pruning institutional numbers will increase the overall efficiency, equity, and effectiveness of the system in fulfilling its various functions and in contributing to national development. The plan is highly interventionist and regulatory in character,[5] with the three-year iterative planning process at its centre. For the purposes of this discussion, three aspects of the merger process illuminate potential pitfalls of policy planning and implementation.

First, unsurprisingly, the merger proposals aroused fierce and passionate opposition. Opposition was particularly strident from historically disadvantaged institutions who interpreted mergers as an attack on and a denial of their historical and potential future role in development. The fundamental rationale for most of the recommended mergers was strongly criticized by many institutions and analysts, as were the criteria and data on which these were based. In motivating the mergers, the min-

ister of education stated the intent to eradicate the anomalous and dupli-
cative proliferation of institutions which were, in the minister's words,
the outcome of 'the geo-political imagination of apartheid planners.' Significantly for this discussion, most policy analysts saw little relation
between the preoccupation with reducing numbers of institutions, on
the one hand, and advancing key policy goals of higher education and
national development priorities, on the other (Subotzky 2002). In the
absence of a compelling rationale, the minister's single-minded focus on
pruning the system appears to be primarily motivated by the political
need to achieve demonstrable change. The ANC is now (2003) approaching the next election, and given the increasingly vociferous criticism of
government's perceived persistent non-delivery on fundamental socio-
economic transformation, this need is understandable. However, making
mergers the priority will absorb enormous energy and resources, with little certainty that these will be cost beneficial. This highlights the danger
of higher education policy being primarily politically, rather than educa-
tionally motivated. Such a tendency augers poorly for the effective contribution of higher education to national development needs.

Second, within this overall framework for change, educational institutions face a bewildering array of somewhat disjointed policy and planning
initiatives and change imperatives, leading to a crippling demand over-
load. Not only do they face multiple aspects of change in policy on higher
education, but they are also subject to various pieces of labour legislation,
including employment equity stipulations. Within this assortment of over
thirty change initiatives, as pointed out by the South African Universities'
Vice-Chancellors' Association (SAUVCA 2002), what is clearly lacking is
the sequential alignment of policy and planning priorities. This is not to
suggest a resort to 'big bang' grand policy approaches but simply to assert
that without sensible policy coordination and prioritization, ongoing
multiple demands will simply exhaust capacity, energy, and compliance.
Ultimately, the result will be resistance to implementation.

Third, in releasing the national plan, the minister insisted that the
period of consultation (which began with the 1996 National Commission
on Higher Education) was over, and the time for decisive intervention
and delivery had arrived. The Department of Education has shown
diminishing patience with what it interprets as obstructive sectoral interests hindering the implementation of the plan and hence of the national
interest. Accordingly, the government has recently adopted an increasingly intolerant and belligerent posture towards the higher education
sector and its stakeholders. Keeping itself at a distance, the government

is forfeiting opportunities to work with intermediate bodies such as the South Africa Universities' Vice-Chancellors' Association. This shift in relations between the government and stakeholders threatens the white paper notion of cooperative governance, and has – significantly for the purposes of this chapter – important consequences for policy implementation, raising a central challenge in this regard. Decisive government action to overcome inevitable contesting interests is necessary in any system. However, needlessly antagonizing stakeholders in this way reveals a short-sighted and potentially counterproductive view of policy. Consultation does not constitute merely a single phase in the policy process. Without an appropriate degree and form of participatory involvement by stakeholders and practitioners in policy-making and implementation, compliance with the government's stronger interventionist approach is unlikely. Indeed, this will simply elicit legal and bureaucratic obstruction of implementation. Change must be managed through finding the appropriate mix of consultative engagement, creating the space for constructive critique, and acting decisively from the centre to avoid reactionary obstruction and ideological recalcitrance. This balance is crucial to successful policy and planning implementation, and in turn to the achievement of the broader purposes of higher education and national development. Otherwise there is the ever-present danger that the government will justify strong intervention to counter opposition in the name of the national interest.

Applications-driven Knowledge Production and Acquisition

South Africa's re-entry into the global arena following years of isolation under apartheid coincided with the increasing homogeneity of globalized economic, cultural, and academic trends. Therefore, it is not surprising that considerable borrowing of seemingly progressive policy has occurred in constructing the framework for transforming the system of higher education. It is argued throughout this chapter that progressive intentions do not always produce desired outcomes in achieving higher education and national development goals. One such case is the recent emphasis on multidisciplinarity in both knowledge production and curricula.

During the implementation vacuum, an important set of responses by many higher education in South Africa institutions involved the restructuring of academic programs. This was based on the assumption, strongly advocated in the DOE's white paper on higher education, that interdisciplinarity was the key to preparing graduates adequately for the new knowledge society and for solving pressing socioeconomic and technical problems. This follows the global proliferation of new organizational and epistemological modes of knowledge production, which has manifested in the shift from 'disciplinary' to 'problem-solving' or 'strategic' research. While various accounts of this change emerged (Etzkowitz, et al., 1998; Rip, 2000), the notion of a shift from 'Mode 1' knowledge production (that is, knowledge produced within conventional disciplinary frameworks, based on peer-review quality criterial) to 'Mode 2' knowledge production (that is, trans-disciplinary knowledge produced to address specific problems, conducted increasingly in transient teams of specialists, based on end-user quality criteria) (Gibbons et al., 1994; Gibbons, 1998) had a major impact in South Africa. According to Gibbons, for institutions – particularly in developing countries – to remain relevant and at the cutting edge of research in the context of a 'new economically oriented paradigm of the function of higher education' (1998, 1), they must develop partnerships and alliances to produce relevant Mode 2 knowledge. They should adjust from being *producers* of mainly disciplinary knowledge to being creative *reconfigurers* of knowledge into interdisciplinary combinations to solve complex problems.

Around the time that the National Commission on Higher Education was doing its work (the mid-1990s), policy-hungry analysts readily seized on the progressive, cutting-edge appeal of the Gibbons thesis. They adopted it rapidly, and rather uncritically, linking it to optimism about an inclusive high-skills path and to meeting national development goals (Cloete et al. 1997; Scott 1997; Subotzky 1999; Kraak 2000). Following this initial optimism, however, Gibbons's version of Mode 2 and its role in fostering development received more circumspect critism (Jansen 2000; Muller 2000; Muller and Subotzky 2001).[6] It was seen as ambiguous as to whether Mode 2 should *replace* Mode 1 disciplinary knowledge or should be an *adjunct* to it (Muller 2000). Although Gibbons and his co-authors would hastily affirm the latter, their account remains equivocal in this regard. It has led to several cases in which interdisciplinary problem-solving curricula have supplanted traditional disciplinary-based curricula. Shifting patterns in knowledge *production* was thus unquestioningly adopted into the realm of knowledge *acquisition*.

Inquiry-rich curricula have a long history and many evident benefits. However, the cautionary concern here is that shifting teaching programs towards interdisciplinarity without a solid foundation of disciplinary training may prove counterproductive. This may be especially so in developing country contexts where the quality of disciplinary training is often suspect. This also runs the risk of setting graduates up for failure by expecting them to contribute to development priorities by means of innovative problem-solving Mode 2 activity without ensuring their prior competence and capacity – which depends on thoroughly grounded discipline-specific knowledge and skills (Muller and Subotzky 2001). Applications-driven research and inquiry-rich instruction may hold much promise for developing countries in meeting their development priorities. However, the potential perils of too-literal interpretations and the uncritical adoption of current trends must be considered.

The key challenge for curriculum development in addressing labour market and development needs in the new knowledge society is, as Schwartzman (2002, 12) argues, 'not with quantitative targets for specific professions, but with the general need to provide society with the proper combination of specialized, generic and "transferable" skills.' Finding this balance remains highly elusive. Employers tend to overemphasize specialized competence above generic high-level competence 'which is a platform for any specialized competence' (Cloete and Bunting 2000, 46). Instead, for skills to remain adaptable, they cannot be too context specific 'or else the knowledge economy will not prosper' (ibid., 47–8). The inculcation of concrete skills precludes the 'kind of adaptability required by an economy characterized by ever-changing cognitive demand' (ibid.) and, without a solid platform of knowledge processing, leaves the student stranded in the particularity of those skills.

In curriculum debates in South Africa, the pursuit of this balance is reflected in two contending positions, framed by the 'disciplinary' and the 'credit accumulation and transfer' positions (Ensor 2001, 273). The latter arises from the advocacy, in recent documents higher education policy, of a 'high skills, high growth' economic development path, aimed at rapid integration into the global world economy. The principal instrument for this is the national qualifications framework (NQF). It is aimed at fostering mobility across the system of education and training through credit accumulation and transfer. NQF rests on the notion of equivalence of forms of knowledge and a series of shifts including the following: from subject-based knowledge of content to student-based generic skills; from courses to credits; from disciplinary curricula to outcomes-based modularized interdisciplinary curricula; and from disciplinary-based departments to interdisciplinary programs, inspired by the Mode 2 thesis. As Ensor (2001) shows, the tension between these discourses has persisted in South Africa throughout the process of making policy on higher education and has led to a current review of the NQF. Tracking some institutional attempts to gear programs to the world of work, Ensor concludes that despite the reorganization and repackaging of these programs, most remain firmly discipline-based and do not constitute integrated interdisciplinary curricula. However, the unintended result of the restructuring is less portability and less flexibility of choices for students than before. In some cases, the process was so extreme that the number of core disciplinary majors were drastically reduced – a situation that had to be rapidly rectified. This is another example of progressive intentions leading to unanticipated outcomes.

These perspectives indicate that far more effort is required to determine the optimal mix of knowledge and skills required in the new knowledge-driven workplace. The task, Ensor argues, is to find common ground between the position favouring disciplinary knowledge and the position favouring transferable skills, thereby addressing the shortcomings of each and combining disciplinary coherence and depth of learning with flexible entry and exit opportunities (and interdisciplinary relevance, it may be added). This remains the principal curricular challenge in preparing graduates for the labour market and thereby in ensuring their effective contribution to development priorities. These experiences suggest the need for caution towards the uncritical borrowing of apparently progressive and innovative policy – especially in the key area of research and curricula – in addressing national development priorities.

Recognition of Prior Learning

Another area of the rapid and problematic uptake of progressive policy and practice has been the adoption of the recognition of prior learning (RPL) as a mechanism to ensure greater equity of access and mobility across education and training. A useful description of RPL and its significance for higher education policy in South Africa is provided by Osman and Castle (2002, 63):

> The recognition of prior learning (RPL) is a tool that assists adults to identify existing knowledge and skills, acquired informally, through work and life experience, while allowing institutions to make judgments about their preparedness for study and eligibility for credit. In South Africa, RPL was introduced to increase the participation of black students in higher education, and to improve the knowledge and skills base of the workforce in the interests of global competitiveness. These intentions link RPL to issues of

equity, redress and social justice, on the one hand, and to lifelong learning on the other. RPL has a prominent place on the national policy agenda, and is one of several initiatives associated with the challenges of globalization and pressures to transform the education and training system.

From this, the attraction of RPL in the South African context is readily apparent. However, while RPL has been widely instituted, this has been largely ad hoc. The first studies monitoring and evaluating the operational challenges and effects of RPL practice are emerging (Shalem and Steinberg 2000; Thaver et al. 2002; Breier 2003). The main challenge for RPL is to facilitate the interface between (both formal and non-formal) varieties of knowledge and experience which arise outside the academy in the world of work, on the one hand, and highly structured formal academic knowledge, on the other. Defending the practice against sceptics who regard it as a soft access option, proponents of RPL do recognize 'that experiential knowledge is distinct from academic ways of knowing, and that learning that occurs in a variety of contexts is not always transferable' (Osman and Castle 2002, 67). In so doing, they optimistically assume that a seamless and meaningful interface can be achieved. However, while paradoxically acknowledging differences in forms of knowledge they do not explain how these can be bridged. This epistemological question is thus reduced to the political issue of attitudes and power relations among different but purportedly equal knowledge workers. It also assumes the equality of all knowledge forms, despite the stated differences: 'the epistemological challenges in RPL relate to whose knowledge is valued and privileged, and whether knowledge outside disciplinary boundaries can be recognized alongside others within the discipline' (ibid.).

Other researchers are more cautious about such claims. Drawing from the work of Bernstein (1990, cited in Breier 2003) on vertical and horizontal knowledge forms in order to develop insights into the complexities of different typologies, it is argued that academic and local forms of knowledge are not reducible to equal status (Breier 2003). In this perspective, academic knowledge is characterized by its vertical structure, that is, the extent to which it generalizes insights beyond local context. Based on this framework, Breier's recent research (ibid.) focuses on combining empirical observations with more sophisticated theoretical modelling of classroom interactions and dynamics between RPL students and teachers within curricula structures. This suggests that, despite the progressive intentions of RPL, access to the highly structured vertical structures and discourses of academic knowledge is not automatic for students whose socioeconomic backgrounds and workplace conditions do not provide opportunities for socialization into these specialized forms of literacy and knowledge.

Other studies show that operationally there are challenges and limits to the effectiveness of RPL as an institutional policy. After sustained efforts to institutionalize the practice at one university, the cost benefits in terms of enrolment remain lower than expected (Thaver et al. 2002). This is not to suggest that the practice will not work without improved approaches, only that initial anticipation of its effectiveness motivated by progressive intent must be moderated in the light of actual experience. In addition, Shalem and Steinberg (2000) identify the enormous load on the educator in facilitating classroom interactions and the interface of the different knowledge forms. The process, therefore, involves far more time and effort than anticipated.

Bernstein's framework remains controversial and contested. Nonetheless, these studies suggest that progressive political motivation to democratize access to academic knowledge, and the interface between the local and academic epistemological forms, must be approached with more circumspection. Democratizing agency and knowledge on the basis of simple equality denies epistemological differences embedded in unequal social relations and knowledge interfaces and, ironically, might disempower those whose positions one seeks to advance.

Conclusion

This chapter addressed the contemporary role of higher education by focusing on the recent higher education policy process in the context of the current political economy of South Africa. The purpose was to draw out possible lessons from the exploration of inter-related themes. One concern is the difficulty of pursuing concerns for equity, redress, and the redistribution of opportunity and wealth – the foundations of national development and transformation in developing countries – within the current hegemony of neo-liberalism in the global discourse. This is evident in the paradox that, despite heightened expectations to the contrary, socio-economic divisions, poverty, and social fragmentation have been exacerbated, rather than alleviated under the new progressive South African government. Another concern relates to how progressive policy intentions and plans do not always lead to desired outcomes. This is apparent in the fact that, despite a comprehensive higher education policy framework for transformation and several progressive policy initiatives, policy implementation and the achievement of policy goals have been delayed and diverted, and have led to unintended and potentially counterproductive consequences.

From this account, various constraints, challenges, and cautionary tales emerge. These can be summarized as follows:

- The dominant political economic context imposes overt and covert conditions on developing countries to adopt prevailing neo-liberal economic policies. These clearly constrain equity, redress, and redistribution – which are central concerns for developing countries.
- The tendency in the prevailing discourse about the role of higher education in the globalized knowledge society is to focus on one pole of the dual development path which developing countries must embrace, that is, engagement in the competitive global economy.
- Linked to this, the current predilection in higher education policy and practice is to focus on the economic purpose of higher education and to advocate the single model of the entrepreneurial university.
- Centralized interventionist policy-making has limited effectiveness. Correspondingly, there is a need to develop ongoing consultative networks between government and higher education stakeholders, without whose meaningful participation in the policy process, lack of compliance and resistance will arise, and this will impede successful implementation.
- To implement complex policy and planning frameworks, the required capacities must exist at the government and institutional levels.
- Assumptions about change and the limits to system-wide and institution-wide grand 'comprehensive' policy and planning may be dangerous.
- There is rapid and often uncritical uptake of global discourses within developing countries.
- A strong disciplinary Mode 1 foundation is important in the trend towards Mode 2 applications-driven knowledge production and acquisition.
- Caution must be exercised concerning the claims of the seamless interface between, and equality of academic and non-academic knowledge forms and agents in recognition of prior learning (RPL) programs.

These challenges and constraints to the effective contribution of higher education towards both global and redistributive development in the context of South Africa may provide instructive lessons for other developing and, indeed, developed countries.

NOTES

1 Exploring this issue requires a fresh look at the theory of the state in the contemporary global, in terms of which examining the case of South Africa as a developing country would be particularly informative. This forms the focus of a proposal for collaborative research in which the author is currently involved.

2 The Symposium Summary acknowledges this bias in stating that studies conducted by higher education institutions in industrialized countries on their impact on local and regional economies have for many years 'concentrated purely on the flow of financial resources in and out of institutions and are often developed with more practical public relations motives. There has been less emphasis on developing similar studies on the contribution of higher education institutions to the human, social and economic development in countries in transition or in the developing world' (University of Toronto 2002, p. 4).

3 The system currently comprises about 600,000 headcount enrolments in thirty-six institutions divided sharply along binary lines, with twenty-one universities and fifteen polytechnic-type 'technikons.' A revolutionary transformation of the student body occurred over the past decade, with the numbers of African students rising sharply, especially in historically advantaged institutions. However, these are generally concentrated at the lower qualifications levels and in the few fields traditionally associated with Africans' role in the divided labour market: the social sciences, the humanities, and public service, especially teacher training. The revolution in student enrolments is thus somewhat skewed (Cooper and Subotzky 2001). Other institutional changes are outlined below.

4 The advisory Council on Higher Education is currently preparing recommendations for developing and implementing a redress policy which has contemporary meaning as well as practical fiscal and operational foundations. In the light of the discursive shifts described here, the government's response to this will be interesting.

5 Ironically, the plan's interventionist nature is directed towards instituting the values of efficiency, competition, and institutional agency associated with the market paradigm. Government intervention is usually associated with countering market values and asserting the public good. Although equity and

redress are symbolically prominently figured in the plan, the effect of its over-all market-related orientation to efficiency is to relegate these concerns to the background.
6 Preliminary findings of research, in which the author is involved, into patterns of knowledge production in South Africa show that innovative organizational forms are evident in serving community development priorities as well as market-related needs, thereby generating income. In most cases, there is evidence of strong continuity between Mode 1 and Mode 2 activities – in both production and dissemination of knowledge. From the cases studied, a broader, richer typology than the dichotomous one advocated by Gibbons has emerged.

REFERENCES

Badat, S., F. Barron, G. Fisher, P. Pillay, and H. Wolpe. (1994). *Differentiation and Disadvantage: The Historically Black Universities in South Africa.* Research Report. Cape Town: Education Policy Unit, University of the Western Cape.
Barnes, T. (2003). Operationalizing Institutional Redress in South African Higher Education. Draft Research Report for the Council on Higher Education. Cape Town: Education Policy Unit, University of the Western Cape.
Bernstein, B. (1990). *The Structuring of Pedagogic Discourse,* vol. 4, *Class, Codes and Control.* London: Routledge and Kegan Paul.
Breier, M. (2003). The Recruitment and Recognition of Prior Informal Experience in the Pedagogy of Two University Courses in Labour Law. Doctoral dissertation, Department of Education, University of Cape Town.
Breier, M., and G. Subotzky. (2003). Organisational Learning and Non-learning: The Contested Dynamics of Higher Education Organisational Change. Paper presented at the annual conference of the South African Association for Research and Development of Higher Education, Stellenbosch, 25–7 June.
Carnoy, M. (2001). The Role of the State in the New Global Economy. In J. Muller, N. Cloete, and S. Badat. *Challenges of Globalisation: South African Debates with Manuel Castells.* Cape Town: Maskew Miller Longman.
Castells, M. (2001). Universities as Dynamic Systems of Contradictory Functions. In J. Muller, N. Cloete, and S. Badat, eds. *Challenges of Globalization: South African Debates with Manuel Castells.* Cape Town: Maskew Miller Longman, pp. 206–23.
Clark, B.R. (1998). *Creating Entrepreneurial Universities: Organizational Pathways of Transformation.* Oxford: Pergamon/Elsevier Science.
Cloete, N., and I. Bunting. (2000). *Higher Education Transformation: Assessing Performance in South Africa.* Pretoria: Centre for Higher Education Transformation.

Cloete, N., J. Muller, H.W. Makgoba, and D. Ekong. eds. (1997). *Knowledge, Identity, and Curriculum Transformation in Africa.* Cape Town: Maskew Miller Longman.

Cloete, N., R. Fehnel, T. Gibbon, P. Maassen, T. Moja, and H. Perold, eds. (2001). *Transformation in Higher Education: Global Pressures and Local Realities in South Africa.* Landsdowne: Juta.

Cooper, D., and G. Subotzky. (2001). *The Skewed Revolution: Trends in South African Higher Education, 1988–1993.* Cape Town: Education Policy Unit, University of the Western Cape.

Department of Education (DOE). (1997). *Education White Paper 3: A Programme for the Transformation of Higher Education.* General Notice 1196 of 1997. Pretoria.

– (2001). *National Plan for Higher Education.* Pretoria: author.

Ensor, P. (200) Curriculum. In N. Cloete, R. Fehnel, T. Gibbon, P. Massen, T. Moja, and H. Perold, eds. *Transformation in Higher Education: Global Pressures and Local Realities in South Africa.* Londsdown: Juta, pp. 270–95.

Etzkowitz, H., A. Webster, and P. Healey, eds. (1998). *Capitalizing Knowledge: New Intersections of Industry and Academia.* Albany, NY: State University of New York Press.

Gibbons, M. (1998). Higher Education Relevance in the 21st Century. Paper presented at the UNESCO World Conference on Higher Education. Washington, DC: World Bank.

– C. Limoges, H. Nowotny, S. Schwartzman, P. Scott, and M. Trow. (1994). *The New Production of Knowledge: The Dynamics of Science and Research in Contemporary Societies.* London: Sage.

Jansen, J.D. (2000). Mode 2 Knowledge and Institutional Life: Taking Gibbons on a Walk through a South African University. In A. Kraak, ed. *Changing Modes: New Knowledge Production and Its Implications for Higher Education in South Africa.* Pretoria: Human Sciences Research Council, pp. 156–81.

– (2001). Explaining Non-change in Education Reform after Apartheid: Political Symbolism and the Problem of Policy Implementation. In J.D. Jansen, and Y. Sayed eds. *Implementing Education Policies: The South African Experience.* Cape Town: University of Cape Town Press.

– and Y. Sayed, eds. (2001). *Implementing Education Policies: The South African experience.* Cape Town: University of Cape Town Press.

Jonathan, R. (2001). Higher Education Transformation and the Public Good. *Kagisano Higher Education Discussion Series* 1. Pretoria: Council on Higher Education, pp. 35–87.

Kassimir, R., Y. Lebeau, and Sall. (2002). The Public Roles of the University in Africa. Background paper for the Social Science Research Council / Association of African Universities research project on the public role of African universities. New York: Social Science Research Council and Accra: Association of African Universities.

Kraak, A. (2003). HRD and 'Joined-up' Policy. In *Human Resources Development Review 2003: Education, Employment and Skills in South Africa*. Cape Town: Human Sciences Research Council Press.

– (2001). Policy Ambiguity and Slippage: Higher Education and the New State, 1994–2000. Presentation in Symposium 11, Higher Education Policy in South Africa, at the international conference Globalization and Higher Education: Views from the South, Cape Town, 27–9 March.

– (2000). ed. *Changing Modes: New Knowledge Production and Its Implications for Higher Education in South Africa*. Pretoria: Human Sciences Research Council.

Motala, E., and J. Pampallis, eds. (2001). *Education and Equity: The Impact of State Policies on South African Education*. Sandown: Heinemann.

Muller, J. (2000). *Reclaiming Knowledge*. London: Routledge-Falmer.

– (2001). Response to A. Kraak, Ambiguity and Slippage: Higher Education under the New State, 1994–2000, and M. Young Contrasting National Approaches to the Role of Qualifications in the Promotion of Lifelong Learning. Papers presented in Symposium 11, Higher Education Policy in South Africa, at the international conference Globalization and Higher Education: Views from the South, Cape Town, 27–9 March.

– and G. Subotzky. (2001). What Knowledge Is Needed in the New Millennium? *Organization* 8(2), pp. 163–82.

National Commission on Higher Education (NCHE). (1996). *A Framework for Transformation*. Pretoria: author.

Osman, R., and J. Castle. (2002). Recognition of Prior Learning: A Soft Option in Higher Education in South Africa? *South African Journal of Higher Education* 16(2): 63–8.

Rhoades, G. (2000). Who's Doing It Right? Strategic Activity in Public Research Universities. *Review of Higher Education* 24(1): 41–66.

Rip, A. (2000). Fashions, Lock-ins and the Heterogeneity of Knowledge Production.' In M. Jacob and T. Hellstrom eds. *The Future of Knowledge Production in the Academy*. Buckingham: Society for Research in Higher Education (SRHE) and Open University Press.

Schwartzman, S. (2002). Public and Private Higher Education in Comparative Perspective. Keynote presentation to the HSRC colloquium Understanding Private Higher Education in South Africa, Johannesburg, 9–10 April.

Scott, P. (1997). Changes in Knowledge Production and Dissemination in the Context of Global competititon. In N. Cloete et al., eds. *Knowledge, Identity and Curriculum Transformation*. Cape Town: Maskew Miller Longman.

Shalem, Y., and C. Steinberg. (2000). Invisible Criteria in Assessment of Prior Learning: A Cat and Mouse Chase. Paper presented at Kenton Education Association conference, Port Elizabeth, 26–7 Oct.

Singh, M. (2001). Re-inserting the 'Public Good' into Higher Education Transformation. *Kagisano Higher Education Discussion Series* 1. Pretoria: Council on Higher Education, pp. 7–21.

South African Universities' Vice-Chancellors' Association (SAUVCA). (2002). *A Vision for South African higher Education: Transformation, Restructuring and Policy Integration*. Pretoria: author.

Subotzky, G. (1999). Alternatives to the Entrepreneurial University: New Modes of Knowledge Production in Community Service Programs. *Higher Education* 38(4): 401–40.

– (2001). Background Report and Analysis for the Annual Report of the Council on Higher Education. Cape Town: Education Policy Unit, University of the Western Cape.

– (2002). The Reconfiguration of South African Higher Education: Some Considerations. *Wits Quarterly Review of Education and Training in South Africa* 9(2): 9–14.

– (2003). Symbolism and Substance: Towards an Understanding Change and Continuities in South African Higher Education. In H. Eggins, ed. *Globalisation and Reform in Higher Education*. London: Open University Press and the Society for Research in Higher Education.

Terreblanche, S. (2003). *A History of Inequality in South Africa 1652–2002*. Scottsville: University of Natal Press.

Thaver, B., M. Breier, and D. Naidoo. (2002). A Review of the Implementation of Recognition of Prior Learning at the University of the Western Cape, 2001. Draft Research Report. Cape Town: Education Policy Unit, University of the Western Cape.

University of Toronto, International Programs Development Office. (2002). Symposium Summary: Creating Knowledge, Strengthening Nations: The changing role of higher education. Toronto: author.

CHAPTER 9

The Role of Technical Education in Enabling the Creation of a Knowledge Economy and Society: The Indian Experience

Ramamurthy Natarajan

Education in general, and professional and technical education in particular, has long been considered an important prerequisite for industrial, economic, and social development. The importance of education has been heightened with the advent of the present information age. In recognition of the importance of education to their national economies, countries around the world have been putting together policies to link education with national economic development.

This chapter describes the relevant features of the Indian experience in regard to developing and harnessing technical education for national economic development. The systems of higher education and technical education in India are among the largest in the world. Moreover, recently there has been a substantial increase in the number of institutions, as well as in the intake capacity in these systems. Especially in the knowledge-based information technology (IT) sector, both enrolments and economic activity have expanded considerably.

The All India Council for Technical Education (AICTE) has statutory authority for promoting and regulating technical education in India. It plays an important role in leading technological and related economic development. Globalization and internationalization policies and initiatives worldwide have an impact on the situation in India, as elsewhere, and efforts are under way to respond to them.

Recently the prime minister of India released a document entitled *A National Vision for a Knowledge Economy and Society.* Its focus is knowledge-related policies and activities, and these have been further elaborated by the planning commission (Government of India 2001). The widening digital divide is a matter of serious concern, and certainly has considerable economic, social and political implications for a large democracy like India.

The emerging challenges, both in higher education generally, and particularly in technical education, in India demand prompt and appropriate responses. Both the challenges and the responses to them will be examined in this chapter.

Universities in India

In the majority of universities in India departments impart education at the postgraduate level and undertake research. Affiliated with them are a large number of colleges offering undergraduate education. Some of the universities have over 100 affiliated colleges and over 100,000 students enrolled. A second type of university is that of the 'unitary' universities (e.g., Aligarh, Annamalai, Banaras, Baroda, Jadavpur, and Lucknow); they do not have affiliated colleges. A new category is the technological or technical university, whose only affiliates are engineering institutions. Some other institutions of higher education have been recognized by the central government as 'deemed-to-be universities'; their aim is to strengthen their activities in specialized fields, rather than to grow into a multifaculty university of the general type. According to the Constitution of India, which came into force in 1951, higher education is as much a responsibility of the central government as of the states.

The National System of Technical Education

The system of formal technical education in India is one of the largest in the world. The numbers of the various types of institutions that comprise the system, as well as their permitted intake capacities, are shown in Table 9.1. The table shows that the intake in the diploma-level polytechnics is substantially below the corresponding figure at the degree-level engineering colleges. The intake capacity in postgraduate programs is less than 10 per cent of that in the undergraduate programs.

The technical education system comprises a wide range of educational and training programs: certificate programs in the industrial training institutes (ITIs), diploma programs in the polytechnics; and degree, postgraduate degree, and doctoral degree programs in the the engineering colleges and higher technological institutions (HTIs), as well as the universities. Some of the HTIs have been granted autonomous status and deemed-to-be university status. As already noted, recently several states have established technological and/or technical universities,

Table 9.1 Technical education institutions in India, by type, number, and permitted intake, in 2002

Type of technical institutions	Number of institutions	Intake
Engineering colleges (degree)	1,195	348,250
Polytechnics (diploma)	1,203	233,296
PGDBM/MBA[a] institutions	872	69,540
MCA[b] institutions	989	49,576
Pharmacy institutions (degree)	274	13,941
Pharmacy institutions (diploma)	354	18,942
Architecture institutions (degree)	107	3,972
Hotel management institutions (degree)	40	2,100
Hotel management institutions (diploma)	74	4,455
Total	5,108	774,072

Source: All India Council for Technical Education (2002).
[a] MBA = Master of Business Administration; PGDBM = Postgraduate Diploma in Business Management
[b] MCA = Master of Computer Applications

whose affiliates are engineering institutions only; this is in contrast to other universities whose affiliates are arts, science, and engineering institutions. Most of the Regional Engineering Colleges, which were under the dual control of the central as well as the state governments, have been granted deemed-to-be university status and are now under the sole control of the central government. They have been renamed National Institutes of Technology. The Indian Institutes of Technology (IITs) are higher technological institutions, created by acts of the Parliament of India. They are research-intensive institutions, whose alumni have distinguished themselves worldwide.

Some Noteworthy Features of the National Technical Education System

Through analysis of the strengths, weaknesses, opportunities, and threats (SWOT) of and to technical education in India, the author has identified the following distinctive characteristics of the system (see Table 9.2).

• A substantial proportion of school-leavers aspire to enrol in professional programs, particularly technical education. This contrasts with the situation in several other countries, such as Germany, the United Kingdom, and Australia which hold education fairs in India to recruit Indian students.

Table 9.2 A SWOT[a] analysis of India's technology education system

Strengths

- Aspirations and enthusiam of youth to pursue technical education
- Private sector initiatives complementing government initiatives
- Increasing interest of industry associations (such as CII, FICCI, ASSOCHAM) and of professional societies to partner and collaborate with academic institutions
- NBA accreditation initiatives promoting quality improvement in the technical education sector
- World Bank funding for TEQIP to upgrade technical education in India
- QIP helped to upgrade the qualifications of faculty in technical institutions, also including non-engineering disciplines
- MODROBS, TAPTEC, and R&D schemes of AICTE,[b] as well as of MHRD, helped modernize the infrastructure, remove obsolescence, and promote work in key areas of endeavour

Opportunities

- Possibly set up quality Indian institutions abroad, as off-shore campuses
- More IT tools becoming available for technology-enhanced learning, thus widening the reach of technical education
- More distance education possibilities, particularly for continuing education
- Networking of technical institutions, at different levels, for mutual benefit, sharing of resources, and jointly undertaking major projects
- Networking of technical institutions with R&D laboratories and industry
- Substantial support coming from many alumni to their alma maters, particularly the Indian institutes of technology

Weaknesses

- Offering technical education perceived as a business opportunity by some
- Shortage of qualified and competent faculty, especially in (hi-tech) ICT areas
- Too few islands of excellence
- Too few graduating engineers interested in teaching careers
- Too little interest in pursuing research-based degrees
- Too few PhD engineers for faculty positions
- Inadequate industry-institute interaction in several institutions
- Industry-perceived mismatch between education and training (knowledge and skills) of graduates and job requirements
- Inadequate assessment and planning of human resources needs
- 'Affiliating system' of India's universities hinders timely curriculum updating and introduction of innovative reforms
- IT industry boom responsible for increased admission capacity in this area but at the expense of other disciplines
- Undergraduate enrolments on the rise but no corresponding growth at the postgraduate level

Threats

- In the emerging GATS scenario, urgent need to address quality concerns
- Competition from international players
- Non-uniform distribution of technical institutions in India, with regional imbalances and interstate migration of students
- Technical institutions in rural and industrially backward areas not as popular with students, thus unfilled capacity in these institutions

Table 9.2 (*Concluded*)

• Role of technology and technology education for national development and prosperity now widely acknowledged	• Tendency of students to prefer IT-related courses, and shun other disciplines • Tendency of research scholars to prefer computer-based research over experimental research • Ratio of diploma to degree programs declining (unlike in some other countries) • Science base in India weakening, will have an adverse impact on country's capacity for technology development

[a] SWOT = strengths, weaknesses, opportunities, and threats
[b] AICTE = All India Council for Technical Education; ASSOCHAM = Association of Chambers of Commerce; CII = Confederation of Indian Industry; FICCI = Federation of Indian Chambers of Commerce and Industry; GATS = General Agreement on Trade in Services; ICT = information and communication technology; MHRD = Ministry of Human Resources Development; MODROBS = Modernization and Removal of Obsolescence Scheme; NBA = National Board of Accreditation; QIP = Quality Improvement Program; R&D = research and development; TAPTEC = Thrust Area Programs in Technical Education; TEQIP = Technical Education Quality Improvement Program

- Most of the recent expansion in the technical education system has occurred in the private sector.
- There is a severe shortage of qualified and competent faculty for technical education.
- Engineering graduates are not attracted to either research and development (R&D) or teaching careers.
- The recent boom in the information technology (IT) sector has caused a distortion in intake capacity and in recruitment; for example, IT companies are ready to recruit graduates from any discipline.
- The IT tools provide a tremendous opportunity both for enhancing the effectiveness of the teaching and learning process and for increasing the reach of education.

Role of the All India Council for Technical Education in the National Technical Education System

The All India Council for Technical Education (AICTE) was set up as an advisory body in November 1945 by the Government of India on the recommendation of its Central Advisory Board of Education (CABE). The general purpose of the AICTE was to stimulate, coordinate, and control the provision of facilities for technical education as needed for industrial development in the postwar period.

The AICTE was given statutory authority through Act Number 52 of 1987, passed by both houses of the Indian Parliament. The act gave the AICTE a three-pronged mandate: the proper planning and coordinated development of technical education throughout India; the promotion of qualitative improvements of such education in relation to planned quantitative growth; and the regulation and proper maintenance of norms and standards in India's system of technical education.

The act also defined the scope of technical education to comprise programs of education, research, and training in engineering, technology, architecture, town planning, management, pharmacy, and applied arts and crafts.

The powers and functions of the AICTE were described in twenty-one sections of the act. These included technical manpower assessment; coordinated development of technical education in the country at all levels; allocation and disbursement of grants to technical institutions; overall improvement of educational processes and promotion of R&D and innovation; formulation of schemes for promoting technical education for women, the handicapped, and the weaker sections of society; promotion of an effective link between the technical education system and other relevant systems; evolution of suitable systems of performance appraisal for technical institutions; formulation of schemes for initial and in-service training of teachers; formulation of norms and standards; fixing of norms and guidelines for tuition and other fees; granting of approval for new technical institutions, and for the introduction of new courses or programs, in consultation with the agencies concerned; advice to the central government regarding grants of charters to professional bodies; formulating norms for granting autonomy to technical institutions; taking steps to prevent commercialization of technical education; formulating guidelines for admission of students to technical institutions; inspecting technical institutions; taking steps to ensure compliance with the directions of the council; giving advice to the University Grants Commission (UGC) for declaring technical institutions as deemed-to-be universities; and establishing a National Board of Accreditation.

The AICTE, after several workshops involving the participation of all its officers, announced the following statement of its vision: 'to be a world-class organization leading technological and socio-economic development of the country by enhancing the global competitiveness of technical manpower and by ensuring high quality technical education to all sections of the society.' The Council has also articulated four mission statements.

The Council has fifty-one members, while its executive committee has twenty-one and meets more frequently. The AICTE has nine statutory boards of studies responsible for the various levels and disciplines in technical education; in addition, five advisory boards have been constituted.

National Education Policies

Since India's independence in 1947, several working groups, commissions, and documents have recognized that the achievement of economic and social development can be facilitated and expedited through proper education, and that the development of human resources has a multiplier effect on the utilization of all other resources. *The Report of the Education Commission* (1964–6) referred to education as the only instrument of peaceful social change.

The first National Policy on Education was formulated in 1968, with the principal aim of creating an 'ethos that would produce young men and women of character and ability, committed to national service and development.' In August 1985, the Ministry of Education prepared a document entitled *Challenge of Education – A Policy Perspective*, which was widely circulated and discussed in several forums throughout India. It resulted ultimately in the formulation of the 1986 National Policy on Education (NPE-1986).

As far as technical education is concerned, the 1968 policy stressed its importance, but dealt with it only briefly. The 1986 document, while recognizing the significant contributions made by technical education to India's economic development, identified several issues requiring immediate attention. These were: obsolescence of machinery and equipment, updating and upgrading of engineering curricula, technician education, the inability to attract good teachers (there was 20 to 30 per cent shortfall, on average), industry-institution interaction, lack of a work ethos in the majority of institutions, industrial investment in R&D, quality assurance in technical education, and the complementary role of management education. The NPE-1986 brought technical and management education in India together for the first time. To ensure efficient implementation of plans enunciated in the national policy, the policy statement was followed up by a 'programme of action,' involving the appointment of twenty-three task forces.

A National Vision for a Knowledge Economy and Society

Prime Minister Vajpayee addressed the Association of Chambers of Commerce (ASSOCHAM) 1999 summit on 'India in the Knowledge Millennium' presenting a vision of India as a 'knowledge superpower' (Vajpayee 1999). His five-point agenda included (1) leveraging existing competencies in IT, telecommunications, biotechnology, drug design, financial services, and enterprisewide management; (2) global networking; (3) gearing education to the creation of a learning society; (4) enhanced interaction among government, industry, and academe in regard to policy and implementation; and (5) strategic alliances among various sectors based upon their capabilities and opportunities.

In moving towards this vision, some specific issues concerning feasibility need to be addressed. It must be determined what precisely India's strengths are and what are the problems that must be overcome if it is to become a knowledge superpower. A feasible timetable should be established to chart progress towards this objective. The key actions that must be taken to achieve this goal need to be identified.

There are some prerequisites that are essential for the realization of this vision. These include a high-quality telecommunications infrastructure; widespread access to and skills in the use of personal computers; extensive education and training facilities; expanded literacy, including basic, functional, scientific, technological, and computer literacy; a reliable and stable supply of electrical power; a government policy regime supportive of these goals; and empowerment of the people, enabling them to realize their potential.

The Planning Commission appointed a task force to develop a strategy for achieving this vision. In 2001, the task force came out with its report entitled *India as Knowledge Superpower: Strategy for Transformation* (Government of India 2001). Among other things, this document emphasized that 'only those nations will survive and succeed, which will build themselves by understanding the dynamics of knowledge and create true knowledge societies' (ibid., 1). The distinct characteristics of a knowledge society are summarized in the report as follows. A knowledge society:

- Uses knowledge through all its constituents and endeavours to empower and enrich its people, creating economic wealth and social good for all;
- Uses knowledge as a powerful tool to drive societal transformation;

- Is committed to innovation;
- Has the capacity to generate, absorb, disseminate, and protect knowledge;
- Enlightens its people so that they may take an integrated view of life to be a fusion of mind, body, and spirit.

In a recent address to the Indian Science Congress, Dr Murli Manohar Joshi, union minister for human resource development and science and technology, elaborated on this vision of society. He paid particular attention to the transformative capabilities of such a society in saying: 'Science and technology have to be rooted in a social, cultural and ethical context, and the question of "Science for whom?" has to be constantly asked. In the national context, science and technology have to frontally address the basic issues of poverty, employment generation, health, environment, education, equity and empowerment at the level of both policy and action, precept and practice. Science and technology must provide hope and opportunities for our youth' (Joshi 2002).

Ensuring Quality Technical Education

For the important role that technical education is to play in India's national economic and social development, technical education must be delivered at a high level of quality. Under the leadership of AICTE, there has been ongoing debate at the national level on how to assess quality in technical education. A major issue continues to be whether academic quality can be measured in quantitative terms. On one side are those who hold the position that quality is a meaningful construct only to the extent that it can be quantified. Those on the other side of this debate hold that quality is important but inherently problematic to measure.

Recognizing validity in both positions, AICTE has set up a National Board of Accreditation. This board defines criteria for assessment of the quality of technical institutions in India that offer post-secondary technical education, at both the undergraduate and postgraduate levels. The accreditation process includes self-assessment by the institution, an assessment based on a site visit by an expert committee, and a subsequent evaluation by a sectoral committee and the board. The requirement for accreditation has been instrumental in making almost all the institutions strive to put in place institutional mechanisms for addressing quality issues.

Challenges in Technical Education – and Responses

Over the past decade or so, there have been a number of changes in the environment of technical education. Some of these are common to the entire realm of higher education of which technical education is but a part. Many of the broader changes relate to globalization and technological change. For example, globalization has increased demands for various types of technical education to enable individuals, firms, and regions to compete effectively in the global economy. The ensuring increase in demand for technical education has put extreme pressure on existing capacity. Moreover, this pressure is exacerbated by further technological changes which threaten to make equipment, as well as the knowledge and skills of the teaching staff, obsolete. Privatization has significantly altered the organization of technical education. Finally, increased pressure for accountability has made quality assurance a priority.

New processes for the development, utilization, and expansion of technical and scientific knowledge have raised questions such as whether and to what extent the qualifications, education, training, and employment of engineers need to be adapted in addressing the changed conditions in which engineers will work. New challenges for the education of engineers and for the engineering professions have arisen from organizational change and the internationalization of business.

Rapid change in information and communications technology (ICT) poses challenging considerations to all educators, especially to engineering educators, worldwide. Traditional and well-entrenched paradigms and practices of education are being thoroughly questioned. Traditionally, access to education is regulated by the requirement that students possess some prerequisite qualifications and (in India) pass entrance examinations. In the emerging information age or knowledge economy, however, it will become impossible to control access to and delivery of educational services, in the ways in which this was done in the past. Information sources are now ubiquitous, and information flows freely to students (and anybody else) wherever they are. Ensuring the quality and credibility of all providers of educational services will be more difficult.

Initiatives such as distance learning, and open and virtual universities, create exciting and innovative opportunities for delivering education without the constraints of time and distance, but they also raise serious questions. What is to become of time-honoured practices and traditions, such as entry-level qualifications, entrance examinations, fixed timetables, 'live' courses, and scheduled examinations? In this context, the need for sophisticated assessment techniques to measure and certify learning and competence will grow. The educational enterprise may need to be oganized around student outcomes, as creative new ways are found to evaluate student achievement. Focus will no doubt shift from course providers, and number of contact hours and credits, to assessment of the extent to which learning has truly occurred.

Summary of the Current Situation

Over the past fifty years, India has created a system of technical education that has considerable size and diversity. Accreditation is a priority. India's National Board of Accreditation provides the criteria and processes for quality assurance and serves to maintain and promote education in India to internationally recognized standards of quality. The board was appointed by the All India Council for Technical Education (AICTE). The AICTE has been given the mandate and authority to maintain and regulate standards, promote quality, and provide direction for planned and coordinated development of technical education throughout India.

Under the auspices of the AICTE, and thorough the actions of various branches of government, India has been responding to the challenges confronting technical education. In January 2002, the Ministry of Human Resource Development (MHRD) announced the establishment of the Technology Education Mission to focus on quantitative expansion of high-quality technical and management education. In another development, 'deemed-to-be university' status has been conferred on the Regional Engineering Colleges, and they have been renamed National Institutes of Technology (NITs) with redefined roles and goals. The MHRD introduced a television channel for technology so that high-quality lectures can be disseminated nationwide. The National Project on Technology-Enhanced Learning (NPTEL) of the Indian Institutes of Technology is another significant initiative in technical education. NPTEL is developing Web-compatible instructional materials, as well as new courses and programs. India has received a loan from the International Bank for Reconstruction and Development (World Bank) for its Technical Education Quality Improvement Project (TEQIP). The TEQIP is upgrading a relatively large number of institutions offering degree-level technical education. A system of registering and licensing engineers is being introduced. These are among the most visible exam-

ples of the many ways in which technical education in India is being rein-
vented in order to address the needs of the worldwide knowledge society
of the early twenty-first century.

REFERENCES

All India Council for Technical Education. (2002). Annual Report. Delhi:
    author.
Government of India. (2001). *India as Knowledge Superpower: Strategy for Transfor-
    mation.* New Delhi: Planning Commission, Task Force Report.
Joshi, Hon. Murli Manohar. (2002). Address delivered on the occasion of the
    89th Indian Science Congress, Lucknow, 3–7 Jan.
Vajpayee, Hon. Atal Behari. (1999). The prime minister's address at the Associa-
    tion of Chambers of Commerce (ASSOCHAM) summit on 'India in the
    Knowledge Millennium.' New Delhi, 18 Dec.

CHAPTER 10

The Role of Universities in Regional Development and Cluster Formation

David A. Wolfe

Introduction

As the economies of the industrial countries rapidly become more knowledge-based, universities are seen as holding the key to regional economic development and cluster formation. The Organisation for Economic Cooperation and Development defines the knowledge-based economy as one in which the production, use, and distribution of knowledge and information are critical to the process of economic growth (OECD 1996). Not surprisingly, the role of the university is central to the emerging knowledge-based economy. Indeed a recent survey in *The Economist* suggests the conception of the knowledge-based economy 'portray(s) the university not just as a creator of knowledge, a trainer of young minds and a transmitter of culture, but also as a major agent of economic growth: the knowledge factory, as it were, at the centre of the knowledge economy' (David 1997, 54).

Closely related to this is the idea that universities can also jump-start the emergence of dynamic regional clusters of firms and thus act as crucial contributors to regional economic development. The well-documented cases of a few highly successful examples, particularly the central role attributed to Stanford University in the growth of Silicon Valley (Gibbons 2000), or MIT in the development of Route 128, have contributed to the widely held view that universities can act as 'engines of innovation' generating new ideas to spur the creation of commercial products, and, indirectly, providing the spark for regional industrial clusters. This overly mechanistic view of the process by which basic scientific research is transformed into economically valuable products places an unacceptable burden on the role that universities are expected to play. At the same time, this piece of conventional wisdom fails to explain the significant number of cases where leading research institutions, such as Carnegie Mellon (Florida 1999) or Johns Hopkins (Feldman and Desrochers 2003), have failed to generate the same kind of spin-offs and regional benefits as those that occurred in Silicon Valley. Clearly these counter-factual cases suggest the need for a more nuanced and contextualized understanding of the actual role that universities play in regional economic development and cluster formation.

The shift to a more knowledge-based economy embodies a number of changes in both the production and application of new scientific knowledge that have critical implications for the processes of knowledge transfer and regional economic development. One of the most significant of these changes involves the relation between the codified and tacit dimensions of knowledge. The dramatic expansion of the higher education sector and the increased funding for research that has, in part, fuelled its growth has generated substantial increases in scientific and research output which largely takes the form of codified knowledge, transmitted relatively easily between researchers through published scientific papers and formal presentations. But as the stock of scientific knowledge grows and becomes more widely accessible through electronic and other means, the relative economic value of that knowledge is diminished by its sheer abundance. Often access to the key elements of the knowledge base depends upon the second or tacit dimension. Following the work of Michael Polanyi (1962), tacit knowledge refers to knowledge or insights which individuals acquire while pursuing scientific work that is ill-defined or uncodified and that they themselves cannot explain fully. It is highly subjective and often varies from person to person. Furthermore, individuals or groups working together for the same firm or organization often develop a common base of tacit knowledge in the course of their research and production activities (Nelson and Winter 1982, 76–82; Dosi 1988, 1126). The tacit dimension of knowledge is particularly significant for regions and communities, for it is the kind of knowledge that tends to be locally embedded. In a knowledge-based economy, spatial proximity is thus a critical factor for accessing this kind of knowledge and exploiting its commercial potential.

The second change concerns the centrality of learning for the innovative process. Lundvall, among others, argues that the knowledge frontier is moving so rapidly that access to, or control over, knowledge assets affords merely a fleeting competitive advantage. It may be more appropriate to describe the emerging paradigm as that of a 'learning economy,' rather than a 'knowledge-based' one. Recent work indicates that innovation is a *social process* triggered by consumers (or users) who engage in a mutually beneficial dialogue and interaction with producers. In this way, users and producers actively *learn* from each other, by 'learning-through-interacting' (Lundvall 1992). It involves a capacity for localized learning within firms, between firms, and between firms and the supporting institutions. Learning in this sense refers to the building of new competencies and the acquisition of new skills, not just gaining access to information or codified scientific knowledge. In tandem with this development, forms of knowledge that cannot be codified and transmitted electronically (tacit knowledge) increase in value, as does the ability to acquire and assess both codified and tacit forms of knowledge, in other words, the capacity for learning (Maskell and Malmberg 1999). The regional level is important for this form of learning because firms within a local region often share a common culture that facilitates learning among them and is supported by a common set of regional institutions.

The Role of Universities in the Knowledge-Based Economy

Despite the growing consensus that the industrial economies are becoming more 'knowledge-based,' there remains considerable controversy over the role that universities should be expected to play. Consistent with the view of universities as 'knowledge factories' for the new economy, many policy-makers view universities as largely untapped reservoirs of potentially commercializable knowledge waiting to be taken up by firms and applied. Policy-makers hope that once this knowledge is harnessed, it will fuel innovation within the firm, thereby increasing the firm's productivity, stimulate the emergence of regional industrial clusters, and, indirectly, contribute to national economic growth. Yet the task of transferring knowledge from universities to industries has proven far more complex than this perspective assumes.

In reality, universities fulfil at least two essential roles in the knowledge-based economy – the performance of research and the training of highly qualified personnel. They thus act both as a primary source of 'knowledge workers,' as well as the key factor of production – knowledge itself. However, a number of changes in other elements of the innovation system have placed new demands and stress on the way in which the university performs these roles. The 'social contract' for science, forged in the aftermath of the Second World War, saw society willing to fund massive investments in basic research in the expectation of long-term economic benefits, while leaving the principal research institutions, the universities, autonomous in the conduct of that research. The social contract for science in postwar society implied a high degree of autonomy for the realm of science, vigorously reinforced by the 'boundary work' of the scientific community itself; it afforded 'expert' status to the role of scientists in the exercise of judgment about most matters relating to the conduct of scientific investigations and the application of the resulting knowledge; and it privileged the role of the universities and other public research organizations as the principal site for the conduct of scientific research, although these arrangements exhibited considerable variation across national innovation systems (Martin 2003).

Underlying this view of the social contract for science was the 'linear model' of innovation that supported the development of postwar science policy in the United States. The model defined the relationship between basic research and more applied forms of technology development as a linear one, involving the progression through a sequence of steps leading eventually to product development – the final stage involving the systematic adoption of research findings into useful materials, devices, systems, methods, and processes. The entire sequence was referred to as the process of technology transfer in an early report of the National Science Foundation. In the idealized linear model, the innovation process commences with basic research conducted without any thought of potential application that leads to discoveries. These discoveries, in turn, open up the possibility of potential applications that are pursued, usually by firms, through applied research, development, design, production, and marketing. The latter stages in this sequence lead to the successful commercialization of the resulting products and processes (Brooks 1996, 21; Stokes 1997, 10–11).

But the essential elements of the social contract for science have been subject to increasing strain in the past two decades as the linear model of innovation has been open to question. These developments are a consequence of major shifts in the relationship between the university and other constituent parts of the national innovation system. The shift results from the modification of the lines demarcating the university from other institutions in society, reflecting the massification and democratization of the post-secondary education system; a questioning of the role of universities and their individual disciplines as the sole, or even primary source, of scientific expertise; the growing internationalization of scientific communities facilitated by the adoption of information and communication technologies; a greater involvement of industry with university research; an increase in interdisciplinary research and a shift in the emphasis of government funding from basic to more applied research; and finally, a greater expectation that university-based research should lead directly to commercializable results (Wolfe 2003).

Increased demands on universities to support the innovation process are partly a consequence of changes in the nature of innovation patterns in the business sector that have limited the ability of private firms to support basic research. Under competitive pressure to introduce new products, processes, and services more quickly, many large corporations have restructured their R&D operations to link research programs more tightly with product development processes. Broader-based inquiries into fundamental science have consequently been scaled back in many firms. At the same time, the globalization of R&D and more widespread sharing of knowledge among researchers and businesses in different countries do not appear to have diminished the importance of a strong domestic knowledge base, or the role of universities/government in helping create it.

Universities have come under increasing pressure in recent years to expand their traditionally dominant role in the conduct of basic research and to supplement their program with more applied research activities, frequently in the form of university-industry partnerships. The changes impacting on the university system are characterized by three trends: (1) the linking of government funding for academic research and economic policy; (2) the development of more long-term relationships between firms and academic researchers; and (3) the increasing direct participation of universities in commercializing research (Etkowitz and Webster 1998). Universities are now expected to generate more applied knowledge of greater relevance to industry, to disseminate knowledge, and to provide technical support to industry. This shift reflects the change in the nature of business R&D described above, but it is also the result of a parallel expectation on the part of government that their investments in basic research should produce a higher economic return. It is reinforced by the political expectation that research funding be tied to broader public policy objectives about promoting national innovative capacity, greater competitiveness and, increasingly, local and regional economic development.

While the shift in policy perspective was partly stimulated by a questioning of the assumptions underlying the linear model, it has yet to be replaced with a more complex and realistic appreciation of the way in which knowledge flows between universities and industry. Conventional approaches to the issue of knowledge flows frequently treat knowledge itself as a universally available commodity, virtually as a free public good, and knowledge transfer as a commercial and legal transaction between clearly defined agents. This view simplifies the complex nature of scientific knowledge and the linkages and processes that facilitate knowledge flows across institutional boundaries and enable firms to absorb and employ that knowledge. Evidence from a growing number of sources, including studies of the economics of innovation and of regional innovation systems, suggests that successful knowledge transfer depends on the type of knowledge involved, and how it is employed. While linkages between universities and industry have proliferated in the past decade and a half, our understanding of the process by which knowledge is transferred from one to the other has not kept pace. As Fumio Kodama and Lewis Branscomb argue,

> disappointment awaits those who expect quick results from university-based high-technology strategies for industrial renewal. First-rank research universities can and most often do make a large and positive contribution to economic performance, regionally and nationally. But to understand the effects we should not focus on the style and content of the transactions with firms but rather look at the university as a pivotal part of a network of people and institutions who possess high skills, imagination, the incentive to take risks, the ability to form other networks to accomplish their dreams. (1999, 16)

The Relationship between Research and Innovation

The preceding discussion suggests that the relationship between publicly funded research and the innovation process is far more complex than indicated by many recent public policy discussions of the role of the university in the commercialization of scientific research. A more accurate understanding of this role requires a sophisticated framework for analysing the character of the institutional and interpersonal linkages between universities and firms and how those linkages contribute to knowledge transfers between the two. An alternative approach to assessing the economic benefits that flow from knowledge transfer focuses on the properties of knowledge not easily captured by the informational view associated with early work on the economics of basic research and the linear model. Keith Pavitt stresses that scientific and technological knowledge often remains tacit, that is, person-embodied in the knowledge, skills, and practices of the researcher (Pavitt 1991). Other scholars in the tradition of evolutionary economics describe knowledge as dynamic and often unarticulated, and claim that firms must invest substantial resources to capture and employ it. This view shifts attention from the applicability of knowledge to the processes that enable a firm to successfully absorb and apply that knowledge.

Pavitt argues that inherent in the traditional rationale for public support of basic research is the danger of confusing the notion of science as a public good (i.e., codified, published, easily reproducible) with science as a free good (i.e., costless to apply as technology). He builds on Nathan Rosenberg's (1990) claim that to assimilate and benefit from external research, firms have to develop a considerable capacity for research themselves. Pavitt maintains that knowledge transfers are mainly person-embodied and that policies that attempt to direct basic research towards specific goals or targets ignore the considerable indirect benefits across a broad range of scientific fields that result from training and unplanned discoveries. This introduces the notion of knowledge as the capacity to acquire and apply research results, rather than as an end in itself. In this perspective, knowledge is the ability to put information to productive use. It provides the basis for understanding new ideas and discoveries and places them in a context that enables more rapid application. The development of such internalized or 'personal knowledge' (Polanyi 1962) requires an extensive learning process. It is based on skills accumulated through experience and expertise. It also emphasizes the learning properties of individuals and organizations. Of crucial importance are the role of skills, the networks of researchers, and the development of new capabilities on the part of actors and institutions in the innovation system.

Analysing this process from the perspective of the firm, Cohen and Levinthal (1990) argue that the process of knowledge transfer from universities and research institutes is strongly conditioned by the capabilities of firms. Firms need to build an internal knowledge base and research capacity to effectively capture and deploy knowledge acquired from external sources. The ability to exploit external knowledge is a critical component of a firm's innovative capabilities. The ability to evaluate and utilize outside knowledge is largely a function of the level of prior, related knowledge within the firm. This prior knowledge includes basic skills or even a shared language, but may also include knowledge of the most recent scientific or technological developments in a given field.

These abilities collectively constitute a firm's 'absorptive capacity.' The overlap between the firm's knowledge base and external research allows the firm to recognize potentially useful outside knowledge and use it to reconfigure and augment its existing knowledge base. Research shows that firms which conduct their own R&D are better able to use externally available information. This implies that absorptive capacity may be created as a by-product of the firm's own R&D investment. A key implication of this argument is that firms require a strong contingent of highly qualified research scientists and engineers as a prerequisite to the ability to absorb and assess scientific results, most frequently recruited from institutions of higher education. The members of this scientific and engineering labour force bring with them not only the knowledge base and research skills acquired in their university training, but often, more importantly, a network of academic contacts acquired during their university training. This underlines Pavitt's point that the most important source of knowledge transfer is person-embodied.

Knowledge Transfer from Universities

One of the difficulties with understanding the nature of the relationship between university-performed basic research and firm-based innovation is uncertainty about how firms in different industry sectors deploy scientific knowledge in the innovation process. One study that cast light on this matter was the Yale survey conducted by Richard Nelson and several colleagues in the early 1980s. The survey queried 650 R&D managers in U.S. firms, representing 130 lines of business. It distinguished between two roles that science plays in supporting innovation: one as an expanding pool of theory and problem-solving techniques deployed in industrial R&D, but not necessarily new science; the other as a direct source of new technological possibilities pointing the way towards new solutions to old problems. Overall, university-based research in a field was reported by the R&D managers as much less important to recent technical advance in industry than was the overall body of scientific knowledge in the field. In most fields, academic research does not provide pilot inventions, but fosters the broad understandings and techniques that industry can later employ for a variety of different purposes. Industrial R&D managers also reported that they value the scientific background and training of their R&D staff more highly than the current research activities of university-based researchers (Klevorick, Levin, Nelson et al. 1995). Nelson expands on the reason why research activity with a direct impact on industrial innovation is limited in research organizations that specialize in the conduct of R&D, such as university research laboratories:

> To do effective industrial R&D generally requires knowledge about the technology of an industry that is not taught in school. It also often requires a certain amount of close and not preprogrammable interaction between the lab and client firm or firms, and complementary work and investment on their part ... Thus effective lab work requires not only industry-specific, but firm-specific, knowledge and sensitivity of the lab to the needs of its client firm. (Nelson 1996, 62)

The findings of the original Yale survey are broadly supported by a 1994 survey of industrial R&D managers conducted at Carnegie Mellon University. The results of the Carnegie Mellon Survey (CMS) reinforce the notion that industrial firms draw upon feedback from their own customers and manufacturing operations as the primary source of ideas for new product and process innovations. Public research is significant in addressing previously identified needs or problems, rather than suggesting new lines of innovative activities, with the exception of a few select industries, such as pharmaceuticals, that draw directly upon the public research base. However a significant proportion, almost a third, of industrial R&D projects do make use of public research findings, and the authors of the study argue that knowledge from public research findings beyond this stated level is transmitted to industrial researchers through a wide range of supplementary channels, such as consulting and informal communications. This insight is supported by an additional finding that the most important mechanisms for communicating research results from public research institutes to industry are the traditional ones of publication and conferences, strongly complemented by informal exchanges and private consulting arrangements between firms and researchers (Cohen, Nelson, and Walsh 2003, 139–41).

The findings of the Carnegie Mellon Survey reinforce the perspective that a key aspect of the process of knowledge transfer from universities and research institutes is through personal connections and that the knowledge being transferred is thus 'tacit' and 'embodied.' To deploy university-generated knowledge in a commercial setting, firms need to capture both its tacit and its more explicit, or codified, component. Another study by Wendy Faulkner and Jacqueline Senker employed a somewhat different research methodology designed to analyse this dimension of knowledge transfer in greater detail. This study explored the relationship from the perspective of the innovating organization, focusing on its knowledge requirements and trying to develop a better understanding of the knowledge flows from academia to industry. The researchers conducted interviews with a number of managers in firms across three science-related industries: biotechnology, engineering ceramics, and parallel computing. They probed for links between the firms and universities and the types of knowledge flowing to the firms. They also attempted to determine the degree of formality of these links and the relative importance of tacit versus codified knowledge. While the findings differ slightly by industry, they conclude that partnering with universities contributes most to firm innovation through an exchange of tacit knowledge and that the channels for communicating this knowledge are often informal. Such informal linkages are both a precursor and a successor to formal linkages and many useful exchanges of research materials or access to equipment take place through non-contractual barter arrangements. The flexibility inherent in such arrangements promotes the goodwill between partners that supports more formal linkages (Senker 1995).

Proximity and Spillovers in Knowledge Transfer

The preceding analysis emphasizes the fact that knowledge transfers between universities and their partners are highly personalized and, as a consequence, often highly localized. This underscores the significance of geographical proximity for the process of knowledge transfer. Proximity to the source of the research is important in influencing the success with which knowledge generated in the research laboratory is transferred to firms for commercial exploitation, or with which process innovations are adopted and diffused. A growing body of empirical research reinforces the finding that the linkages and benefits that flow from public investments in basic research are localized in this manner. The most frequently cited explanation for this proximity effect is the need to gain access to tacit knowledge, or at least knowledge that is not yet codified. Conversely, the role of proximity declines when useful knowledge is readily available in more codified forms that can easily be transmitted and accessed across broad distances. Proximity may also be more important for the transfer of relatively new research results in science-based fields, where personal access to those conducting the research is critical for the effective transfer of its insights (Feldman 2000; Adams 2001; Arundel and Geuna 2001).

One prominent line of research has investigated the geographic spillovers from government funding of scientific research to other types of activities, such as industrial R&D. Access to the U.S. Patent Office database enabled researchers to assemble large volumes of patent data with geographic precision. These data provide a rich geographic time series, which has been further broken down into patent families, patents that reference or cite each other and are used to indicate the flows of knowledge from one intervention to another. Using patents as a proxy for innovative output, Jaffe related the incidence of patents assigned to various corporations in different states with industrial R&D and university research. He found an important indirect or induced effect. There is also an association between industrial R&D and university research at the state level (Jaffe 1989). In a subsequent study, Acs et al. (1991) replaced the number of patents with the number of announcements of new or improved products found in newspapers and trade journals. Their analysis indicated that spillovers from university research to industrial innovation were greater than Jaffe described.

Employing the same data used by Acs et al., Feldman and Florida's model showed that the process of innovation is highly dependent on the underlying technological infrastructure of an area, consisting of both university and industrial R&D, agglomerations of related firms, and business services. Furthermore, these innovative capabilities tend to be highly specialized in regional concentrations distributed across the United States. 'In the modern economy, locational advantage in the capacity to innovate is ever more dependent on the agglomerations of specialized skills, knowledge, institutions, and resources that make up the underlying technological infrastructure' (Feldman and Florida 1994, 226).

Jaffe et al. (1993) also used patent citations to analyse the spillover effects of academic research. The results indicated that knowledge flows from universities to firms are highly localized at the regional or state level. They found evidence that patents cite other patents originating in the same city more frequently. Citations are five to ten times as likely to come from the same city as the control patents. This research highlights some of the factors that condition localization. Citations are more likely to be localized in the first year following the patent. This effect fades with time: citations show fewer geographic effects as knowledge diffuses. In a slightly different approach, Audretsch and Feldman (1996) used innovation citations that represent the market introduction of new commercial products. These data consist of new product announcements compiled from technology, engineering, and trade journals. They found a direct relationship between the propensity for industries to concentrate geographically and the knowledge intensity of the industries' activity. They also used survey data to identify the disciplines that form a common science base that contribute to cross-industry increasing returns. This work found that industries relying on the same science base also tend to cluster geographically.

Knowledge Transfer and Cluster Formation

The proximity effect of knowledge transfer provides a strong clue as to why universities are increasingly seen as an essential element to the process of regional economic development and for stimulating the formation of clusters, especially in knowledge-intensive industries, such as biotechnology and information and communications technology. But a critical issue that has been less well explored in the literature involves both the degree to and the way in which the proximity effect of university research on innovativeness contributes to the process of cluster formation. Another matter requiring further attention is the question of which of the university's central roles in the knowledge-based economy – the performance of scientific research or the training of highly qualified personnel – exerts the dominant influence on the process of regional economic development and cluster formation. Clusters are defined as 'a geographically proximate group of interconnected companies and associated institutions in a particular field, linked by commonalities and complementarities' (Porter 1998, 199). They can include concentrations of interconnected companies, service providers, suppliers of specialized inputs to the production process, customers, manufacturers of related products, and governmental and other institutions, such as national laboratories, universities, vocational training institutions, trade associations, and collaborative research institutes.

The mutually beneficial activities of the firms in a cluster generate a number of cluster assets that can be viewed as quasi-public goods. The general level of knowledge and information built up in the cluster can act as such a good, if the level of trust is sufficient to generate an easy and mutual exchange of both tacit and codified knowledge. Similarly, the mobility of personnel between firms in a cluster can constitute a similar source of knowledge flows. Even more important, the strength of the cluster can provide an important stimulus to public investment in specialized infrastructure, such as communication networks, joint training and research institutions, specialized testing facilities, and the expansion of public laboratories or post-secondary educational institutions. As the depth and value of such investments increase, so do the economic benefits flowing to firms located in the cluster. Thus the strength of the cluster and its supporting infrastructure of quasi-public goods and public institutions creates a mutually reinforcing positive feedback loop (Porter 1998, 218–19).

Clusters have an additional effect on improving the capacity of member firms to innovate and thus enhance their potential for productivity growth. Membership within the cluster affords firms a clearer view of current and prospective technology trends, allowing them to identify more rapidly new market opportunities for product or process enhancements through better information about buyer needs. On the supply side of the equation, cluster participation provides firms with early information about new technology trends and component and machinery capabilities, allowing them to perceive opportunities for improving or enhancing their own products or firm capabilities. Even more important than these valuable sources of information, membership in the cluster allows firms to act quickly by providing them with the ready source of supply that they need to bring new products or services to the market. These advantages are strongly reinforced by the competitive pressure that comes with location in the cluster. The presence of multiple rivals in the cluster, competing to take advantage of similar market opportunities and supply capabilities, pushes firms to excel at the innovative process. However, these internal competitive pressures are strongly reinforced by the potential for cooperation. Competition and cooperation are both present within the cluster because they work on different dimensions and between different economic actors (Porter 1998, 220–3; Best 1990).

A number of recent studies have also identified the finding and retaining of talent as a critical factor influencing the development of clusters and the growth of dynamic urban economies. Locations with large talent pools reduce the costs of search and recruitment of talent – they are also attractive to individuals who are relocating because they provide some guarantee of successive job opportunities. In Richard Florida's interviews, numerous executives confirmed that they will 'go where the highly skilled people are.' Highly educated, talented labour flows to those places that have a 'buzz' about them – the places where the most interesting work in the field is currently being done. One way to track this is through the inflow of so-called star scientists, or by tracking the in-migration of tomorrow's potential stars (post-docs). Another approach, employed by Florida and colleagues (Florida 2002; Gertler, Florida, Gates et al. 2002), utilizes a more broadly defined measure of 'talent,' and attributes strong geographical attraction to the presence of other creative people and activities locally. Inbound talented labour represents knowledge in its embodied form flowing into the region. Such flows act to reinforce and accentuate the knowledge assets already assembled in a region.

Knowledge and Learning in Clusters

Much of the literature on the economic benefits of clusters stresses the fact that the key advantages are derived from the agglomeration economies afforded by the cluster. These agglomeration economies arise primarily from the ready access afforded to firms by co-locating with key suppliers. Porter stresses that the location of a firm within a cluster contributes to enhanced productivity by providing it with superior- or lower-cost access to specialized inputs, including components, machinery, business services, and personnel, as opposed to the alternative, which may involve vertical integration or obtaining the needed inputs from more remote locations. Sourcing the required inputs from within the cluster reduces the need to maintain costly inventory and the consequent delays that can arise with shipments from distant locations. It also facilitates communication with the key suppliers in the sense that repeated interactions with the supply firms in the value chain create the kind of trust conditions and the potential for conducting repeated transactions on the basis of tacit, as well as more codified, forms of knowledge. Clusters also offer distinct advantages to firms in terms of the availability of specialized and experienced personnel. The cluster itself can act as a magnet drawing skilled labour to it or, conversely, the location of specialized training and educational institutions in the region provides a steady supply of highly qualified labour to the firms in the cluster (Porter 1998).

While not diminishing the importance of these agglomeration economies, a more recent stream of analysis suggests that the underlying dimension which confers competitive advantages on the firms located in the cluster is ready access to a common knowledge base. The central argument in this literature is that the joint production and transmission of new knowledge occurs most effectively among economic actors located close to each other. Proximity to critical sources of knowledge, whether they are found in public or private research institutions or grounded in the core competencies of lead or anchor firms, facilitates the process of acquiring new technical knowledge, especially when the relevant knowledge is located at the research frontier, as in the field of biotechnology research, or involves a largely tacit dimension. Knowledge of this nature is transmitted most effectively through interpersonal contacts and interfirm mobility of skilled workers. From this perspective, 'a key feature of successful high-technology clusters is related to the high level of embeddedness of local firms in a very thick network of knowledge sharing, which is supported by close social interactions and by institutions building trust and encouraging informal relations among actors' (Breschi and Malerba 2001, 819). This argument is strongly supported by empirical findings in the literature on the impact of proximity on knowledge flows, discussed above.

Building on this stream of the literature, Peter Maskell has proposed that we require a knowledge-based theory of the cluster, but extends this approach to both high-technology and conventional clusters. He suggests the primary reason for the emergence of clusters is the enhanced knowledge creation that occurs along two complementary dimensions. The cluster affords firms benefits along a horizontal dimension through coordinating dispersed sources of knowledge and overcoming the problems of asymmetrical access to information for different firms. It also facilitates the actual flow of knowledge between firms along the vertical dimension. The horizontal dimension of the cluster consists of those firms that produce similar goods and compete with one another. The advantages of proximity arise from continuous monitoring and comparing of what rival firms are doing, which act as a spur to innovation as firms race to keep up with, or get ahead of, their rivals. The vertical dimension of the cluster consists of those firms that are complementary and interlinked through a network of supplier, service, and customer relations. Once a specialized cluster develops, firms within it increase demand for specialized services and supplies. Further, once the cluster has emerged, it acts as a magnet drawing in additional firms whose activities require access to the existing knowledge base or complement it in some significant respect (Maskell 2001, 937).

A knowledge-based theory of the cluster recognizes the fact that knowledge flows present in a cluster frequently involve a combination of both local and global sources. Bathalt, Malmberg, and Maskell (2002) maintain that successful clusters are effective at building and managing a variety of channels for accessing relevant knowledge from around the globe. However, the skills required when dealing with the local environment are substantially different than the ones needed to generate the inflow and make the best use of codified knowledge produced elsewhere, and these differences must be managed by the cluster. They maintain that an accurate model of the knowledge-based cluster must account for both dimensions of these knowledge flows. They refer to these two kinds of knowledge flows as 'local buzz' and 'global pipelines' respectively.

According to Storper and Venables (2003) buzz arises from the fact of physical co-presence. It incorporates both the broad general conditions that exist when it is possible to glean knowledge from intentional face-to-face contacts, as well as the more diffuse forms of knowledge acquisition that arise from chance or accidental meetings and the mere fact of being in the same location. Buzz is the force that facilitates the circulation of information in a local economy or community and it is also the mechanism that supports the functioning of networks in the community. Pipelines refer to channels of communication used in distant interaction, between clusters and external sources of knowledge. Important knowledge flows are generated through network pipelines. The effectiveness of these pipelines depends on the quality of trust that exists between the firms in the different nodes involved. The advantages of global pipelines derive from the integration firms located in multiple selection environments, each of which is open to different technical potentials. Access by firms to these global pipelines can feed local interpretations and the use of knowledge that developed elsewhere into a cluster. Firms need access to both local buzz and the knowledge acquired through international pipelines. The ability of firms to access such global pipelines and to identify both the location of external knowledge and its potential value depends very much on the internal organization of the firm, in other words, its 'absorptive capacity.' The same can be said of local and regional clusters (Bathalt et al. 2002).

Path Dependency and the Creation of Clusters

According to a number of observers, clusters are seeded by a variety of methods; however, their growth can only be facilitated by building upon existing resources. There is considerable disagreement over whether they can be built just anywhere from scratch. The key assets that determine the viability of a cluster are firm-based. Of particular importance is the emergence of an anchor firm for the cluster. Whole clusters can develop out of the formation of one or two critical firms that then feed the growth of numerous smaller ones. Examples of the role played by this kind of anchor firm can be found in the case of MCI and AOL in

Washington, DC, or Nortel in Ottawa, or NovAtel in the case of the Calgary wireless cluster. In other instances, the presence of major anchor firms in a local cluster can act as a magnet, attracting both allies and rivals to locate in the region to monitor the activities of the dominant firm. This is the case with San Diego, where Nokia, Ericsson, and Motorola have all located their CDMA wireless research efforts to benefit from Qualcomm's leadership in the field, or in Ottawa, where Cisco and Alcatel both acquired local firms to benefit from the optical and telecommunications expertise in the region. This process can require decades to take root, a point not well recognized by many of the localities currently engaged in developing cluster strategies. And while universities and public research institutes can play an important part in the development of the cluster, as was the case with the NRC's laboratories and the Communications Research Centre's role in attracting the Bell Northern Research Laboratories to Ottawa, or UC San Diego's becoming home to the research that led indirectly to the founding of Qualcomm, the relationship is far less direct or instrumental than is often presumed.

Other analysts emphasize the role that highly skilled labour, or a unique mix of skill assets, often produced by the post-secondary educational institutions, plays in seeding the growth of a cluster. However, this process also requires a long time to take root. The presence, or absence, of key institutional elements in a local or regional economy may affect both their innovative capacity and their potential to serve as nodes for cluster development. Other studies underscore the importance of local governments and economic development agencies adopting sustained development strategies and the key role played by civic entrepreneurs in those strategies. Similarly, the ability, or inability, of the local or regional economy to develop the underlying conditions of trust and social capital that contribute to the presence of a learning economy may inhibit its capacity to sustain the growth of dynamic clusters. A critical question that remains unexplored through most of this literature is how the conditions that influence the trajectory of growth for specific regional or local economy can be altered by direct intervention.

Many clusters enjoy the knowledge assets and research infrastructure that are necessary for the development of an innovation-based development strategy, but they differ dramatically in their capacity to mobilize these assets in the pursuit of such a strategy. Similarly, experience suggests that local communities can formulate strategies to alter their economic trajectory and improve their chances of economic development. The successful initiation of this kind of process depends upon the ability to collaborate across boundaries – both geographic and social. Even in established clusters, the mere concentration of a large number of firms is not sufficient to transform a particular locale into a vibrant and dynamic regional economy. It also requires the presence of an 'economic community' – strong, responsive relationships between the economy and community that afford both companies and the community a sustained advantage. These relationships are mediated by key people and organizations that bring the economic, social, and civic interests in the community together to collaborate (Henton, Melville, and Walesh 1997). Henton and his colleagues argue that social capital is a critical ingredient in the success of the most dynamic clusters and regional economies. Social capital *can* be created and the basis for doing so is the establishment of collaborative networks between various elements of the business and civic communities, including the university research institutions:

> The presence of *collaborative institutions and organizations,* such as cluster organizations, professional networks, research-industry consortia and entrepreneurial support networks, greatly facilitates this environment. These alliances, networks and other relationship-building mechanisms create connections and linkages vital to economic development in a technology-driven world ... many regions fortunate enough to have university research assets underuse these knowledge economy resources, precisely because relationships have not been established to connect the university and local industry ... Relationships matter. (Montana, Reamer, Henton et al. 2001, 10)

Successful clusters are built on local institutions of collaboration, which are both formal and informal organizations that facilitate the exchange of information and technology, and foster cooperation and coordination. They create social capital and improve competitiveness within clusters by creating relationships and establishing trust, facilitating the organization of collective action, developing collective institutions that benefit the members of the cluster, identifying common strengths or mutual needs and contributing to the development of a common economic agenda. Collaborative organizations and institutions embody values and attitudes that are intrinsic to the region. This element of the regional culture is an important, but overlooked, component in the design of cluster development strategies. The essential criterion for success is finding the appropriate mechanisms to engage key members of the community in a sustained effort to advance its opportunities. The recruitment of a committed, creative, and collaborative leadership is the most essential element for the success of a strategic planning process in regional economic development. These collaborative leaders share certain characteristics: they can see the opportunities opened by the emergence of the knowledge-based economy; they exhibit an entrepreneurial personality, in both a business and a 'civic' sense; they are willing to cross functional, political, and geographic boundaries in pursuit of their strategic goals and they are committed to and comfortable working in teams (Montana et al. 2001, 31–5). Universities can play, and have played, a critical role as sources of this dynamic, far-sighted community leadership and in building collaborative institutions at the local level.

Universities as Knowledge Poles for Cluster Development

As we saw at the outset, the mere presence of leading research universities in a community is not sufficient to stimulate the formation of a dynamic and innovative cluster, or to sustain the process of regional economic development. However, their presence can play a vital role in contributing to cluster development. That role should not be viewed simply as a source of scientific ideas for generating new technology to transfer to private firms, or as a source of new firm formation as research scientists spin findings out of their laboratories into new start-ups. While successful research universities perform these functions, overall they play a more fundamental role as providers and attractors of talent to the local and regional economy and as a source of civic leadership for the local community.

At the same time, communities located around the research institution cannot simply rely upon the presence of a leading research university as the 'engine of innovation' that will drive economic growth in their region. They must display both the capacity to absorb and utilize the knowledge and the skilled labour produced by the institution – in other words, a 'regional absorptive capacity' (Mallet 2002, 605) – and the social cohesion to build an economic community around their research infrastructure. Ultimately, the most valuable contribution that universities make to this process is as providers of highly skilled labour or talent. If knowledge is rapidly becoming the central factor of production in the emerging economy, the ability to absorb and use that knowledge or to learn is the most essential skill or process. Learning processes are eminently person-embodied in the form of talent. 'Universities ... are a crucial piece of the infrastructure of the knowledge economy, providing mechanisms for generating and harnessing talent' (Florida 1999, 72).

This means that the role of public policy in seeding cluster development, particularly as it applies to research-intensive universities, is critical. The impact of public sector interventions on cluster development can be positive, negative, or inadvertent in character. On balance, however, the public interventions which have the most effect in seeding the growth of clusters are those that strengthen the research infrastructure of a region or locality and contribute to the expansion of its talent base of skilled knowledge workers. These points were strongly emphasized in a recent report prepared for the Ontario government:

> Basic university research advances fundamental understanding and provides a substantial rate of economic return through the preparation of a highly skilled workforce, contributing to the foundation of many new technologies, attracting long-term foreign (and domestic) investment, supporting new company development and entrepreneurial companies and participating in global networks. Government funding is the primary support for virtually all investment in truly frontier university research. (Munroe-Blum 1999, 14)

Recent research on the growth and development of three major information and communications technology (ICT) clusters in Ontario – Ottawa, Toronto, and Waterloo – documents the important contribution made by the research infrastructure in all three communities, in both public research laboratories and post-secondary educational institutions (Wolfe 2002). However, the findings underline the fact that direct seeding of the cluster by post-secondary institutions is the exception, rather than the rule. The case studies of the three clusters suggest that universities and research institutes act primarily as attractors of inward investments by leading anchor firms interested in tapping into the knowledge base of the local community, or its 'local buzz,' and as providers of the talent pool that firms in the cluster draw upon, rather than as direct initiators of cluster development. In this respect, universities also act as part of the network linking actors in the local cluster to the global pipelines that are also essential to the knowledge flows in the cluster. Successful research universities also attract leading scientists, further reinforcing their linkages to external knowledge flows through the extensive network of contacts they bring to their new location.

Several examples from the case studies serve to illustrate this point. Among the three cases, the one which most clearly represents a central role for the university is Waterloo. All accounts of the origins of this cluster link its roots to the far-sighted vision of a key group of business leaders to create a new university in the region in the late 1950s in a period when the provincial government (with financial support from the federal government) was expanding the post-secondary education system. Even more influential were subsequent decisions to focus the core strengths of the university in the sciences and engineering and to establish what has become one of the most successful co-op education programs in North America. The founders of many of the firms that populate this cluster are graduates of the university and many started their companies with core technologies developed while they were at the university. Even the most internationally successful of these firms maintain their primary research base in the Waterloo area because of their ability to draw upon a highly trained group of science and engineering graduates from the university.

An illustration of the inadvertent role that public policy can sometimes play is provided in the case of the telecommunications cluster in Ottawa, which originated partly with the judicial decision in the United States to force the Western Electric Company to divest itself of its subsidiary, the Northern Electrical Manufacturing Company (now Nortel) in the late 1950s. Cut off from its sources of innovation and research, Northern Electric searched for a location to establish its own facility. It eventually bought a substantial tract of land on the outskirts of Ottawa to be the home of Bell Northern Research, largely because it viewed the presence of the National Research Council laboratories and the Communications Research Centre in the nation's capital as a substantial draw for the highly skilled research scientists and engineers it expected to populate its research facility. Many of the leading entrepreneurs in the Ottawa telecommunications and photonics cluster began their careers as researchers for BNR or another subsidiary, Microsystems International. Although the research universities played a secondary role, the official genealogy of Ottawa high-tech companies credits Carleton University as contributing substantially to the development of firms in the community:

> The Ottawa story emphasizes the critical importance in cluster development of deeply rooted R&D strength. It also clearly underscores the fact that access to technology demands the presence of world-class scientific research institutions. Only through the combined impact of public and private sector research activity could Ottawa have spawned its own home-grown high-tech industry. (Mallet 2002, 6)

In a series of interviews conducted for the case studies, universities were identified as a source of strength for the sector, both in terms of their ability to provide a steady stream of highly skilled personnel, a prime driver of sector growth in Ontario, as well as a strong base of research with close links to industry.[1] Industry representatives feel that specific programs, such as the co-op program at Waterloo, have been effective at moving students into industry settings. In addition to providing a strong talent base for firms located in the clusters to draw upon, the university research infrastructure is important for the clusters in two additional respects – as a key source of new ideas for domestic companies, both in terms of spin-offs and knowledge transfer, and also, as a factor contributing to the reputation of the key clusters in Ottawa, the Greater Toronto Area, and Waterloo, thus helping to attract large foreign firms to invest in the province. The case of Cisco (both with respect to the Ottawa cluster and more recently Waterloo) was widely cited as the most significant inward investment to the regional clusters, but Alcatel, Lucent, and other leading IT firms were also mentioned. Most recently, IBM, with one of its Centres for Advanced Studies located in its software laboratories in Markham, just north of Toronto, has expanded its presence in the Ottawa cluster as well. Through the acquisition of two local software companies – Tarian Software and Rational Software Corporation – IBM tripled the size of its Ottawa laboratories to 300 employees. This expansion was furthered with the opening of a new Centre for Advanced Studies in the Ottawa laboratories to give graduate students from Carleton and the University of Ottawa experience in working with experienced software engineers in the development of new programs for database management (Pilieci 2003). The growing presence of these large multinational players is seen as evidence that the Ontario clusters have emerged as a major player on the international scene owing, in part, to the growing reputation of their research infrastructure.

Many companies are expanding their investments in the university research base through direct funding of basic research, affiliation with federal and provincial Centres of Excellence, or partnering on more applied research initiatives. Companies cite the positive benefits that have flowed from recent federal and provincial increases in university funding through programs such as the Centres of Excellence, the Canada Foundation for Innovation, or the Ontario Research and Development Challenge Fund. The two largest players in the sector, Bell Canada and Nortel Networks, have both launched major research initiatives in the past several years, principally at the University of Toronto and the University of Waterloo. In 2000, Nortel was funding $15 million of research at eleven Ontario universities and had invested an additional $18 million to create two dedicated institutes, the Nortel Institute of Optical Electronics at the University of Toronto and the Software Institute at the University of Waterloo. For its part, Bell Canada invested $35 million over three years in its Bell University Laboratories program at the Universities of Toronto and Waterloo. Although the level of Nortel research funding has declined in the recession, its strong links to the research base remain intact. Representatives of the business and industry association sectors cite the strong entrepreneurial culture at the University of Waterloo and the encouragement that faculty receive to develop and exploit their innovations as critical factors in the growth of the ICT cluster in Canada's Technology Triangle. They recognize the driving role that the university's research base has played in the recent growth and expansion of the ICT cluster in their region. The region is currently reaping the benefits of investments in the post-secondary research and education base made in the late 1950s and 1960s.

While the Waterloo case suggests that far-sighted investments in post-secondary education and the research infrastructure can seed cluster development, more often universities are followers, rather than leaders, in cluster formation – as they respond to the demands of local firms for an expanding talent pool by increasing their own teaching and research activities in areas of technical competence critical for the growth of those firms. One of the key factors cited repeatedly as crucial for the current and future well-being of the ICT sector in Ontario is the availability of a continuing supply of highly skilled personnel. A number of new federal and provincial initiatives address this issue directly. Foremost is Ontario's Access to Opportunities Program with $150 million in new funding over three years, designed to increase the number of students enrolled in computer science and related engineering programs by 17,000 a year. Virtually all the province's universities and colleges submitted proposals under this program and the Council of Ontario Universities noted that the universities exceeded the initial target, resulting in the creation of 23,000 new places. While employment in the sector fell from 2000 to 2002, the decline was largely limited to the manufacturing sector, as employment in the service sector continued to grow. Over the longer period from 1997 to 2001, employment in the ICT sector increased by 32 per cent, suggesting that demand remains strong for the graduates from these programs.

Conclusion

The strength and vitality of universities remains essential for growth in
the knowledge-based economy. Universities perform vital functions both
as generators of new knowledge through their leading-edge research
activities and as trainers of highly qualified labour. As most research universities will attest, the two functions are integrally linked, and when they
are most effective, they contribute strongly to regional economic growth
and development. As such, they provide the essential infrastructure from
which clusters can develop. But it is important to be clear about the precise role they play. Strong research-intensive universities feed the growth
of clusters by expanding the local knowledge base and providing a steady
stream of talent that supports the growth of firms in the cluster. They also
serve as magnets for investments by leading or anchor firms, drawing
them into the cluster to gain more effective access to the knowledge base
and the local buzz. In some instances, successful research efforts can
expand the cluster by spinning off research results into new products and
firms, but it is a mistake to view this as their primary purpose. But it is dangerous to assume that the economic returns to this investment be judged
solely on the success with which research findings are transformed into
commercial products. Recent policy initiatives which aim to elevate the
commercialization of technology to equal status with research and teaching as mandates of the university fundamentally miss this point. Universities must also be a vital part of the local 'economic community' by
building the region's social capital and taking a leadership role in activities designed to enhance the region's absorptive capacity. Continued
public support for both the teaching and research mandates of the university are essential if they are to succeed in these roles and contribute to
the growth of their local and regional economies.

NOTE
1 The following discussion draws upon a number of confidential interviews with
   business, education, and industry association leaders conducted as part of a
   study of ICT clusters in Ontario (Wolfe 2002).

REFERENCES
Acs, Zoltan J., David Audretsch, and Maryann P. Feldman. (1991). Real Effects

of Academic Research: A Comment. *American Economic Review* 82: 363–7.

Adams, James D. (2002). Comparative Localization of Academic and Industrial Spillovers. *Journal of Economic Geography* 2: 253–78.

Arundel, Anthony, and Aldo Geuna. (2004). Proximity and the Use of Public Science by Innovative European Firms. *Economics of Innovation and New Technology* 13: 559–80.

Audretsch, David, and Maryann P. Feldman. (1996). R&D Spillovers and the Geography of Innovation and Production. *American Economic Review* 86: 630–42.

Bathalt, Harald, Anders Malmberg, and Peter Maskell. (2004). Clusters and Knowledge: Local Buzz, Global Pipelines and the Process of Knowledge Creation. *Progress in Human Geography* 28: 31–56.

Best, Michael H. (1990). *The New Competition: Institutions of Industrial Restructuring.* Cambridge, U.K.: Polity Press.

Breschi, Stefano, and Franco Malerba. (2001). The Geography of Innovation and Economic Clustering: Some Introductory Notes, *Industrial and Corporate Change* 10(4): 817–33.

Brooks, Harvey. (1996). The Evolution of US Science Policy. In Bruce L.R. Smith and Claude E. Barfield, eds. *Technology, R&D, and the Economy.* Washington, D.C.: Brookings Institution and the American Enterprise Institute, pp. 15–48.

Cohen, Wesley M., and Daniel A. Levinthal. (1990). Absorptive Capacity: A New Perspective on Learning and Innovation. *Administrative Science Quarterly* 35:128–52.

Cohen, Wesley M., Richard R. Nelson, and John P. Walsh. (2003). Links and Impacts: The Influence of Public Research on Industrial R&D. In Aldo Geuna, Ammon J. Salter, and W. Edward Steinmuller, eds. *Science and Innovation: Rethinking the Rationales for Funding and Governance.* Cheltenham, U.K.: Edward Elgar, pp. 109–46.

David, Peter. (1997). The Knowledge Factor: A Survey of Universities. *Economist,* 4 Oct., 53–5.

Dosi, Giovanni. (1988). Sources, Procedures and Microeconomic Effects of Innovation. *Journal of Economic Literature* 26: 1120–71.

Etkowitz, Henry, and Andrew Webster. (1998). Entrepreneurial Science: The Second Academic Revolution. In Henry Etkowitz, Andrew Webster, and Peter Healey, eds. *Capitalizing Knowledge: New Intersections in Industry and Academia.* New York: SUNY Press, pp. 21–46.

Feldman, Maryann P. (2000). Location and Innovation: The New Economic Geography of Innovation, Spillovers and Agglomeration. In Gordon L. Clark,

Maryann P. Feldman, and Meric S. Gertler. eds. *The Oxford Handbook of Economic Geography.* Oxford: Oxford University Press, pp. 373–94.

– and Pierre Desrochers. (2003). Research Universities and Local Economic Development: Lessons from the History of the Johns Hopkins University. *Industry and Innovation* 10(1): 5–24.

Feldman, M., and R. Florida. (1994). The Geography of Innovation: Technological Infrastructure and Production Innovation in the United States. *Annals, Association of American Geographers* 84(2): 210–29.

Florida, Richard. (1999). The Role of the University: Leveraging Talent, Not Technology. *Issues in Science and Technology,* Summer, pp. 67–74.

– (2002). *The Rise of the Creative Class: And How It's Transforming Work, Leisure, Community and Community and Everyday Life.* New York: Basic Books.

Gertler, Meric S., Richard Florida, Gary Gates, and Tara Vinodrai. (2002). *Competing on Creativity: Placing Ontario's Cities in North American Context.* A report prepared for the Ontario Ministry of Enterprise, Opportunity and Innovation and the Institute for Competitiveness and Prosperity. Toronto. Http://www.utoronto.ca/progris/Competing%20on%20Creativity%20in%20Ontario%20Report%20(Nov%2022).pdf.

Gibbons, James F. (2000). The Role of Stanford University: A Dean's Reflections. In Chong-Moon Lee, William F. Miller, Marguerite Gong Hancock, and Henry S. Rowen. eds., *The Silicon Valley Edge: A Habitat for Innovation and Entrepreneurship.* Stanford, Calif.: Stanford University Press, pp. 200–17.

Henton, Douglas, John Melville, and Kimberly Walesh. (1997). *Grassroots Leaders for a New Economy: How Civic Entrepreneurs Are Building Prosperous Communities.* San Francisco: Jossey-Bass.

Jaffe, A. (1989). Real Effects of Academic Research. *American Economic Review* 79: 957–70.

– M. Trajtenberg, and R. Henderson. (1993). Geographic Localization of Knowledge Spillovers as Evidenced by Patent Citations. *Quarterly Journal of Economics* 63: 577–98.

Klevorick, A.K., Richard Levin, Richard Nelson, and Sidney Winter. (1995). On the Sources and Significance of Inter-Industry Differences in Technological Opportunities. *Research Policy* 24: 185–205.

Kodama, Fumio, and Lewis M. Branscomb. (1999). University Research as an Engine for Growth: How Realistic Is the Vision? In Lewis M. Branscomb, Fumio Kodama, and Richard Florida, eds. *Industrializing Knowledge: University-Industry Linkages in Japan and the United States.* Cambridge, Mass.: MIT Press, pp. 3–19.

Lundvall, Bengt-Åke. (1992). Introduction. Bengt-Åke Lundvall, ed. In *National*

Systems of Innovation: Towards a Theory of Innovation and Interactive Learning.
London: Pinter Publishers, pp. 1–19.

Mallet, Jocelyn Ghent. (2002). *Silicon Valley North: The Formation of the Ottawa Innovation Cluster.* Toronto: Information Technology Association of Canada. Http://www.itac.ca.

Martin, Ben. (2003). The Changing Social Contract for Science and the Evolution of Knowledge Production. In Aldo Geuna, Ammon J. Salter, and W. Edward Steinmuller. eds. *Science and Innovation: Rethinking the Rationales for Funding and Governance.* Cheltenham, U.K.: Edward Elgar, pp. 7–29.

Maskell, Peter. (2001). Towards a Knowledge-Based Theory of the Geographic Cluster. *Industrial and Corporate Change* 10(4): 921–43.

– and Anders Malmberg. (1999). Localised Learning and Industrial Competitiveness. *Cambridge Journal of Economics* 23: 167–85.

Montana, J., Andrew Reames, Doug Henton, John Melville, Kim Walesh, John McNamee, Kay Fonk, John Feiser, and Kelly Robinson. (2001). *Strategic Planning in the Technology-Driven World: A Guidebook for Innovation-Led Development.* Washington, D.C.: Collaborative Economics and the Economic Development Administration, U.S. Department of Commerce.

Munroe-Blum, Heather. (1999). *Growing Ontario's Innovation System: The Strategic Role of University Research.* Report prepared for the Ontario Ministries of Colleges, Training and University, Energy Science and Technology, and the Ontario Jobs and Investment Board. Toronto.

Nelson, Richard R. (1996). Capitalism as an Engine of Progress. In *The Sources of Economic Growth.* Cambridge: Harvard University Press, pp. 52–83.

– and Sidney G. Winter. (1982). *An Evolutionary Theory of Economic Change.* Cambridge, Mass.: Belknap Press.

Organizqation for Economic Cooperation and Development (OECD). (1996). Special Theme: The Knowledge-Based Economy. In *Science, Technology and Industry Outlook 1996.* Paris: author.

Pavitt, Keith. (1991). What Makes Basic Research Economically Useful? *Research Policy* 20: 109–19.

Pilieci, Vito. (2003). IBM Unveils Cutting-Edge Lab: Ottawa Facility a Boon to Graduate Students. *Ottawa Citizen,* 4 June, p. D1.

Polanyi, Michael. (1962). *Personal Knowledge: Towards a Post-Critical Philosophy.* New York: Harper and Row.

Porter, Michael E. (1998). Clusters and Competition: New Agendas for Companies, Governments, and Institutions. In *On Competition.* Cambridge: Harvard Business Review Books, pp. 197–288.

Rosenberg, Nathan. (1990). Why Do Firms Do Basic Research (with Their Own Money)? *Research Policy* 19: 165–74.

Senker, Jacqueline. (1995). Tacit Knowledge and Models of Innovation. *Industrial and Corporate Change* 4(2): 425–47.

Stokes, Donald E. (1997). *Pasteur's Quadrant: Basic Science and Technological Innovation.* Washington, D.C.: Brookings Institution.

Storper, Michael, and Anthony J. Venables. (2003). Buzz: Face-to-Face Contact and the Urban Economy. Paper presented at the. DRUID Summer Conference on 'Creating, Sharing and Transferring Knowledge: The Role of Geography, Institutions and Organizations,' Copenhagen/Elsinore, 12–14 June.

Wolfe, David A. (2002). Knowledge, Learning and Social Capital in Ontario's ICT Clusters. Paper presented at the Annual Meeting of the Canadian Political Science Association, Toronto, 29–31 May.

– 2003. Commentary on Part I: The Evolving Research Environment. In Aldo Geuna, Ammon J. Salter, and W. Edward Steinmuller, eds. *Science and Innovation: Rethinking the Rationales for Funding and Governance.* Cheltenham, U.K.: Edward Elgar, pp. 93–100.

CHAPTER 11

Campus and Community: Partnerships for Research, Policy, and Action

Beth Savan

Partnerships between universities and local community groups are proliferating, because they confer significant benefits on all participants (Loka Institute 2002; Sclove et. al. 1998; Campus Compact 2000). Academics are working with non-governmental organizations (NGOs) to give their research a local grounding, to respond to urgent community needs, and to gain the satisfaction of seeing research recommendations actually implemented in the form of new policies, programs, and activities (Reardon 2000; Garvin 1995). Students gain exciting applied experience, contacts, and job prospects through their involvement in such applied research projects, and community groups gain access to otherwise inaccessible intellectual and human resources. These partnerships can take a variety of forms, to meet different objectives, including research, service delivery, and advocacy, on the part of the community groups, and education, training, public service, and enhanced image on the part of the academic institution. This chapter focuses on partnerships that join universities with community-based NGOs to achieve specific research and action outcomes. Research partnerships that harness academic resources and rigour to meet community development goals are collectively termed 'community- based research' (Loka Institute 2002), and the literature on this kind of research work is growing (Sclove et al. 1998).

Community-based research is distinguished from more traditional applied research in that the community groups have an important role in defining the research topic and sometimes in managing the research itself. In other words, community members are not research subjects to be studied by academics to advance knowledge in a particular field; they are, instead, research directors, working in partnership with university-based scholars (and occasionally on their own) to identify and pursue original research trails. Invariably, these research goals are intimately tied to action or advocacy outcomes, which contribute to community development and environmental improvements or enhanced population health. Research partnerships are variously called action research (Garvin 1995; Greenwood and Levin 1998, 2000; Puckett and Harkavy 1999; Stringer 1999), participatory action research (Reardon 2000; Smith et al. 1997; Fals-Borda and Rahman 1991), collaborative inquiry (Bray et al. 2000), science shops (Lurson 2001), or service learning (Campus Compact 2000). These different collaborative methodologies are described and discussed elsewhere, in another publication by this author (see Savan and Sider 2003). Suffice it to say, here, that community-based research, action research, participatory action research, and collaborative inquiry all have a research focus which involves dedicated, multiyear partnerships, and long-term research, policy and/or action goals.

Alternatively, partnerships can be devised primarily to provide direct service to community groups, to develop a sense of civic responsibility in students, and to support experiential learning. These rather different kinds of partnerships usually involve undergraduates serving in short-term placements or carrying out course work in off- campus agencies. The community groups, again, have control over defining student tasks, but the responsibilities of the students are also constrained by course- or program-related obligations. These experiential learning programs are usually termed 'service learning' (in North America) or 'science shops' (in Europe), and have been widely documented (Lurson, 2001; Campus Compact 2000). They build on shorter-term partnerships which support much more limited objectives; they are more similar to term papers, in scale, as opposed to the longer-term community-based research, already described, which often results in substantial reports, theses, and books. The case study described below involves elements of both the action research / participatory action research tradition, as well as the science shops / service learning model.

Introduction to Sustainable Toronto

Sustainable Toronto is an example of campus-community collaboration. This project is a community-based research initiative hosted by the University of Toronto, in partnership with York University and several local environmental organizations, as well as the City of Toronto. It was funded for three years by the Community University Research Alliance Program of the Social Sciences and Humanities Research Council of Canada (SSHRC). The aim of this project is to promote community sustainability in the City of Toronto. This general project goal is being advanced through a series of eleven sub-projects that link research with policy and action to advance sustainability (see Sustainable Toronto 2003). A partners committee, which includes all sub-project directors and academic advisers, was established to guide all project plans.

Each sub-project is directed by a community partner, who is someone based in an environmental NGO or in the city government, and this community partner works with a faculty academic adviser. Together, with one or more graduate research assistants assigned to each sub-project, they identify the specific research topic and then design and supervise implementation of the research. Students carry out the bulk of the research work, through a variety of paid and unpaid positions and course-related requirements. Graduate Research Assistants and undergraduate or graduate work-study students are the only students who are paid for this work. Other students doing the research include undergraduate and Master's students preparing research theses; students in a professional experience course (an off-campus placement course conferring academic credit for a full year undergraduate course); undergraduate students working on short-term course assignments; and students in applied research courses, which involve teams of students working on research projects for off-campus organizations. These arrangements are described more fully in another publication by this author (Savan and Bell 2002).

Sub-projects address a range of issues, and have produced diverse outputs. One team is assessing the potential of urban agriculture to address the nutritional needs of urban dwellers. It has established several community gardens and measured their production, and is publishing reports and a scholarly article. Another group engages citizens and youth in monitoring environmental quality. They are using bioindicators, and the results are posted on an interactive Web-based geographic information system (GIS) map. This team has prepared two academic articles, as well as diverse conference presentations to scientific experts and government policy makers (see Savan 2003). Still other teams have prepared a directory of ethnocultural and environmental groups and a Web site publicizing health promotion measures. These diverse outcomes generally link research, action, and often policy, although each sub-project has a unique focus and balance among these three objectives.

Partnership Models, Benefits, and Barriers

The sub-projects in Sustainable Toronto represent a range of different partnership relationships, which cover the spectrum from long-term institutional research partnerships to shorter-term annually renewable arrangements. The Sustainable Toronto project as a whole evolved from a series of experiential learning initiatives, which used the service learning (or science shop) model to link students with off-campus organizations. The benefits and challenges presented by this approach are described below. Then they are contrasted with the longer-term, more research-oriented community-based research model adopted by Sustainable Toronto. In addition, the barriers to their more widespread application are explored, with recommendations made to encourage and enhance productive relationships between campus and community.

Service Learning or the Science Shop Model

Collaborations between university programs and off-campus groups and agencies have multiple aims. Generally, these are intended to foster civic engagement, education, and skills development; introduce a network of professional contacts to students; and provide a significant resource to underfunded community groups and agencies (Campus Compact 2000; Jorgensen 1999; Owens and Wang 1996; Pearce and Lynch 1998). In service learning or the Science shop model, a student works on a project for a single term or, perhaps, one academic year. Such projects depend on placement courses and co-op terms and can also use applied research or thesis courses and internships to engage students on relevant work for NGOs and other community groups. Often these projects have circumscribed goals because the time and resource constraints inherent in this model require that research and action projects be well developed when presented to the university partners. Furthermore, their successful outcomes often depend on mastery by students of new skills, such as teamwork, using meetings effectively, project planning, and financial management. Our own experience indicates that experiential learning projects can, nevertheless, provide great benefits to students, strengthen the links between particular programs or departments on campus and the community, and enhance the capacity of community groups – and the long-term prospect of further engagement in community work on the part of the involved students (Lerner et al. 1998).

Significant resources are required to maintain these partnerships. Co-op terms and professional experience courses, as well as applied research, practical theses, and internship courses are particularly demanding of faculty and administrative time. Often they require an application and matching process in the previous term and off-site visits by university faculty for guidance and evaluation. Student projects must combine the needs of the off-campus agency, as well as the academic requirements of the relevant course. Projects which may form part of a larger program have to be sub-divided to give each student some independent area of responsibility which can be reported on and evaluated. Administrative, implementation, or outreach work has to be formulated in such a way that a reflective exercise can complement it, to ensure that the experience is placed in a larger academic context. Of course, the goals of the university faculty, the students, and the community groups involved are likely to vary widely. Negotiation of projects which meet everyone's needs can be challenging and is usually time consuming. As a result of all of these factors, experiential learning courses demand more resources than typical university courses. They require ongoing departmental support to develop, maintain, and enhance partnerships, as well as to administer the courses in such a way that all parties benefit and partnership relationships are strengthened.

Community-Based Research Model

Community-based research projects like Sustainable Toronto are generally longer-term endeavours. Usually these projects go on for several years. In this way, they differ markedly from the short-term, largely course-based partnerships formed to foster service learning and science shops. Collaborative research projects, lasting for more than one academic year, are more likely to attract outside funding for graduate research assistantships. They will be more attractive to graduate students, who might be able to integrate work on a multiyear project with their theses requirements. Moreover, these more ambitious projects are able to accommodate the advanced planning required for paid undergraduate positions, like the part-time work-study employment available to Ontario students who qualify for student aid but do not receive sufficient funding. These and other subsidized or fully funded positions often require a significant lead time to ensure that the resources can be applied to work relevant to the partnership project.

Multiyear partnership projects permit greater student and faculty engagement in the research design than the short-term projects, as often the latter are defined and planned in some detail before students or even their supervising faculty become involved at all. Ideally, the trust and cross-fertilization fostered by strong shared interests and project collaboration can lead to joint development of new research projects and even new research trails. For university researchers, the collaboration with community groups can provide access to foundation funding, which might otherwise not be available, since it is often tied to action outcomes. For community groups, partnership with a university allows them to benefit from the dedicated research funding that is the usual support for academic work.

The potential for innovation in both the definition of problems and in the research approaches is another well-documented benefit of cross-sectoral collaboration (Lerner et al. 1998). Research productivity and economic development spin-offs are spurred by enduring partnerships between university faculty and off-campus organizations (Markey and Roseland 2001). Jointly designed undertakings, such as Sustainable Toronto, often result in policy and action outcomes as well as scholarly publications (Sustainable Toronto 2003). These outcomes may be reported in the popular media or in non-academic journals, greatly enlarging the audience for the research and the profile of the institution and the community. The benefits for short-term partnership projects, described above, are also all enhanced by longer-term partnerships. Universities develop a stronger bond to the host community, enhancing both the university's reputation with the public, as well as the credibility of the community group.

Multiyear partnerships face considerable challenges, both on and off campus (Jackson et al. 2000; Santiago-Rivera et al. 1998; Perkins and Wandersman 1990). The applied and interdisciplinary scholarship demanded by community-based research does not always enjoy the support of departments, faculties, and senior university administrations who are accustomed to rewarding theoretical research and only those publications that appear in peer-reviewed scholarly journals. Policies for hiring and promotion, and resource allocation to traditional academic courses, also frequently neglect this emerging area of academic interest (Lerner et al. 1998). Lack of administrative experience in development and maintenance of institutional partnerships can retard or even prevent these initiatives.

Community groups have experienced difficulties in pursuing collaborative research projects. Non-governmental organizations usually have meagre resources and cannot subsidize community-based research.

Their staffs are often overcommitted, working on several projects. Thus, they have difficulty finding the time to undertake the lengthy negotiations, planning, and meetings required for collaborative research. Unlike university programs, community organizations do not always have a learning culture, and the supervision and guidance of students can present a challenge for them. Immediate advocacy and action goals often preoccupy community groups, and this reduces the priority of long-term research projects for them.

Government and foundation funding programs are providing a strong incentive to overcome these barriers. Many, if not most Canadian foundations encourage partnership undertakings to reduce overlap and promote efficiency in their funding programs. Federal research funders are actively promoting academic collaboration with off-campus groups through programs like SSHRC's Community University Research Alliance Program, which funded Sustainable Toronto. Institutional leadership is critical to overcoming these barriers (Holland 1997). Encouraging applied research; funding for community-based research initiatives; and revision of hiring, tenure, and promotion guidelines so that they recognize the virtues and benefits of community-based research will go a long way towards encouraging long-term community research partnerships.

Discussion

It is evident that projects with different kinds of objectives may lend themselves to different models of community-based research. Indeed, these types of partnership may represent an evolution in the relationship between partners. Our experience began with short-term consultative relationships, in which students carried out four to six months of research on projects with predetermined topics for off- campus agencies. This work was largely undertaken on campus, using traditional academic research techniques. Over time, as the relationships between the university faculty and the community groups strengthened, a professional experience course was developed. In this course, students were placed in off-campus agencies to carry out a variety of tasks, often with much of the nature and focus of the work having been predetermined. Much greater advance planning was required for the interviews to match students with agencies and for contractual agreements that had to be reached regarding the balance of academic and practical work required in the course and the obligations outlined for all parties. In this course, students spent most of their time off campus. Based on the success of this experiment, a much larger collaboration was planned that would involve outside funding for project directors and graduate research assistants. From this collaboration, the Sustainable Toronto project was developed.

Conclusion

Innis College's Environmental Studies Program, at the University of Toronto, has been very successful in its experiments with experiential learning. Through various courses we now engage approximately thirty undergraduate and graduate students each year in coursework requiring collaboration with off-campus agencies. Sustainable Toronto shows considerable promise as a multiyear community-based research project. It retained over ninety students during the first two and one half years of its operation, through experiential learning courses, work-study positions, and graduate research assistantships. We are actively pursuing eleven sub-projects with nine different off-campus groups. Finally, we are applying for follow-up grants, building on our existing partnerships and expanding them to involve more participants, including new community groups and two other academic units at the university – the School of Graduate Studies and the Joseph Rotman School of Management. Nonetheless, we have encountered many difficulties, both within the university and in relation to the off-campus groups. Maintaining healthy partnerships is very difficult, and some of our collaborative sub-projects have been more productive and cordial than others. Furthermore, at the University of Toronto we still fall well short of the institutionalized links to the community that would most benefit faculty, students, and off-campus groups. We would all be best served by a university that is seen as a public resource – one that is an active partner in solving urgent social, environmental, and economic problems and engages its members in highly rewarding service to the wider community.

NOTE
The author is indebted to David Sider, Mary McGrath, and Gaby Binette for their very constructive comments on a draft of this chapter. Countless Sustainable Toronto staff, students, and volunteers developed and carried out the projects reported here; for their continuing dedication and creativity I am especially grateful. Further development of those ideas is presented in a recent paper by the author in the *Community Development Journal*, 39 (4): 372–84. Funding provided by the Community University Research Alliance Program of

the Social Sciences and Humanities Research Council of Canada to the Sustainable Toronto project permitted preparation of this work.

REFERENCES

Bray, J.D., J. Lee, L.L. Smith, and L. Yorks. (2000). Collaborative Inquiry: A Paradigm for Adult Learning through Research. In *Collaboarive Inquiry in Practice: Action, Reflection and Meaning Making.* Thousand Oaks, Calif., London, and New Delhi: Sage Publications, pp. 1–18.

Campus Compact. (2000). Introduction: Creating a Framework for the Engaged Campus. In *Campus Compact: The Engaged Campus.* post-meeting workshop at the American Association of Colleges and Universities U annual meeting. Washington, D.C.: author.

Fals-Borda, O., and M.A. Rahman. (1991). *Action and Knowledge: Breaking the Monopoly with Participatory Action Research.* New York: Apex Press.

Garvin, T.G. (1995). We're Strong Women Building a Community University Research Partnership. *Geoforum* 26(3): 273–86.

Greenwood, Davydd J., and Morten Levin. (1998). *Introduction to Action Research: Social Research for Social Change.* Thousand Oaks, CA: Sage.

– (2000). Reconstructing the Relationships between Universities and Society through Action Research. In: Norman K. Denzin and Yvonna S. Lincoln, eds. *Handbook of Qualitative Research,* 2nd ed. Thousand Oaks, CA: Sage, pp. 85–106.

Holland, B. (1997). Analyzing Institutional Commitment to Service: A Model of Key Organizational Factors. *Michigan Journal of Community Service Learning* 3: 30–41.

Jackson, E.T., K.A. Graham, and A.M. Maslove. (2000) Enhancing University-Community Partnerships: Challenges in Retooling the Academy for More Effective Engagement with Civil Society. *Education through Partnership* 4(2): 16–30.

Jorgensen, M.S. (1999). Science Shops: An Introduction to the Concept of Science Shops and to the Science Shop at the Technical University of Denmark. The Science Shop, c/o Department of Technology and Social Sciences Technical University of Denmark, Lyngby.

Lerner, R.M., L.K. Simon, and D.B. Mitchell. (1998). Creating Outreach Universities: Challenges and Choices. In Jacqueline McCroskey and Susan Einbinder, eds. *Universities and Communities: Remaking Professional and Interprofessional Education for the Next Century.* Westport, CT: Praeger, pp. 268–82.

Loka Institute. (2002). *About the CRN: What Is Community Based Research?* Available online http://www.loka.org/crn/About%20CRN.htm.

Lursen, M. (2001). A Science Shop Network under Construction, *Living Knowledge: Journal of Community Based Research,* 1: 4–7.

Markey, S., and M. Roseland. (2001). *Reaching across the Divide: The Role of Univer-*

sities in Building Capacity for Community Economic Development. Burnaby, BC: Community Economic Development Centre, Simon Fraser University.

Owens, T.R., and C. Wang. (1996) Topical Synthesis No. 8. Community Based Learning: A Foundation for Meaningful Educational Reform. Northwest regional Educational Laboratory. Available online http://www.nwrel.org/scpd/sirs/10/t008.html)

Pearce, J., and J. Lynch. (1998). Addressing Controversial Environmental Issues. *Council on Undergraduate Research Quarterly* (Sept.): 10–14.

Perkins, D.D., and A. Wandersman. (1990). You'll Have to Work to Overcome Our Suspicions: The Benefits and Pitfalls of Research with Community Organizations, *Social Policy* 21(1): 32–41.

Puckett, J., and I. Harkavy. (1999). The Action Research Tradition in the United States: Toward a Strategy for Revitalizing the Social Sciences, the University, and the American City. In Davydd J. Greenwood, ed. *Action Research: From Practice to Writing in an International Action Research Development Program.* Amsterdam and Philadelphia: John Benjamins Publishing Company, pp. 147–67.

Reardon, K.M. (2000). An Experiential Approach to Creating an Effective Community-University Partnership: The East St Louis Action Research Project. *Cityscape: A Journal of Policy Development and Research* 5(1): 59–74.

Santiago-Rivera, A.L., G. Skawennio Morse, A. Hunt, and H. Lickers. (1998). Building a Community-Based Research Partnership: Lessons from the Mohawk Nation of Akwesasne. *Journal of Community Psychology* 26(2): 163–74.

Savan, B.I., and D. Bell. (2002). Teaching Sustainability at Universities: Towards Curriculum Greening. In W. Filho, ed. *Environmental Education, Communication and Sustainability* 11. Berlin: Peter Lang, pp. 303–21.

Savan, B.I., A. Morgan, and C. Gore. (2004) Shifts in Environmental Governance in Canada. How are Environmental Groups to Respond? *Environment and Planning.*

Sajan, Beth and David Sider. (2003). Contrasting Approaches to community-based research and a case study of community sustainability in Toronto, Canada. *Local Environment,* 8(3), pp. 303–16.

Sclove, R.E., M.L. Scammell, and B. Holland. (1998). *Community Based Research in the United States: An Introductory Reconnaissance.* Amherst, Loka Institute. MA:

Smith, Susan E., Dennis G. Willms, and Nancy A. Johnson. eds. (1997). *Nurtured by Knowledge: Learning to Do Participatory Action-Research*: Ottawa: Apex Press and International Development Research Centre.

Stringer, Ernest T. (1999) *Action Research,* 2nd ed. Thousand Oaks, CA: Sage.

Sustainable Toronto. (2003). *Promoting Community Sustainability: Linking Research and Action, Projects and Partnerships.* Available online http://www.sustainabletoronto.ca).

CHAPTER 12

Global Cities, Local Knowledge Creation: Mapping a New Policy Terrain on the Relationship between Universities and Cities

Patricia L. McCarney

Cities worldwide are undergoing tremendous transformation because of globalization and rapidly increased rates of urbanization. On this global economic grid, global cities serve as strategic sites both for propelling their nation's international competitiveness, and by virtue of the functions they perform, for driving globalization itself. Numerous attempts have been made to define and rank global cities. Usually, these are based on attributes that include, among others, the presence of head offices of the largest banks, headquarters of the largest corporations, market valuation of companies listed on the stock exchange, and large numbers of foreign banks. Global cities are rightly regarded as centralized points of control for the management and finance of this transnational system. Not as well articulated is the role of new scientific and technological knowledge that is being generated by institutions of higher learning located in these cities. This knowledge is an essential part of the economy of the global city.

The interconnectedness of global cities – how global cities are bound to each other – has been examined, largely with a focus on the hypermobility of capital. Much less attention has been given to the interconnectedness globally of the knowledge economy. The knowledge economy is globally connected through international research networks; traded information, ideas, and innovations; and strategic university partnerships. The global knowledge economy suggests an alternative way in which cities are bound together globally. From these considerations, this chapter will take an exploratory track in mapping a framework for future research to improve understanding of this emergent and vital relationship between global cities and higher education.

Global Urban Development in Perspective

The twenty-first century is our first 'urban century' – for the first time in human history the majority of the world's population will live in cities. It is anticipated that in just a few more years, by 2007, the so-called rural-urban divide will have been crossed, and the world's population will have become predominantly urban. By 2030, more than three-fifths of the total population will be resident in urban areas (U.N. Population Division 2001).

Furthermore, the world is now characterized by tremendously large cities. A mega-city, by definition, has eight million or more inhabitants. In a ranking of city agglomeration by population, made by the United Nations, there are now twenty-eight mega-cities in the world. Some of these largest ranked cities, for example, New York, London, Paris, and Tokyo, have always been in the higher income parts of the world. Now, however, the majority of them are located in the low-income countries. Twenty-two mega-cities are in the developing world, with only six remaining in the developed countries.

Today's cities are tremendously large relative to cities in the recent past. In 1950, only one city in the world, New York, had more than ten million inhabitants. By 2001, seventeen cities had more than ten million people each. Now the largest five cities in the world have more than fifteen million people: Tokyo, with 26.5 million; Sao Paulo, with 18.3; Mexico City, 18.3; New York, 16.8; and Mumbai (Bombay), 16.5 million. Of the seventeen largest cities, all but four – Tokyo, New York, Los Angeles, and Osaka – are in the less developed regions of the world. The thirteen remaining cities with population of more than ten million each are Sao Paulo, Mexico City, Mumbai, Calcutta, Dhaka, Delhi, Shanghai, Buenos Aires, Jakarta, Beijing, Rio de Janeiro, Karachi, and Metropolitan Manilla. It is predicted that by 2015 four cities will join this list, and remarkably, Dhaka will have moved up in rank to become the second largest city in the world, at 22.8 million people.

Almost all of the world population growth between 2000 and 2030 is expected to be concentrated in urban areas. Thus, the urban population will have increased by 2.1 billion persons – which is nearly as much as will have been added to the world population, 2.2 billion – and almost all of this will be absorbed by the urban regions of the less developed countries (U.N. Population Division 2001).

Mega-cities, and rapid rates of urban growth, may be regarded as engines of growth. They will drive our future prosperity and cultural development, with global cities serving as essential modernizing nodal points of the information age. Such cities also introduce enormous problems, particularly with the delivery, functioning, and maintenance of urban services. In many of the more developed countries, cities are underfunded and struggling to balance budgets, deliver basic urban services, and meet demands for improved infrastructure, education, and health care services. Meanwhile, dramatic demographic changes in the developing world are occurring in a context of low economic growth, burdensome debt, and acute urban poverty. This situation has led to the seemingly perpetual incapacities of cities worldwide to meet the rising demand for basic services, and physical, economic, and social infrastructure. Access to services poses tremendous problems for people in mega-cities, particularly with sanitation, collection of solid waste, urban transport, health care services, and education.

Another problem for mega-cities is the critical challenge to supply increasingly sophisticated infrastructure so that they may be globally competitive. Global cities have the dual mandate to perform as global centres of production that must compete internationally for corporate location, information, and innovation, and at the same time, be generators of local economic development opportunities for their own citizens.

Globalization has focused attention on the significance of ensuring robust global cities. The expanding role of transnational corporations operating in urban centres throughout the world, construction of newly integrated trading blocs, globalization of spheres of economic and sociocultural development, and the persistence of international debt and attendant austerity measures, all find expression in the city. In this context, too, the knowledge economy is producing new spatial formations (detailed below) in cities which are connected globally while being locally bound. Often at the core of the knowledge economy network are the city's universities.

The worldwide network of global cities is in a period of dynamic transformation. These cities are functioning as platforms for the post-Fordist economy and as important nodal points for the operations of transnational corporations. They are centres for innovation, and important locations for higher learning, flexible manufacturing, high-technology industries, and related services, especially media and finance. These cities are embedded in dense global distribution networks that increasingly override nation-state boundaries. Global cities, in rich and poor countries alike, are becoming the privileged channels for engaging with the global economy. They are attractive centres for immigration, creative arts, new employment opportunities, and the development of local (and regional) enterprise. Global cities are also centres of mass poverty, substandard housing, and homelessness. Finally, global cities are vast political economic centres that are facing precarious levels of service delivery with limited fiscal capacity – being the third tier of government – to correct these problems.

In global terms, global cities are rightly deemed the dominant engines of growth, and the staple of the global economy is the knowledge economy. It thus becomes important to consider global cities and higher education at their local interface, in the spatial context in which the city and the university coexist. The literature on global cities tends not to focus on the role of higher education in its frame of analysis. Likewise, the literature on higher education and the knowledge economy tends not to focus on the role of cities, although many of the leading universities reside in cities. In this chapter, each will be examined in turn, with a view to constructing a framework for future research on this emergent and vital relationship between global cities and higher education.

A Global Cities Framework

The terminology associated with measuring and defining cities, in keeping with the rapid trends of urbanization, is in flux. Urban settlements, as defined by the United Nations, have 20,000 or more people, whereas cities have 100,000 or more people. Now, there are cities with populations of ten or twenty million people, or more, and so new terms and definitions have emerged. Some of these are 'mega-city,' 'megalopolis,' and 'ecumenopolis,' – reflecting the sheer size of these cities. In the past decade the term 'global city' has emerged to describe not just population magnitude, but also the strategic role of a large city in its relationship to the rest of the world. A global city is differentiated from other large cities by virtue of the functions it performs, functions that drive globalization. Although the knowledge economy often gets mention as a basic feature of globalization, analysts of the global city fail to address the role of institutions of higher learning in the global city in defining its core qualities and functions.

Saskia Sassen has done seminal work in the evolution of examining the global city. Sassen defines global cities as command points in the organization of the world economy, since they are key locations and key marketplaces for the leading industries of the current period, that is, finance and specialized services for firms (Sassen 1994). They are also production sites: global cities are 'sites for (1) the production of special-ized services needed by complex organizations for running a spatially dispersed network of factories, offices and service outlets; and (2) the production of financial innovations and the making of markets, both central to the internationalization and expansion of the financial indus-try' (Sassen 2001, 5).

Peter Hall has also been instrumental in developing the field of study on global cities. Hall (2001) suggests that 'high-level global cities' can be distinguished by a high degree of concentration of four particular clus-ters of advanced services. These are command and control functions such as government, international agencies, and the headquarters of major private corporations; financial and business services, from com-mercial services such as accountancy, law, and advertising to public rela-tions, management consultancy, and the design professions, including architecture, civil engineering, fashion, and interior design; tourism, both for leisure and business; and cultural and creative industries, which can include the live performing arts, museums and galleries, and the print and electronic media (newspapers, magazines, books, film, televi-sion, and radio). Hall argues that these activities prove to be highly sym-biotic: thus, London is simultaneously a business centre, a cultural centre, and a tourist centre (ibid., 61–4).

Over the past thirty years, various scholars studying the world's cities have tended to position them hierarchically – usually ranking them according to various types of attributes. Again, the list of such attributes fails to include institutions of higher learning. Short and colleagues (1996), in countering the generally held assumption that global city pri-macy rests with simply London and New York, offer the following list of attributes for global cities: (1) the head office location of the largest banks ranked by assets; (2) the headquarters of the world's largest indus-trial corporations; (3) the market valuation of companies listed on the stock exchange; and (4) headquarters of the top fifty foreign banks in the United States. This list expands the number of global cities, toppling London and New York in terms of global city primacy, by adding Tokyo, Paris, Frankfurt, Chicago, Seoul, Osaka, and Toronto.

Taylor (1997) and Beaverstock et al. (1999) criticise this ranking-by-attribute approach for ignoring the critical importance of the mutual relationships between individual global cities. In doing so, they draw on Sassen's (1991) identification of 'advanced producer services' or corpo-rate services, which tend to be highly concentrated in a limited number of leading cities. All of these services have specific multicity, multistate locations and a specific role in the current world economy. Beaverstock et al. (1999) inventory the services in 122 cities in terms of their external relations with and connections to other cities and according to four types of firms: advertising, banking and finance, accountancy, and law. They give these cities 'Alpha,' 'Beta,' and 'Gamma' status and rank them accordingly.

Beaverstock et al. produced a ranked list. On it are ten 'Alpha world cities': London, Paris, New York, Tokyo, Chicago, Frankfurt, Hong Kong, Los Angeles, Milan, and Singapore. There are also ten 'Beta world cities': San Francisco, Sydney, Toronto, Zurich, Brussels, Madrid, Mexico City, Sao Paulo, Moscow, and Seoul. Finally, thirty-five 'Gamma world cities' are listed: Amsterdam, Boston, Caracas, Dallas, Dusseldorf, Geneva, Houston, Jakarta, Johannesburg, Melbourne, Osaka, Prague, Santiago, Taipei, Washington, Bangkok, Beijing, Rome, Stockholm, Warsaw, Atlanta, Barcelona, Berlin, Buenos Aires, Budapest, Copenhagen, Hamburg, Istanbul, Kuala Lumpur, Manila, Miami, Minneapolis, Montreal, Munich, and Shanghai. All of the other cities that they studied are listed in an additional category called 'Evidence of World City Formation.' In this latter group are sixty-eight cities. A few of them are in South Asia (e.g., Mumbai, New Delhi and Bangalore), and some are in the Middle East (e.g., Tel Aviv, Abu Dhabi, Cairo, Dubai, Riyadh, and Tehran). African cities are rare, with only Cape Town appearing here (although Johannesburg is listed as a Gamma world city). As Beaverstock et al. point out, significant about this listing is the regional concentration. Their list reflects an 'uneven globalization' with 'evidence of world city formation' largely concentrated in three regions: the northern portion of the Americas, western Europe, and Pacific Asia. Beaverstock et al. call these the world's major 'globalization arenas.'

The firm, or more precisely, advanced producer services are definitive for global city status, although institutions of higher learning are not entered into the calculation. Nevertheless, of interest here is spatial analysis of global cities undertaken by Peter Hall (2001). Hall argues that, although it is important to define global cities in terms of their external linkages, global cities should also be defined in terms of corresponding internal linkages. To make his case, Hall traces the movement of information electronically, and among people, in city regions. He submits that increasingly sophisticated systems of electronic exchange permit flexible kinds of exchange. This observation has implications for the internal geography of global cities and their immediately proximate regions. Hall points to the higher demand for fast transportation networks, including highways, high-speed rail links, and frequent one- to two-hour commuter flights between nodes. Most important for our purposes here, however, is that Hall's depiction of the internal geography of global city regions brings educational sub-centres, at least in spatial terms, into the matrix.

Hall notes that global cities are becoming increasingly complex and sophisticated: 'high-level intelligence and control functions of the global cities are increasingly dispersed across a wide geographical area' and are highly interconnected. This creates new urban forms on a vast scale, networked externally on a global scale, and internally over thousands of square kilometres. 'The resultant geographical structure is quintessentially polycentric' (2001, 73). Hall calls these global cities 'the precursor of a new scale of urban organization' (ibid., 74). This polycentric regional structure is composed of:

- *The traditional downtown centre* – based on walking distance, served by radial public transportation, serving the oldest informational services (banking, insurance, government) and located in the old city cores (e.g., downtown Manhattan, the City of London);
- A *newer business centre* – serving newer services which have expanded in the twentieth century, such as corporate headquarters, the media, and new services such as public relations, design, advertising (e.g., London's West End, midtown Manhattan);
- An *internal edge city* – resulting from pressure of space in traditional centres and on old industrial or transport land (e.g., London Docklands or Canary Wharf and the World Financial Centre);
- An *external edge city* – often located on the axis of the main airport (e.g., London's Heathrow, Paris's Charles de Gaulle, Washington's Reagan Dulles Corridor);
- An *outermost edge city complex* – for research and development (R&D), usually twenty to forty miles (thirty to sixty kilometres) from the core (e.g., Reading, Greenwich Connecticut); and,
- *Specialized subcentres* – usually education centres, entertainment and sporting complexes, convention centres, waterfront centres, and the like.

Centres of education are recognized as being part of the polycentric regional structure of global cities, albeit as one among many specialized subcentres. Nevertheless, it is significant that Hall describes these education subcentres of the global city in the following terms: 'These take a

great variety of forms and locations ... some are older centers, formerly
separate and independent, that have become progressively embedded in
the wider metropolitan area (Oxford, Cambridge, Uppsala, New Haven).
Some of these may take on new functions, witness the emergence of the
Cambridge region as a major high-technology center ("Silicon Fen")
since 1970' (2001, 74).

In constructing a framework for the global city within which to consider
the role of higher education, an important aspect is the notion of global
cities as 'technopoles' (Borja and Castells 1997; Castells and Hall 1994).
'Technopolises' (Borja and Castells) have taken root in large metropolitan areas, often on the suburban periphery, such as Silicon Valley near
San Francisco, the Research Triangle in North Carolina, and Route 128
around Boston. These sites represent localized agglomerations in a new
global context. These technological industrial complexes stemmed
from the spatial articulation of specific factors of production: capital,
labour, and raw materials. In the kinds of examples just given, the raw
materials are new scientific and technological knowledge. This knowledge is generated by research institutions such as Stanford University,
the California Institute of Technology, the University of North Carolina
at Chapel Hill, and the Massachusetts Institute of Technology. In their
extensive study of technopoles, Castells and Hall (1994, 476) describe
cities or areas within cities that are devoted to research and innovation
in high technology:

> They are promoted by central or regional or local governments, often in
> association with universities, together with the private companies that
> occupy the resulting spaces. And these technopoles, the more interesting
> ones, are invariably more than just plots to rent. They also contain signifi-
> cant institutions of a quasi-public or nonprofit type, such as universities or
> research institutes, which are specifically implanted there in order to help in
> the generation of new information. For this is the function of the techno-
> pole: it is to generate the basic materials of the informational economy.

Despite all of the activity in planning, developing, and incubating new
technopoles, 'most of the world's actual high-technology production
and innovation still comes from areas that are not usually heralded as
innovative milieux, and indeed may have few of their physical features:
the great metropolitan areas of the industrialized world.' Tokyo, Paris,
and London are 'quintessential innovative milieux,' according to Castells and Hall (1994, 483).

Global cities today are not like their predecessors of the nineteenth century, which concentrated industries that produced manufactured goods such as textiles and steel. Global cities emerged at the end of the twentieth century as new centres producing information, research, knowledge, and innovative ideas. These new forms of economic production rely on science, technology, new knowledge, and information. These have become the inputs to a city's growth and competitiveness globally. This argues for an examination of the role of higher education in the economics of the new global city.

Universities, Intellectual Capital, and the Economy

Economists who use productivity and competitiveness as their starting points, employ indicators such as levels of education of segments of the workforce to determine prosperity. The increase in earnings associated with higher levels of education is seen as evidence of the positive impact of education on productivity (see, e.g., Institute for Competitiveness and Prosperity 2003, 20). In addition, levels of education are calculated within what Richard Florida (2002) has termed a 'Talent Index' which is a measure of human capital in a region based on the region's share of adults with a bachelor's degree or higher. Universities play an important role in building a strong base of human capital, and in granting degrees. This human capital determines a nation's competitiveness in the global economy.

In addition to generating higher levels of education and intellectual capital, and thereby contributing to the index of productivity, an important and central role of the university is that of creating knowledge and information and generating new ideas for research and innovation. The link between innovation and transferring this knowledge and information into high-technology production processes has increasingly come under scrutiny.

Although new knowledge is generated in many places, relatively few people or organizations can absorb and apply that knowledge (Fogarty 1999). There appears to be a consistent pattern in the flow of patented information from universities. Fogarty (1999) shows how intellectual property migrates from universities to high-technology regions such as the greater Boston area, the San Francisco Bay Area, and the New York metropolitan area. The specific types of high-technology production are well catalogued in a 'Tech-Pole Index,' created by the Milken Institute, that is based on the output of the city-region in high-tech goods and services. The Tech-Pole Index reflects a city-region's level of specialization in technology-intensive output, and the absolute value of the city-region's high-technology economy. The index includes the following items: drugs and pharmaceuticals; computer and office equipment; electronic components and accessories; aircraft and parts; guided missiles, space vehicles and parts; search, detection, navigation, guidance, and aeronautical systems, instruments and equipment; laboratory equipment and instruments, medical and dental instruments and supplies; telephone communications and services; computer programming, data processing, and other computer-related services; motion picture production and allied services; engineering, architectural, and surveying services; research, development, and testing services (DeVol 1999, 34).

Governments, as well as institutions of higher learning, are seeking reliable connections between higher education and the creation of wealth. South-east Asian economies attach tremendous importance to the generation of knowledge and the development of commercially exploitable ideas, as evidenced by their massive investments in higher education. Malaysia, for example, intends to become a net exporter of higher education by 2020, while China plans to be producing nearly ten million graduate scientists and engineers by the same date (Robertson 1999, 30): 'Developed and emerging economies alike have been seduced by the prospect that the successful exploitation of a society's intellectual capital – the untapped stock of ideas and inventions which the most academically endowed possess – will deliver competitive advantage through improved productivity and economic growth' (ibid., 18).

'Academic capitalism' is a term developed by Slaughter and Leslie (1997). It is particularly instructive in that it addresses both the commercialization of the research relationship and the shifting power relationships inherent in this new process – fields and disciplines closely aligned to the market gain influence within the university.

The opinion is emerging that universities must provide a 'suitable return on public investment by producing both greater volumes of high-skilled labor and the innovations necessary to refresh the economy. They have learned to emphasize the spillover effect of their work into commercially viable ventures, greater productivity, and economic competitiveness' (ibid. 1999, 19). The relationship between universities and the private sector can bring real benefits to the latter. Drawing on the results of a 1995 report by Coopers and Lybrand, on 400 American companies and entitled *Report on University-Business Joint Ventures*, Robertson suggests that academic entrepreneurs can intervene and add value to businesses. Companies with university partnerships had productivity rates 59 per cent higher than companies without such relationships; they also had 21 per cent higher annual revenues and 23 per cent more capital investments. All in all, companies involved with research universities earn substantial benefits in increased productivity, profitability, and innovation (ibid., 26).

In *Creating Entrepreneurial Universities*, Burton Clark (1998) examines five case studies of universities in Great Britain, the Netherlands, Sweden, and Finland that have been 'transformed' so that through greater partnerships with the private sector, they have reduced their dependence on state funding. These universities are the University of Warwick and the University of Strathclyde in Great Britain, University of Trente in the Netherlands, Chalmers of Technology in Sweden, and the University of Joensuu in Finland. In the case of the University of Warwick in England, Clark observes: 'The idea [for reducing dependence on outside funding] was sharpened with a strategic decision not to generate new income by "fundraising" – "we would not go begging for money" – but to actually earn it ... As put later by the much-involved registrar, Michael Shattock, "We had to find ways to generate funding from other sources; we did not see why people or companies would simply give us money so we decided to earn it"' (1998, 16).

Clark points to the successful efforts of Warwick's engineering department, beginning in 1980, to foster close collaboration with major companies and to act as the research and development arm of such companies. This close association with industry at Warwick, enshrined in the establishment of the Warwick Manufacturing Group, is in Clark's opinion a model for other universities to follow. He refers to the establishment of the associated Warwick Science Park, which is a partnership with Barclays Bank, as another model for similar settings elsewhere. Clark points out that 'Barclays wanted a relationship with the university that would link the bank to high technology companies and their activities' (ibid., 19).

The creation of new ideas, and their commercial exploitation for creation of wealth is at the centre of the debate over the role of the university in the new knowledge economy. Whereas universities traditionally served in the production and dissemination of knowledge, now technology transfer and the formation of firms places the university in a new alignment with the business community and the global market. Etzkowitz and Leydesdorff contend that a new social contract between the university and the larger society is being negotiated in terms much more specific than the old ones: 'The former contract was based on a linear model of innovation, presuming only long-term contributions of academic knowledge to the economy. Now both long- and short-term contributions are seen to be possible, based on examples of firm formation and research contracts in fields such as biotechnology and computer science. A spiral model of innovation is required to capture multiple reciprocal linkages at different stages of the capitalization of knowledge' (1997, 1).

The tension between the necessity to generate wealth and the simultaneous necessity of civic advancement has become increasingly evident over the past decade in a divide in the literature on higher education. Views on the role of the university are divided along the above lines in Canada, the United States, and some European countries. Some celebrate the entrepreneurial university and the links of the university to the knowledge economy as one of the key engines of economic growth and a nation's competitiveness in the global economy. Others are opposed to what they see as takeover of the university by corporate interests. They are concerned about the problems that poses for the freedom of speech and assembly and the cultivation of critical consciousness and enlightened dissent.

A number of Canadian academics have recently taken that perspective. What they see as the corporate takeover of higher education is leading to curtailment, in their view, of free and critical inquiry, with implications for the freedom of speech and assembly (see, e.g., Pocklington and Tupper 2002; Noble 2002; Turk 2000; Tudiver 1999).

In his book entitled *The Great Transformation in Higher Education 1960–1980*, Clark Kerr examines the issue of the current and ideal functions of the university. He is steadfast in his call for protecting the right of dissent and he states:

> Basic to the new consensus should be the absolute and total protection of the right to dissent. Dissent is not something which should be cherished for sake of the faculty members or students alone. Dissent on campus should be cherished for the sake of society. I have often thought that the rules on academic freedom are really basically for the protection of society, so that it will be assured that there will be freely placed before it a variety of points of view from which it might choose – some viewpoints being quite critical. A greater effort to develop understanding on the part of the American people of the positive role played by dissent is necessary. Society can only renew itself adequately if there are people who will criticize it on the basis of scholarship. (Kerr 1991, 194)

New forms of local economic development strategy and consideration of the place of the university in the cities in which they are located are taking on new importance.

Studies of universities and their relationship with local knowledge economies are growing in both number and detail. In the most known case of Silicon Valley, we now understand that the initial start-up companies in micro-computing were born from in-house university projects by researchers at Stanford University. The joint founders of Hewlett-Packard were Stanford graduates (Robertson 1999, 31). Much of the entrepreneurial talent in the area had initially arrived to attend one of its major universities such as the University of California at Berkeley and Stanford University. After graduation, they are staying in the area, generating appreciable wealth (Huffman and Quigley 2002). Firms spawned by MIT graduates, including Gillette, Digital, and Campbell's Soups, are now generating U.S.$230 billion in revenues, which is more than the gross national product (GNP) of many countries, and employ 1.2 million people. Half of these firms were established by alumni within fifteen years of graduation, but 15 per cent within six years (Robertson 1999, 31). The Boston area is exceptional for its concentration of knowledge-intensive institutions, with sixty-five universities and colleges, and also because it is a place in which 'higher education and local industry mingle seamlessly in knowledge work and wealth creation.'

Policy-makers and university leaders the world over are striving to understand this seamless relationship between knowledge creation and wealth creation. In part, this quality can be attributed to planning and local leadership in the city itself and its universities. But that is not all of it. In the case of Boston, 'researchers at MIT regard the transfer of academic ideas from the university to the business environment as a natural feature of their professional lives' and in California, 'the transfer of the outcomes of intellectual capital from "ideas" to commercial product was, and continues to be, iterative throughout Silicon Valley to the extent that the results of academic research are meshed seamlessly with venture capital in the pursuit of commercial viability' (Robertson 1999, 31).

The essential argument that emerges from this dual examination of both global cities and higher education is that universities are a vital local asset in global cities, where intellectual capital is produced and ideas are transferred to a market for wealth creation. A strong resonance has been revealed, as well as the need to improve knowledge on this emergent and vital relationship between global cities and higher education.

Inroads are being made, and the work of Richard Florida offers a critical beginning. He draws on the work of Fogarty, to argue that to turn intellectual property into economic wealth, creative communities surrounding the universities must be able to absorb and utilize it within a social structure of creativity. The surrounding community must have the capacity to absorb and exploit the innovation and technologies that the university generates, and also help put in place the broader lifestyle amenities and quality of place sought by the 'creative class' (Florida 2002, 293). His main thesis is that the 'creative class' has certain preferences that cities and regions must accommodate if they seek to remain competitive. These include diversity and bohemian lifestyles. Florida sees the important role played by universities, noting that they can act as magnets for attracting high-level technological talent: 'Regions with top-flight universities, like Stanford and MIT, can ... draw the best and brightest high school grads from everywhere and hold onto many of them after graduation' (ibid., 30). The presence of a major research university thus becomes a critical advantage in terms of economic development. Florida posits a triple role for the university, in what he refers to as 'the 3T's of creative places – technology, talent and tolerance' (ibid., 292):

1 *Technology* – Universities are centres for cutting-edge research in various fields, from software to biotechnology, and important sources of new technologies and spin-off companies.
2 *Talent* – Universities are amazingly effective attractors of talent and their effect is 'truly magnetic.' Eminent researchers and scientists attracted to the universities, in turn, attract graduate students, generate spin-off companies, and encourage other companies to locate nearby, creating a cycle of self-reinforcing growth.
3 *Tolerance* – Universities help create a progressive, open, and tolerant climate for people that helps attract and retain members of the creative class. For example, many college towns, from Austin, Texas, to Iowa City, Iowa, have always been places where gays and other 'outsiders' could find a home.

All of these observations have implications for policy. The need for alliances across the concerned policy community is recognized. Etzkowitz and Leydesdorff (1997) suggest a 'triple helix' of university, industry, and government relations as one framework for the construction of alliances. At the municipal level, it is critical that local leaders, both in the mayor's office and in council, adopt a strategic role and become entrepreneurial and innovative in building such alliances. Muncipal leaders will need to draw on a wider network of resources than was normally the case in the past and build alliances with not only local and other tiers of government but also universities, private sector interests, civil society groups, and non-profit organizations. In creating innovative local economic policy, civic leaders must be cognizant of the differing cultures, social structures, and politics of these institutional networks and the economic trajectory each is seeking to influence.

Another consideration for local economic policy is how to keep graduates from leaving the area. Graduate retention initiatives should be promoted as a way of upgrading the stock of higher-level skills in the local economy. Universities used to be regarded simply as institutions that produced graduates for a national labour market, and there was little concern for retaining graduates for the region's own labour market. Little is known, however, about the flow of students through universities and into the local workforce. The figures for Boston cited earlier were striking in that U.S.$230 billion in revenues was generated by firms established by MIT graduates and half of these firms were established by alumni within the first fifteen years after graduation from MIT. The need for the city to retain its university graduates in the local economy is critical for its long-term prosperity in the global economy.

The university is the magnet that attracts top talent. But it is up to the city, in coalition with its citizens and its business community, to ensure a quality of place to retain that talent. Stanford University did not turn the Silicon Valley area into a high-tech powerhouse on its own; regional business leaders and venture capitalists built the local infrastructure that this kind of economy needed. The City of Palo Alto, bordering Stanford University, functions as a hub in providing office space for start-up companies, venture capitalists, and high-technology service providers, as well as a wide range of amenities. On the east coast of the United States, the Kendall Square area around MIT has been an important new site for urban renewal. Old warehouses and factories have become home to start-up companies, venture capital funds, restaurants, microbreweries, cafes, and hotels. Regional leaders in Austin, Texas, have taken aggressive measures to create not only incubator facilities and venture capital but also outdoor amenities and the quality of place that creative people demand. University and regional leaders in Philadelphia, Providence, and New Haven are also actively trying to generate such quality of place in and around their universities (see, e.g., Florida 2002).

Identifying a New Policy Terrain for Global Cities and Universities

Universities now face the multiple challenges of building research competitiveness to facilitate commercialization and the generation of wealth, while fulfilling their social mandate to reach out to their local communities and offer access to students of all incomes, and their political mandate to ensure open debate, dissent, and freedom of thought, while also teaching students and producing new research results. Cities now face the challenges of being globally competitive while also meeting the demands of their local citizens, particularly those less privileged. A disjuncture is arising in this policy environment that reflects society's ongoing debates over whether to promote growth or equity; over what is to be considered to be in the public domain and what are private interests; and over notions of exclusivity and inclusivity. Further research on the nature of the relationship between global cities and the role of the university ought to proceed in this context. Cities and universities are alike in that both are seen as places that engender civic tolerance, democratic values, and civilizing forces. In other words, together cities and universities can become the mediating front on which to consider the broad debates on the implications of global change.

In the policy environment, local leaders are mediating demands associated with building competitive global cities and improving the lives of the city's residents, in particular, the lives of their poor. This situation often manifests itself as a duel between a set of demands that are externally driven both by foreign firms and national levels of government concerned with the creation of competitive cities for enhanced macroperformance and a set of demands that are more internally driven by the city's local constituencies. The dilemma for local government policymakers, occupying as they do the pivotal local space of urban politics, is how to reconcile these opposing pressures.

Identification of this policy disjuncture allows us to connect debates about the entrepreneurial university to an interesting new policy terrain, internal to the city. The more sophisticated business interests and knowledge-rich human capital seeking urban improvements for enhanced competitiveness are in competition with organized low-income communities, small enterprise associations, and civic groups demanding improved access to livelihoods, basic services and the new economy. New jobs in information-based services, technology, finance, and law are available to very few citizens in the global cities. In the less-developed countries, numbers of city workers resorting to the informal sector of the economy are rising. Increasingly polarized groups are occupying cities: on one side is a new 'talent class' with jobs at the core of the global economy and, on the other, an expanding poorer population of informal workers, while wages for the so-called under-valorized job sector are falling ever more behind.

In the university, some students, faculty, and graduates are entrepreneurs, innovators, and inventers and a strong part of the high-level talent spoken of so much in this chapter. Many, however, are not. The university will continue to be home to theorists, humanists, and social advocates. Indeed, many of these people will continue their work to ensure a quality of life in their city that is inclusive and tolerant.

Discontinuities are also emerging. The categorization of Alpha, Beta, Gamma, and soon-to-be Gamma cities, described in detail at the beginning of this chapter, indicates that a larger and larger urban system, networked with cities of various sizes, is forming, with most of that system located in a few and economically dominant geographical regions of the world. The question of who is in and who is out of this network is looming greater. This sharpening inequality is also troubling within single countries between their key global cities and their other regions.

In this policy terrain, the question of agency arises. What influence do local people, local leaders, smaller businesses, NGOs, and simple individual citizens have in shaping the development course for their city? For locally elected political leaders, how much manoeuvrability is there? How much voice does urban civil society have in setting the agenda for these local leaders to shape their city and allocate resources? Effective agency is highly dependent on the political process and the form of governance. Who influences the urban agenda in global cities? Will the powerful elites continue to dominate the local political agenda, or are the majority, low-income, and often marginalized sectors of the city gaining influence, either through urban social movements or other forms of civic action?

In presenting the global cities framework, as it has recently evolved, this chapter argues for the importance of situating universities and examining the role of higher education in analyses of the global city. It argues that the spatial location of universities in cities is too often overlooked as a crucial context in studies of innovation. New research that better examines this essential relationship is called for. The new policy terrain that this subject encompasses has been shown to be complex and difficult to navigate because of deep divides and disjunctures. Analysts of global cities and higher education need to zoom out and develop a more broadly based perspective. We know that universities are much more than creators of wealth in the narrow sense of commercializing ideas. We also know that cities are much more than just competitive financial empires or the hearts of capitalism. Louis Wirth once stated that urbanism could be conceived of as a way of life (1938). Such an interpretation defies reductionism in analysing cities. So, too, the relationship between global cities and universities is more than just economically determined. Cities and universities each represent core political values, associated with civic tolerance, diversity, democratic freedoms, inclusiveness, community, and equity.

The form of governance in both cities and universities becomes critical if this complex policy terrain is to be successfully manoeuvred. In cities, this means an effective decentralization of responsibilities and fiscal powers, political legitimacy, as well as open forums for groups in civil society to engage meaningfully in making decisions on local policy. In universities, this means open management structures in which the central role of the university in this shifting policy terrain continues to be debated, and the ability to build alliances globally in ways that create inclusiveness for their students and faculties in a broadly based, transdisciplinary manner. In a global context of profound change, our cities and our universities will continue to undergo fundamental reform. This climate creates both the potential and the space for new considerations on innovation, more inclusive alliances, and a more broadly based trajectory redirected towards prosperity for all.

REFERENCES

Beaverstock, J.G., R.G. Smith, and P.J. Taylor. (1999). *A Roster of World Cities*. GaWC Research Bulletin 5. Loughborough: University of Loughborough, Department of Geography. http://www.lboro.ac.uk/gawc.

Borja, Jordi, and Manuel Castells. (1997). *Local and Global: The Management of Cities in the Information Age*. London: Earthscan Publications.

Castells, Manuel, and Peter Hall. (1994). Technopoles, Mines and Foundries of the Informational Economy. Reprinted from *Technopoles of the World*. In Richard T. LeGates and Frederic Stout, eds. (1996). *The City Reader*. London: Routledge.

Clark, Burton R. (1998). *Creating Entrepreneurial Universities: Organizational Pathways of Transformation*. International Association of Universities. Guilford, Surrey: Biddles Ltd.

DeVol, R. (1999). *America's High-Tech Economy: Growth, Development and Risks for Metropolitan Economics*. Santa Monica, CA: Milken Institute.

Etzkowitz, Henry, and Loett Leydesdorff, eds. (1997). *Universities and the Global Knowledge Economy*. London: Cassell.

Florida, Richard. (2002). *The Rise of the Creative Class*. New York: Basic Books.

– (2003). The New American Dream. *Washington Monthly* (March).

Fogarty, Michaels, with Amit K. Sinha. (1999). University-Industry Relationships and Regional Innovation Systems – Why Older Industrial Regions Can't Generalize from Route 128 and Silicon Valley. In Lewis M. Branscomb, Fumio Kodama and Richard L. Florida, eds. *Industrializing Knowledge: University-Industry Linkages in Japan and the United States*. MIT Press, pp. 473–509.

Hall, Peter. (2001). Global City-Regions in the Twenty-first Century. In Allen J. Scott, ed. *Global City-Regions: Trends, Theory, Policy*. Oxford: Oxford University Press.

Huffman, David, and John M. Quigley. (2002). The Role of the University in Attracting High-Tech Entrepreneurship: A Silicon Valley Tale. *Annals of Regional Science* 36: 403–19.

Institute for Competitiveness and Prosperity (2003). *Missing Opportunities: Ontario's Urban Prosperity Gap*. Working Paper 3. Toronto: author.

Kerr, Clark. (1991). *The Great Transformation in Higher Education, 1960–1980*, Albany: State University of New York Press.

Noble, David F. (2002). *Digital Diploma Mills: The Automation of Higher Education*. Toronto: Between the Lines.

Pocklington, Tom, and Tupper Allan. (2002). *No Place to Learn: Why Universities Aren't Working*. Vancouver: UBC Press.

Robertson, David. (1999). 'Knowledge Societies, Intellectual Capital and Economic Growth.' In Harry Gray, ed. *Universities and the Creation of Wealth*. Buckingham: Open University Press.

Sassen, Saskia. (1991). *The Global City: New York, London, Tokyo*. Princeton, NJ: Princeton University Press.

– (1994). *Cities in a World Economy*. Thousand Oaks, CA: Pine Forge Press.

– (2001). *The Global City: New York, London, Tokyo*, 2nd ed. Princeton, NJ: Princeton University Press.

Short, J.R., Y. Kim, M. Kuus, and H. Wells. (1996). The Dirty Little Secret of World Cities Research – Data Problems in Comparative Analysis. *International Journal of Urban and Regional Research* 20: 697–719.

Slaughter, Sheila, and Larry L. Leslie. (1999). *Academic Capitalism: Politics, Policies and the Entrepreneurial University*. Baltimore: Johns Hopkins University Press.

Taylor, P.J. (1997). Hierarchical Tendencies amongst World Cities: A Global Research Proposal. *Cities* 14: 323–32.

Tudiver, Neil. (1999). *Universities for Sale: Resisting Corporate Control over Canadian Higher Education*. Toronto: James Lorimer.

Turk, James L., ed. (2000). *The Corporate Campus: Commercialization and the Dangers to Canada's Colleges and Universities.* Toronto: James Lorimer.

U.N. Population Division. (2001). *World Urbanization Prospects: The 2001 Revision.* New York: United Nations.

Wirth, Louis. (1938). Urbanism as a Way of Life. *American Journal of Sociology* 44 (1938): 1–24.

Creating Knowledge:
New Challenges and Roles

CHAPTER 13

Creating Knowledge, Strengthening Nations: The Role of Research and Education in Humanities and Social Sciences in Government Agendas for Innovation

Shirley Neuman

I take as my starting point a phenomenon that does **not** foreground the humanities and social sciences. Indeed, my starting point often leaves humanities and social science scholars and teachers in the defensive posture of pariahs in technoland. My subject is the agendas that governments develop to improve global competitiveness and gross domestic product (GDP). These agendas are published as government documents, can easily be found on government Web sites, are launched with gravity and hoopla, and are touted as government initiatives and priorities designed to strengthen the nation's economy. They sally into the world garbed in the rhetoric of whatever qualities business schools, politicians, and lesser pundits of the moment deem most essential to economic success.

Today many national agendas, including those of Canada, Australia, the European Union and many of its constituent members such as France and the United Kingdom stress 'innovation.' In Canada's innovation strategy (Government of Canada 2001a, 2001b), in the European Union's 'Sixth Framework' (European Commission Research Centre 2002), and in the United Kingdom's 'Science and Innovation Policy for the 21st Century' (2002) definitions of 'innovation' are narrowly tailored, if far from uniform.[1]

The European Union draws close links between innovation and 'technological innovation,' taking as a fundamental assumption that 'the role of R&D as a driving force for a competitive and dynamic knowledge-based economy is linked to the economy's capacity to turn new knowledge into technological innovation' (Commission of the European Communities 2002, 3). The United Kingdom's June 2000 white paper presenting its 'science and innovation policy' asserts that 'innovation is the motor of the modern economy, turning ideas and knowledge into products and services ... The innovation process is a cycle in which ideas, talent and design skills, money and management, come together to create products and service which consumers want.' Like many innovation agendas, that of the United Kingdom is clear that 'the cycle of innovation must be fed by ideas and basic knowledge' and it emphasizes the need for 'basic curiosity driven research' (Government of the United Kingdom 2000, 'Foreword').

A discussion paper put out by the Government of France (via the Internet, but no longer available) for the period October 2002 through February 2003, defined 'innovation' as a largely psychological environment which creates a rapprochement between researchers, on the one hand, and business and industry, on the other. In this 'environment,' researchers would value 'enterprise, commercialization and profit,' and the public would develop an 'image' of researchers 'turned less exclusively to the lab and more towards industry.' (See Gouvernement de France [2002] for the innovation plan that resulted from the national exercise in consultation.)

However a government frames the question of innovation, the energy it seeks to set loose under this rubric has two preconditions: research and development and the 'transfer' of research findings from bench to business by applying research findings in the development of new technologies to be used in producing new products and services. Innovation agendas give rise to national research priorities that are framed in thematic rather than disciplinary terms.[2] In any event, these agendas cannot and should not be lightly dismissed for, well thought out and adequately implemented, they do much to improve our standard of living and quality of life. Poorly thought out, and badly implemented, they have unintended and sometimes damaging consequences.

Most innovation agendas pay scant attention to the possible contributions the humanities and social sciences might make. Documents that do intimate a role for the knowledge from these disciplines do not articulate precisely what that role might be. This holds even in the EU documents, which list the 'human sciences' as one of six priorities. At the best, government innovation policies are open enough in their language that a social scientist or scholar working in the humanities could adapt the government agenda to his or her own research program, as is the case with Canada's innovation strategy. An innovation policy may allude to 'opportunities in new and emerging fields of research that will provide social, cultural, and economic benefit' (Kemp 1999). However, such openings, with their emphasis on 'new' and 'emerging' areas of research, as opposed to traditional disciplinary research, offer scant hope or honour for the humanities or social sciences.

My subject is the very legitimate role the humanities and social sciences can play and should play in such agendas – an honourable role that neither trivializes nor inappropriately commercializes humanities and social science research and education and that can contribute immeasurably to the quality of our lives, our 'innovation,' and our governments' agendas for innovation. My strategies are simple. By examining Canada's innovation agenda, I shall point to the social science research that underpins many such documents and then cite some areas of education and research in the social sciences and humanities that are critical to what we now call innovation.

Canada's Innovation Strategy: Its Foundation in Social Science Research

The Government of Canada lays out its innovation strategy in two documents under the brave banners of *Knowledge Matters* (2001a) and *Achieving Excellence* (2001b). The logic of the strategy is that if Canada improves its global competitiveness, and hence its national wealth, it will have the resources to improve health care, social services, and education programs for its citizens. And these improvements, in a virtuous circle, will make Canada and Canadians more productive and, therefore, more globally competitive. The nation's citizens will be healthy, wealthy, and wise, and, although *Achieving Excellence* does not quite say so, they might even be happy.[3]

These documents define the role of universities in two ways. First, universities are the 'dominant players in terms of training the highly qualified people who create and apply knowledge' (2001b, 9). Secondly, universities do research: applied research (often in partnership with industry) and basic research (financed by the federal granting councils, provincial research and matching grant programs, and by the universities themselves). 'Leverag[ing] the commercialization' of both basic and applied research ranks high among the government's priorities, and its innovation agenda is clear about its expectations for universities in this regard: 'Academic institutions would be expected to manage the public investment in research as a strategic national asset by developing innovation strategies and reporting on commercialization outcomes. An evolving partnership would see universities more aggressively contribute to innovation in Canada, in return for long-term government commitment to their knowledge infrastructure' (2001b, 52). The relevance to this mandate of research in the fields of pharmaceuticals, biotechnology, advanced materials, industrial and chemical engineering, laser optics, computer engineering, biochemistry, and a host of related fields is clear and important; that of the humanities and social sciences is less evident.

In the section of *Achieving Excellence* titled 'The Knowledge Performance Challenge,' text boxes highlight inspirational examples of innovation by Canadians. These models of innovation – and they are inspiring – include Canadaarm2 on the international space station, high-tech communications equipment on board commercial trucks, longer-life cellphone batteries, CA*NET 3, three-dimensional imaging systems to detect concealed items in cargo and luggage.

They include the development of the first heat recovery ventilator for homes, commercialization of new agricultural products, research and production of marine-based natural health and nutritional products, technology to reduce acidic drainage from mine wastes, the development of the ultraviolet index, wildlands fire information systems, the use of satellite technology for greater precision in monitoring sea ice conditions, and use of geographical information system (GIS) technology to calibrate applications of pesticides and water to crops, as well as to map seabeds in targeting scallops for harvesting. They include therapy for age-related macular degeneration, an innovative wheelchair drive mechanism, and development of an artificial spider silk fine enough to use in making sutures and tough enough to protect spaceships from celestial debris.

Finally, they include a single example that does not involve any significant component of engineering technology – the development by a First Nations community of a successful business plan to realize new revenue.

I do not cite this emphasis on engineering technology in order to dispute its critical importance to our industrial, health, and knowledge economies. Nor am I indulging in a complaint about how humanities and social science research is not included in national innovation strategies, for, in fact, the document opens space for such research at several points, although admittedly without great precision. I cite it to point to the comparative absence of examples from the humanities and social sciences, and to the difficulty the authors of the innovation agenda seem to find in articulating a role for the knowledge of these disciplines in a national research agenda. This is the case, even though Prime Minister Jean Chrétien, in introducing *Achieving Excellence*, said: 'In the 21st century, our econimic and social goals must be pursued hand-in-hand. Let the world see in Canada a society marked by innovation and inclusion, by excellence and justice.'

Nevertheless, there is one way in which social science research is everywhere in the innovation strategy – a kind of palimpsest, a writing not quite erased but also not quite recovered and articulated, over which the innovation strategy is inscribed. I refer to the footnotes of *Knowledge Matters* (Government of Canada 2001a). *Knowledge Matters* makes its case for skills, training, and research education on the basis of evidence drawn from reams of social science research studies and statistics on population and labour supply, as well as on the basis of indicators of productivity, economic status, and educational achievement. Social science research tells the Government of Canada that there are problems to be addressed and what those problems are: that, for example, GDP per hour worked is 19 per cent lower in Canada than in the United States and that 25 per cent of Canadian high school graduates are insufficiently literate to work in the knowledge economy. Without social science research, the Government of Canada – indeed, any government – would be hard put for evidence that the country needed an 'innovation' agenda.

If social science research provides the evidence that nations need 'innovation' agendas, then what can social science and humanities research contribute to that agenda? In the next sections, I want to recover at least the outlines of the palimpsest to name some of the areas of social science and humanities research and education that critically underpin nations that are to remain or to become prosperous, peaceful, just, productive. Let me begin with the question that drives innovation agendas: competitiveness in a global economy.

Global Competitiveness

Let us assume that there are really only three large categories of knowledge that a country needs so that it can begin to develop strategies for global competitiveness (although it will assuredly need many more kinds of knowledge to realize those strategies). It needs to know what the conditions for success in a global environment and economy are. It needs to know the conditions of productivity in its own country and the ways in which they measure up or fall short. At least as important, it needs to know about other countries to which it is intending to take its goods and services to market – about their peoples, cultures, governments, economies, and values.

For a country to know these things, it needs the research and academic programs of the social science darlings of innovation agenda setters, the economists and the professors of finance and marketing, to be sure. But it also needs research in management practices, business processes; in demographics, sociology, comparative politics, diasporas, in the meaning of nations' cultural productions, in history, in religions. Moreover, researchers often will be better able to explain the movement of labour, capital, goods, and knowledge, and will be better able to understand political and social problems, if they work in interdisciplinary teams. Closer links between research in economics and comparative politics, for example, could further enormously our understanding of global markets and of the social and national – as well as economic – conditions that determine those markets. So, too, might intensified forays into 'behavioural' political science and economics, linking these disciplines to those of sociology and psychology, but also to history and religion, and asking about cultural and individual adaptation and motivation in relation to economic conditions.

If, for example, Canada's GDP is 19 per cent less per hour worked than that of the United States, it is reasonable to assume that this may not be entirely a function of technology lag, higher taxes, or even the level of employee training or R&D spending. Might there be assumptions in Canada about what constitutes a reasonable, or good, life that lead to lower productivity? Are there modes of management or employee interaction in Canada's organizations that are deeply ingrained by virtue of Canadian value systems or the Canadian legal context but that inhibit productivity and innovation or, perhaps, reduce motivation? Do the social values enshrined in Canadian legislation, as opposed, let us say, to the values of American individualism, lead to different aspirations, goals, and levels of productivity for both individuals and firms? These are questions existing in the realm of speculation merely, and readers may well decide that to connect Canada's Constitution with national productivity is stretching it. I ask them, however, in all seriousness to indicate something of the role that research into issues of organization, cultural practices, social structures, education, and values might play in understanding why Canadians do or do not innovate and why Canadians might choose not to – even if this means forgoing the economic advantages of doing so.

As for the knowledge that individuals – the businessmen in the field – need if they are to engage successfully in the cross-cultural interactions that sustain the global economy, let me take as my example (an anecdotal one) an American vice-president of Solomon Smith Barney, a man who often spent his days brokering deals between Paris and Tokyo or Hong Kong and New York. He had majored in economics as an undergraduate and then gone on to complete a Master of Business Administration degree and to his very successful career. When I asked him if he now felt that there were subjects he should have studied but had not, which might have provided him knowledge that would help him in his current work, he answered unhesitatingly: 'religions and history.'

What this man needed to know, in order to interact effectively with the team on the other side of the video conference table, on the other side of the world, was something of the social, political, and cultural history of the people with whom he was attempting a conversation. He needed to understand something of their religious beliefs, their education, and the assumptions and priorities to which history, religion, and education had led them. He needed to know these things because he needed to understand the cultural, intellectual, and emotional formation of his counterparts and the ways that formation shaped their approach to problems, questions, concerns, style of negotiation, and expectations for outcomes at the international table. As he very simply put it, 'when they think about a time frame, do they think about their grandchildren or the next quarter?' He would need to know this whether he worked in international finance, international diplomacy, or international trade.

If we do not understand the ethical, philosophical, religious, and historical assumptions underlying the belief systems of the people we deal with, we can sometimes run over them or walk around them (or they will run over or walk around us), but we cannot work with them and we can seldom compete with them. Education in the humanities and social sciences and research into history, religion, and cultural productions are fundamental to that understanding.

Innovation as Phenomenon, Process, and End

Innovation as phenomenon, process, and end should, in any nation wishing a thoughtful and empirical basis for its policy and research priorities, be an important object of study. Is innovation only a matter of new technologies and the education of the workforce needed to invent, produce, and use them? Or is innovation, as Roger Martin has suggested in his paper 'The Demand for Innovation in Canada,' also a matter of business processes (2002a, 2)? Might innovation be a matter of social and cultural knowledge and, if it is, how and where do we learn that knowledge and how do we teach it?

How do innovative people think? How do we educate people to ask constantly 'What if?' or to think across the synapse – connecting two seemingly unrelated ideas, observations, events, anecdotes, phenomena, or facts – to suggest new and creative ways of doing things, making something, or conceptualizing an issue? When people think in terms of patterns and processes, and from such thinking identify underlying problems, propose new and often more efficient ways of doing things, or new alignments of people, processes, and responsibilities, what are they actually doing? How do we teach others to do it?

These are questions for educational practice and for research. They are questions for anthropologists to answer by observation of human behaviour in social and organizational settings; for psychologists to test; for economists to explore in terms of behavioural responses to incentives; for sociologists and historians to investigate in relation to specific societies and cultures; for scholars of literature, music, and art to explore through analysis of cultural production; and for scholars in education faculties to explore in relation to learning.

Shaping the Effects of Technology

I began by noting how frequently 'innovation' is identified with 'technological innovation.' One of the consequences of that identification is that we hear a good deal these days about the need to study the impacts of technology, especially information technology and new media. That deterministic formulation of the research question makes us the passive objects of something called 'technology,' when in fact, we have a great deal of power to shape technologies to have the political, psychological, social, cultural, communications, learning, and aesthetic effects we desire. Research in the social sciences and humanities can enable us to identify and describe what it is we want from technologies other than productivity and increased GDP. By doing so, this research can help us invent technologies that make our lives better in many new respects, and it can help us avoid technologies that come with unintended consequences and unanticipated 'collateral damage.'

Management

National innovation policies all emphasize people: a well-educated workforce and an entrepreneurial management class. If innovation –

and much else – critically depends on leadership, as well as on individual workers, then we can ask a related question: how do we develop a creative, entrepreneurial management class?

Robert Allen (2004) has shown that a high proportion of Canada's current management class have an undergraduate education in the humanities or social sciences. Allen also shows that these managers, in their maturity, receive the same salaries as those educated in the professional fields, suggesting that they are at least as valuable to their firms as their more technically trained colleagues. Recent calls from Canadian chief executive officers (CEOs) asking governments to support undergraduate education in the arts and sciences, as well as increasingly diverse recruiting practices of firms in North America,[4] suggest a growing recognition that the broad-based, complexity driven education of an arts and science degree, with its emphasis on analytic, research, and communications skills, produces a management capability that more narrowly tailored technical training often does not

At the Rotman School of Management at the University of Toronto, researchers have identified this capability as *integrative thinking*, by which they mean the ability to make decisions in a complex environment in which one must weigh many interacting variables. They visualize this as a multi-directional, multi-dimensional grid. The manager's task is to find a way to a solution in this complex topography by looking at the whole environment, problem, or situation, and not merely at one or a few of its constituent parts (Martin 2002b).

When I read descriptions of integrative thinking, I recognize the activity of a trained reader of a novel.[5] Between page 1 and the end of a novel, a trained reader charts her way through another society and culture, or through some particular manifestation of her own – its politics, laws, customs, religion, history, and values. She masters the more or less extended kinship system and the professional and friendship networks of the characters that populate the fiction, often in historical circumstances quite different from her own. She comes to understand the psychological makeup of the characters, their motivations, and their relations with one another; the situation or plot in which they find themselves; the alternatives open to them; the inevitability of their end, if it is inevitable, and the alternatives their author has denied them, if it is not. A well-trained reader will also understand the place the novel holds in the author's national literature and in the history of literature itself. She will be able to define the ways in which the novel draws on well-established traditions and the ways in which its language, form, characterization, or plot map out new territory in the national psyche or advance new answers to the question of how writers represent lives, cultures, communities, and histories.

A novel, in short, is a highly complex and integrated system. Students who are taught to read novels carefully, analytically, and holistically – like those who can approach music or a painting or a philosophical treatise in this manner – have been taught the basics of integrative thinking. Research that examines exactly what it is we do when we read a novel, look at a picture, make a philosophical argument, or listen to a complex musical composition could tell us what it is we do when we think integratively.

Learning

Innovation agendas stress not only the rapprochement of research and business, and not only technology, but also learning, skills, and lifelong learning. Of the two documents (discussed earlier) outlining Canada's innovation strategy, for example, one is a program for developing 'skills and learning for Canadians.' The United Kingdom's innovation strategy stresses the need for science, math, and technology learning.

The learners needed to sustain innovative – and just – nations are not only those in the workforce today. They are being conceived this very moment. They are the two-year-olds, who in telling their caregivers a story meet with their encouragement or rebuff. They are the baby-boomers, whose use of their retirement will have a profound impact on the new economy.

It is worth pausing over the exciting discoveries in neuroscience and psychology of the past years in relation to development (see, e.g., Keating and Mustard, 1993, for an early summary of this research). This research tells us that a child's physical, social, and cognitive development is strongly influenced by early nutrition and physical activity but also by the quality of early interactions with other people. This research tells us that a child in a supportive, interactive environment becomes more linguistically, physically, and socially adept than does a child in a silent, unsupportive envirnment devoid of interaction. Research also tells us that these differences are a function not only of learning, but also of the development of the neural pathways that depend on interactive learning. This is research with the profound implications for national policies affecting childcare in an economy that relies on the work of both parents, for early childhood education, and for the long-term success of any nation that wants to succeed in the knowledge economy.

What this means is that not only 'skills training' but also **research** around learning, pedagogy, and public education must be a foundation of any society aspiring to join the knowledge economy. We need to know how very young children develop not only their capacity to learn language, but also to learn mathematical and spatial reasoning and integrative thinking, and we need to know much more about what the predisposing conditions are to that learning. We need to know what the most effective pedagogies are for teaching textual and visual literacy as well as numeracy at different ages; for teaching technological aptitude; for fostering creativity, invention, open-mindedness, and collaboration.

In economies and societies that require workers to return again and again to the educational well for refreshment and renewal, we need research about how adults of different ages learn, what they can learn well and what they cannot, and we need research to tell us what the most effective strategies and pedagogies are for teaching them. In economies and societies in which social, employment, and health policies that apply to the elderly will determine dramatically how much these citizens drain from the GDP and how much they contribute to it, we need research about what and how the elderly learn and continue to contribute to society. In a society in which health care, financial services, and commerce are increasingly delivered via technology, we need research to determine the most effective ways of keeping an elderly population technologically competent.

Our innovation agendas, indeed our nations, can be no stronger than the discovery and application of knowledge about how we learn, how we know what we know, and how we think creatively. This is the research of educators and education faculties; of neuroscientists and cognitive scientists; of scholars of literature, music, and fine art; of philosophers and linguists.

Immigration

Some immigrants in some countries are needed, but unwanted – migrant workers who do work that others will not, but who for all that remain illegal, ill-tolerated, ill-educated, ill-housed, ill-fed, and ill-served. Some immigrants are ostensibly welcomed, but their skills and education go unaccredited and unused in their new country. And some immigrants are enabled to contribute fully to the new society they have chosen.

One specific goal of Canada's innovation strategy is to assess, accredit, and employ the skills of immigrants. That will require assessment of learning outcomes and the establishment of comparative benchmarks among training regimes from different countries. It will require the kind of social science research that is done in our education faculties, in combination with the expertise of our humanities scholars, demographers, sociologists, and others, who can bring to understanding the contexts of immigrants' knowledge.

To enable immigrant citizens to become fully productive and innovative members of our societies we also need to understand much more. We need more research about how adults learn second, third, and even fourth and fifth languages. We need research that analyses the ways in which immigrants can most effectively learn the tacit and unexpressed knowledge that underpins so much behaviour and so many expectations in the host culture. We need to understand more about the importance of the connections diasporic populations maintain with their homelands and with their ethnic communities in other countries and in their new country, and what these networks mean for the circulation of family members, goods, knowledge, culture, and political and social values. Most of all, we need to understand the conditions under which migrant populations adapt and succeed, to be as fully strengthened by our new citizens as we might be.

Moreover, this understanding cannot be a one-way street. For if Canada is to become, as its innovation strategy asserts it shall, a truly inclusive society, if Canadians are to avert ethnic tension and be enriched by the multicultural diversity that immigration has produced in the world's most prosperous nations, we need to cross cultural bridges in the other direction. Each one of us will prove to be a better citizen for our capacity to see, understand, and acknowledge the different cultures, histories, and religions that others bring to our common citizenship. Each of us will also prove more reflective, more analytic, and more responsible citizens as we work and live with the ways in which these diverse citizens help shape national policy, national legislation, national priorities, and national discourse. The research of humanities scholars, political scientists, and anthropologists proves invaluable, for it not only elucidates for us the histories, politics, religions, cultures, and cultural productions that have shaped the new citizenry of our nations, but it also helps us understand how the cultural experience that immigrants bring to their new country is shaped and modified by their new context. To understand this is to understand ourselves better.

Policy and Regulatory Regimes

Policy and regulatory regimes have long been at the heart of governments' approaches to stimulating innovation and economic growth.

The questions are familiar. Can productivity be increased by new tax policy? Can GDP be increased by free trade policies? Or is protectionism better? Should immigration be encouraged or discouraged? Which immigrants should be encouraged?

Social science and humanities research can contribute to the development of policy and regulatory regimes in ways that improve policy, improve technological innovation, and improve the quality of our lives. Let us take two examples in which government is, or will be, highly involved in the development of policy and regulatory regimes.

One is in science policy. In Canada, the United States, and Europe, governments quite rightly consult physical and life scientists on a great range of environmental, health, and other policy issues, such as those around clean air and safe food, water, and drugs. Perhaps more often than one could wish, the result is of the kind succinctly summarized in the title of a lecture series sponsored by the Faculty of Science at the University of British Columbia some years ago: 'Surprise! Unintended Consequences of Public Policy.' If a nation wants to be surprised, let it make policy based on sound science but without addressing the aspirations and belief systems of the people to whom the policy applies or their possible motivations and means to adapt the policy to ends that will defeat it – without thinking through the ways in which policy can be 'gamed,' walked around, used to ends contrary to those intended, ignored, and covertly and overtly resisted. In short, we need solid research about the social and cultural contexts in which public policy is meant to be effective if we do not wish to read the headline '*Surprise!*' in our morning paper.

Biotechnology provides the most obvious example of the need for social and ethical research in our contemporary world. One of the technologies governments most seek to attract, the applications of human genomics research, perhaps more than any other innovation, call on our analytic and interpretive skills as humanities and social science scholars. From a marketing point of view, the human desires to live well and not to die just yet, and to keep our loved ones well beside us, will prove powerful incentives for individuals and societies to buy gene therapies and gene technologies. Nevertheless, the push to human 'perfection,' which some celebrate as the Utopian possibility of biotechnology, raises some of the most deeply troubling questions we have faced as human beings. How will we define intellectual property when we are dealing with human genes and the 'cures' they might offer? We need the research of both legal and medical scholars, as well as of ethicists. How do we establish the appropriate balance between creating genetic 'perfection' (however conceived) and human life? We need not only our medical researchers, but also our philosophers, historians, sociologists, psychologists, and scholars of Greek tragedy, among others. How do we prevent – or regulate – traffic in human genes? Economists, legal scholars, sociologists, and criminologists will all have expertise to bring to bear. Thinking about the opportunities biotechnology, and particularly human biotechnology offers, I recall the remark a medical researcher made to me at the time the media were full of news of Dolly: 'We can clone Dolly the sheep,' she said, 'but we need the philosophers to tell us what it means.' That task is as difficult as any a humanities scholar has ever addressed. If we do not address it well, biotechnology will certainly lead us not only to medical miracles but, at least some of the time, into the zones of '*Surprise!*' and human tragedy.

Communities

By now my argument is no doubt becoming overly insistent: innovation is a matter of people. People innovate in large and significant ways when they work and think and live together. They innovate when the conditions of their lives enable them to do so. Famine, poverty, disease, illiteracy, war, discrimination, and authoritarian regimes we know to be poor prognosticators of innovation.

If we turn, however, to the social conditions that create positive indicators for innovation, we meet some provocative social science research. Richard Florida, for example, locates innovative economic growth in what he calls 'the creative class' in which he includes 'people in science and engineering, architecture and design, education, arts, music and entertainment, whose economic function is to create new ideas, new technology and/or new creative content' and a secondary group of professionals in fields such as health – about 30 per cent of the U.S. population (2002, 8). Florida finds a strong correlation between high-tech industries of the kind that governments seek to attract and large urban populations of immigrants, gays, and 'bohemians' (by which he means artists, musicians, designers, and writers). What the convergence of gays, bohemians, and immigrants in cities that prove attractive to those working in the knowledge economy tells Richard Florida is that creative talent is attracted to certain kinds of urban environments: those with a lively street scene and an easy and varied consumerism, as we might expect, but also those with the broad diversity and concomitant tolerance and interaction signalled by large populations of the immigrants, gays, and bohemians who precede the high-tech knowledge workers. Florida's work tells us that, because people do not live to work, but work to live, place matters, and that, if we want to attract the educated, creative people who are innovators, we need to think about our cities – about their culture, their population, and their social 'climate,' as well as their built environment.

Creating urban places has become an art and an evolution, relying on a great deal of research and large international conferences attended by mayors and city planners. Urban geography, which studies the movement of different populations, is critical – I'd cite the Metropolis project, which studies the movement within cities of ethnic groups in relation to assimilation and social mobility, as exemplary.[6] Urban planning in all its aspects – architecture, landscape design, transportation, environmental considerations, cultural attractions and cultural vitality, education, sectoral development, municipal policy – enables or cripples a city's capacity to attract the 'creative class.' At its best, urban planning is highly driven by social science and humanities research about traffic movement, population movement within built and open and commercial and private space, the revitalization of downtown cores, cultural production of many kinds, the economics of the cultural industries and public policy that will foster them, professional and business incentives, care of the homeless, crime prevention, multiculturalism, education and dozens of other issues.

At their best, cities and nations depend not only on the social diversity that shapes the cities to which the 'creative class' is attracted, but on social cohesion. They depend on the extent to which we can forge, out of populations with diverse historical, social, religious, and cultural backgrounds, common understandings, common cause, and common values. Literature, art, films and music, patterns of voting, religious observance, and consumerism can signal our common understandings (or their absence) long before such cohesion is fully articulated in a nation's educational system, laws, policies, or constitution. The research of social scientists and humanities scholars teases those understandings out into the light of social and policy discourse in order to lay the foundations for the preservation of democratic values on which worthwhile innovation and economic and social well-being rest.

Et al.

The list does not end here. Most of the urgent issues in our world – from food and environmental sustainability to the sociocultural determinants of health and well-being – require the knowledge and the research not only of medical and physical scientists and of engineers, but also of humanities scholars and social scientists, if they are to be understood in all their complexity. The tentative, incompletely articulated gestures towards humanities and social science research that can be found in some of the most recent agendas for innovation, such as those of Canada and some of the countries of the European Union such as France, are the first faint dawn of that recognition.

Coda

Technology and innovation help a nation earn its collective living. Education and research in the humanities and social sciences tell us how we are living and behaving, why we are living and behaving as we are, how we might live and behave to different and perhaps better ends, what makes life worth living and for whom and why. The research of the humanities and social sciences teaches us how others live and what others believe and value. Analysing cultural, social, political, and economic behaviour, events, and productions, and developing paradigms for ethical reasoning, humanities and social science scholarship offers us ways of thinking through the very difficult questions the global economy, agendas for innovation, and technological developments have laid at our collective door. If our innovation policies are to serve what should be the agenda of any great nation – to ensure that its citizens are healthy, wealthy, and wise – they will draw evidence, sustenance, and wisdom from the education and research of the social sciences and humanities.

NOTES

1 The United States has not developed an umbrella 'innovation' policy or an umbrella national research agenda. The scientific advisory groups to the president and various federal government departments post to their credit long lists of policy papers advising on research agendas relative to particular topics, but no coordinated approach that crosses topics or departments. The phenomenon by which governments develop overarching national research agendas, and tie these into 'innovation' agendas of other aspects of economic development such as tax incentives and education and training, could be construed as a direct response to the power of the U.S. economy in the global marketplace. Indeed, some of these documents (and most notably those of Canada) take U.S. data as their benchmark and define 'innovation' as the necessary quality that will enable a country to compete globally in a market dominated in many ways by the United States.

2 Research priority is generally given to the following subject areas: genomics and biotechnology, information and communications technology, environmentally sustainable development, and food quality and safety. The United Kingdom also emphasizes the promotion of mathematics and science research. For the European Union one of the priorities is 'citizens and governance in a knowledge-based society.' Billed as 'the return of the human sciences,' the aim of this priority is to 'restore ... relations between science and the citizen, between research and society' (European Commission Research Centre 2002). This EU priority is much more closely aligned with the 'psychological environment' which the discussion paper put out by the Government of France defines as 'innovation' than it is with social science and humanities research as those of us in the *sciences humaines* have understood it.

3 Those interested in government-sponsored R&D, and possessed of some memory for the ins and outs of policy on this front, will detect in this description an earlier draft report of a federal Advisory Committee on Science and Technology which presented its conclusions under the title of *Healthy, Wealthy and Wise*. The report was not released and its recommendations did not immediately shape the government's agenda. Several years later, however, and considerably reworked, much of what this advisory report had to say has found its way into Canada's 2002 'innovation strategy.'

4 Many 'new economy' firms – ranging from software developers to investment firms such as the New York based Blackrock – now hire a mix of 'techies' (computer scientists in the case of software developers, economists, and MBAs in the case of investment firms) and humanities and social science graduates. Walk into Blackrock and meet new young hires, for example, and you will find graduates of comparative literature, philosophy, and English programs hired because of the particular abilities their humanities education allows them to bring to the job.

5 This analogy comes from my work as a scholar of literature. However, some months subsequent to the conference on Creating Knowledge, Strengthening Nations, I found myself at a symposium sponsored by the Conference Board of Canada at which a management guru suggested that one of the latest trends in the human resource management sector was the advice to read novels rather than management literature. The tenor of the advice, which viewed novels as case studies of human interaction, suggested that much of what novels had to offer the practical as well as the imaginative mind was going unremarked.

6 The Metropolis project is the result of a partnership between the Social Sciences and Humanities Research Council of Canada and Citizenship and Immigration Canada. The project has established four centres of excellence

(Montreal, Vancouver, the Prairies, and the Maritimes) to study issues of population migration, cultural diversity, and integration of immigrants into Canadian cities and has established at least twenty international partnerships for the purposes of drawing international comparisons. Information about the project and its centres can be found at http://canada.metropolis.net.

REFERENCES

Because some of the government policy and discussion documents I cite in this article may well prove difficult to retrieve from libraries, I have cited (in parentheses) Web sites where these are available. Where the Web site has been my only access to the document, it is cited without parentheses.

Allen, Robert C. (2004). Education and Technological Revolutions: The Role of the Social Sciences and Humanities in the Knowledge Based Economy. In Jane Gaskell and Kjell Rubenson, eds., *Educational Outcomes for the Canadian Workplace: New Frameworks for Policy and Research.* Toronto: University of Toronto Press, pp. 56–88.

Commission of the European Communities (2002). More Research for Europe: Towards 3% of GDP. Communication 499. Brussels: European Union. http://europa.edu.int/eur-lex/pri/en/dpi/cnc/doc/2002/com2002_0499en01.doc

European Commission Research Centre (Nov 2002). The Priorities of the Sixth Framework Programme 2002–2006. *RTD Info: Magazine for European Research.* Special Edition. http://europa.edu.int/comm/research/rtdinfo/en/special-fp6/index.html

Florida, Richard (2002). *The Rise of the Creative Class and How It's Transforming Work, Leisure, Community and Everyday Life.* New York: Basic Books.

Gouvernement de France. (2002). Plan innovation. http://www.recherche.gouv.fr/plan-innovation/presentation5.htm

Government of Canada (2001a). *Knowledge Matters: Skills and Learning for Canadians: Canada's Innovation Strategy.* Ottawa: Industry Canada, Government of Canada. (http://www.innovationstrategy.gc.ca)

– (2001b). *Achieving Excellence: Investing in People, Knowledge and Opportunity: Canada's Innovation Strategy.* Ottawa: Industry Canada, Government of Canada. (http://www.innovationstrategy.gc.ca)

Government of the United Kingdom (2000). *Excellence and Opportunity: A Science and Innovation Policy for the 21st Century.* London: Department of Trade and Industry, Government of the United Kingdom. http://www.science.gov.uk/enterprise/dtiwhite/index.html

Keating, Daniel P., and J. Fraser Mustard (1993). Social Economic Factors and

Human Development. In D. Ross, ed. *Family Security in Insecure Times*. Ottawa: National Forum on Family Security, pp. 87–105.

Kemp, D.A. (1999). Knowledge and Opportunity: A Policy Statement on Research and Research Training. Canberra: Ministry for Education, Training and Youth Affairs, Government of Australia. http://www.dest.gov.au/archive/highered/whitepaper/default.asp

Martin, Roger L. (2002a). The Demand for Innovation in Canada. Unpublished paper. http://ctdirect.com/economics/standard/full/Martin.pdf.

– (2002b). Integrative Thinking: A Model Takes Shape. *Rotman Management* (Fall 2002): 8–11.

CHAPTER 14

Harnessing Genomics for Global Health: The Role of Higher Education

Abdallah S. Daar and Peter A. Singer

The International Development Research Centre (IDRC) is a public corporation created by the Canadian government to help communities in the developing world find solutions to social, economic, and environmental problems through research. In the mid-1990s, together with two other Canadian organizations, the International Institute for Sustainable Development (IISD) and the North-South Institute (NSI), the IDRC sponsored a landmark study. The results of it became known as 'the Strong report,' after its chairman, Maurice Strong. Published in 1996, the report is entitled *Connecting with the World: Priorities for Canada Internationalism in the 21st Century* (IDRC 1996). It contains recommendations aimed at moving Canada towards being a 'knowledge broker' to developing countries. The Strong report argues that the 'greatest challenge in the future – for Canada and industrialized countries – will be to bridge the gaps between what we know we can do and what needs to be done. That bridge building will need to become far more inclusive and pluralistic than current efforts that are conducted primarily by and for rich countries and for the growing numbers of rich within poor countries.' Furthermore, the report points out that 'the Canadian academic community has played an important role in the development of Canada's position in the world, but it has not done enough to translate knowledge into practical tools for sustainable development or useful instruments for policymakers at home and abroad. Canadian universities are important players in this field and, regardless of Canada's future abroad, they will remain a permanent feature of the landscape. Bringing Canadian universities into a meaningful partnership with other like-minded institutions will be an urgent challenge in the coming months and years.'

In this chapter, we will highlight how universities can respond to this challenge. We begin by identifying what we consider to be the crucial role of a great university in incubating development-oriented, research-based programs aimed at improving global health. We argue that, among public institutions, only universities can play such a role. We then provide, as a case example, an examination of our own program, the Canadian Program on Genomics and Global Health (CPGGH) at the University of Toronto to illustrate some of the themes discussed in the early sections.

The World's Great Universities: Innovative, Interdisciplinary, International

We propose that in the future the world's truly great universities will need to emphasize 'three I's': innovation, interdisciplinarity, and internationalism. Innovation means tapping into the creativity of those people who do basic research in fundamental disciplines like physics, chemistry, and biology. As pointed out by Birgeneau (see Introduction to this volume), of three great recent discoveries – the Internet, global positioning systems (GPS), and biotechnology – none was preplanned, and all three arose through freedom of inquiry – adequately financed – on fundamental questions.

Universities should play a leading role in innovation policy by working cooperatively with government, private industry, and civil society. Innovation is important to economic development, and universities have several important roles in a country's system of innovation. They produce discoveries that are commercialized. They produce highly skilled workers. Perhaps, however, most innovatively, universities can contribute to the design of the innovation system itself.

Innovation also means paying attention to the findings of social scientists and humanities scholars. One, among several important roles for the social sciences and humanities in innovation (see the chapter by Shirley Neuman), is the fostering of cross-cultural understanding in our increasingly globalized world. Scientific discoveries can raise profound ethical questions. We find help towards answers to such questions in the humanities and social sciences.

Interdisciplinarity means that problems or issues are examined from the standpoint of several disciplines working together. Easton provides what is probably the best description of the potential of interdisciplinarity (1991, 12):

> Herein lies one of the major crises of modern knowledge. It is what I have called the Humpty Dumpty problem. To understand the world it has seemed necessary to analyze it by breaking it into many pieces (i.e. the disciplines and their own divisions). But to act in the world, to try to address the issues for the understanding of which highly specialized knowledge was presumably sought, we need to somehow reassemble all the pieces. Here is the rub. Try as we may, we are no more able than all the king's horses and all the king's men to put our knowledge together again for coping with the whole real problems of the world.

As Easton has observed, the challenges that confront us do not neatly arrange themselves into traditional academic disciplines. Scientific fields are converging: for example, NBIC is a new field which is informed by nanotechnology, biotechnology, information technology, and cognitive neuroscience (see, e.g., National Science Foundation 2002). Even more challenging are interdisciplinary connections between the sciences, social sciences, and humanities. These are essential connections because societies have to strike the appropriate balance between reaping the benefits and managing the risks of any new technology.

Take as an example nanotechnology. Most industrialized countries are investing heavily in nanotechnology research and development (R&D), and such investment has grown from U.S.$678 million worldwide in 1997 to more than U.S.$2.2 billion in 2002. Meanwhile, the ethical, environmental, economic, legal, and social implications of nanotechnology have not yet been addressed seriously nor pursued on a large enough scale. The unique equity, privacy, security, environmental, legal, and metaphysical questions raised by nanotechnology require detailed discussion now and, perhaps, specific regulations in the future. Demands for a moratorium on the deployment of nano-materials should be seen as a wake-up call for developers of nanotechnology. A confrontation, like the one around genetically modified (GM) foods, can only be avoided if immediate steps are taken to close the gap between the science and the ethics of nanotechnology. In short, either the ethics will catch up or the science will slow down (see Mnyusiwalla et al. 2003). To address these issues there is no viable alternative to interdisciplinarity.

Interdisciplinarity is much touted, but seldom practised. Some examples of interdisciplinary research organizations are Rockefeller University, MacArthur Foundation research networks, and more recently, the Pasteur Institute. However, the vast majority of universities are organized into departments representing traditional disciplines, and so interdisciplinary work does not always flourish. (A) radical proposal to change this state of affairs is made by Gazzaniga in an article in *Science* (1998 237):

> The university administration [should] announce to its faculty that while continuing to function as they are for 1 year, they are free to reorganize themselves in any way they see fit, planning new curricula, graduate programs, special emphasis groups, and all the rest. For instance, faculty from different departments could combine to teach about an area, such as the mind. They would request space for their new venture and spell out the teaching load they would share. At the end of the year, the new organization of the university should reflect the new configurations of the academic world. After regrouping, people would be better prepared for the intellectual work of the next century.

That is not likely to happen at most universities. However, to promote interdisciplinarity, it is not required to abolish departments. The issue is one of balance. The bedrock of a university is its disciplines. But management incentives could be introduced to spur interdisciplinary work. For example, support for interdisciplinary centres – and positive feedback from directors of such interdisciplinary centres – could be used as a criterion in the dean's annual performance appraisal of department chairs and the provost's annual performance appraisal of deans.

Internationalism recognizes that our world is becoming smaller and increasingly globalized. For the university, this provides three distinct opportunities. First, universities will want to benchmark themselves against the best international universities in the world: the Harvards, MIT's, Stanfords, and Oxfords. Second, universities will want to ensure that their students are exposed to the cross-cultural experiences that come with an international outlook. Third, a commitment to internationalism helps universities address global inequities in education, health, and other basic human needs. For example, in Canada today life expectancy is about eighty years and rising; in several countries in sub-Saharan Africa life expectancy is less than thirty years. This, and similar discrepancies, are among the greatest ethical issues now facing the world.

As an example of a response to these problems is the 'Grand Challenges in Global Health' competition sponsored by the Bill and Melinda Gates Foundation. It was announced in January 2003 at the World Economic Forum. Inspired by Hilbert's Grand Challenges in mathematics, this is a competition for grants worth U.S.$ 200 million, conducted in partnership with the U.S. National Institutes of Health, in support of highly innovative scientific research that addresses critical challenges in global health. A board of scientists, chaired by Nobel Laureate Harold Varmus, will identify the grand challenges. Then, the world's most innovative researchers will compete by submitting proposals to solve them.

Will universities rise to meet these and similar important challenges? Have they the ability to create interdisciplinary platforms to address global health inequities? Research universities bring together accomplished faculty members, highly talented students, interdisciplinary capacity in its various centres, research resources, (including competitive grant funding), and their international reputations. All these are necessary ingredients for success. Indeed, we believe that no institutions other than universities are capable of undertaking this kind of enterprise. Consider the other possible contenders:

- *Governments.* Competing priorities and short attention spans are the characteristics of governments. Their bureaucracies do not allow for critical original ideas, let alone rapid and flexible implementation. Thus, with few exceptions, governments generally depend on short-term external contracting for policy development, or they create agencies (such as the Canadian Institutes of Health Research or Genome Canada) to fund long-term research or institutions (such as Canada's National Research Council) that have in-house research capacity.
- *Industry.* Although it may have long-term research agendas, industry is driven, naturally and efficiently, by the imperative of profits. Thus, by nature, industry is not able to undertake the kind of research and create the partnerships described here, and should it try to do so, it would most likely not have the needed legitimacy or trust.
- *International organizations.* Even when they do have the financial resources and legitimacy, international organizations rarely have in-house research capacity, and so they often depend on academics for this type of research.
- *Think tanks.* Especially the large think tanks do have the in-house research capacity, but they are often identified with specific political

agendas, and this, once again, raises issues of legitimacy and trust.

Technology and Development: Setting the Scene for Genomics

Technically, genomics is the study of whole genomes. However, in our operational definition, genomics is 'the powerful new wave of health-related life sciences (biotechnologies) energized by the human genome project and the knowledge and tools it is spawning.' This definition crosses over to biotechnology broadly, and in a narrower but liberating sense, it encompasses transcriptomics, proteomics, metabalomics, and ultimately, systems biology.

The previous major wave of technologies, and one that is still running its course, was the information and communications (ICT) wave. It was enabled by the digital revolution. The impact of ICT has, on the whole, been very positive, despite the dotcom bust. ICT enabled the creation of hugely successful firms, for example, Intel and Microsoft. In developing countries with the right mix of capacities, the digital revolution created wealth and allowed some local companies to become players on the global scene, for example, Infosys in India: 'No longer mere "body shops," Indian software outfits are grabbing lucrative business from Western companies' (Kitchens 2002). The potential of the ICT wave is amply demonstrated by the fact that many developing countries 'leap-frog' forward for example, by using mobile phone technology to bypass obsolete land line technology (U.N. Development Program 2001; BBC 2002). Even in poor villages in Bangladesh, women have been able to set up small, profitable businesses based on the use of cellphones (Ahmed 2000), established using microcredit (see U.N. 1995). However, ICT has also created a digital divide: half the world's population has probably never made a telephone call, let alone been in possession of a computer or connected to the Internet.

Genomics is the next technological wave after ICT. Based on scientific and technological innovations dating back to the early 1970s, the whole field became energized by the enormous sums of money put into it by the U.S. government and the Wellcome Trust, initially, followed later by other governments. The first phase culminated in the draft sequencing of the human genome by 2001. Equally impressive was the sequencing of the genomes of a number of species of pathogens. The genomics wave holds great opportunities for improving the health of people all over the world.

The Genomics Initiative at the University of Toronto: Background

In 1998 one of us (Daar) was asked by the World Health Organization (WHO) to prepare a report examining the implications of all genetic manipulations on global public health (see Daar and Mattei 2000). In doing that work, we identified the potential for improving health in developing countries and the 'rays of hope' that these countries possess in terms of negotiating their position. Such rays of hope include the following:

• Much of the globe's biodiversity and genetic resources are in the developing world.
• Many of the population and disease groups of interest to genetic researchers are in the developing world.
• In terms of numbers, in the twenty-first century, the developing world is likely to be the main consumer of genomics/genetics technologies and their products.
• Genomics/genetics technology is easily transferred, provided the population is appropriately educated and trained.

This work was followed by the WHO report entitled *Genomics and World Health* (WHO 2002a), which essentially makes the point that genomics is relevant to improving health in developing countries. However, it warns that numerous ethical issues remain to be studied and addressed and that a focus on genomics should not detract from the application of tested and proven public health measures. Nevertheless, in the Foreword of the report, WHO Director General, Dr Gro-Harlem Brundtland states: 'The Report focuses on the expectations, concerns and possibilities for the use of new genomic knowledge in improving world health. The specific challenge is how we can harness this knowledge and have it contribute to health equity, especially among developing nations. It is a reality that most genomic and biotechnology research is presently carried out in the industrialized world, and is primarily market-driven. Genomics also needs to be applied to the health problems of the developing world. It is crucial that we actively seek means to involve developing country scientists in innovative biotechnology.' At the event launching the report, Brundtland said: 'Genome research, if we handle it correctly, can change the world for all health care. In particular, it has the potential to allow developing countries to leap-frog decades of medical development and bring their citizens greatly improved care and modern methods in the much more immediate future' (WHO, 2002b).

In its 2001 *Human Development Report*, the United Nations Development Program (UNDP) took the position that technology can be made relevant and useful to poor countries, as long as the risks are managed. This report examined three areas: food, medicine, and information systems. In its Introduction, perhaps in response to the debate on the relevance of genetically modified (GM) crops for food security in developing countries, Mark Malloch Brown, a UNDP administrator, points out that the report 'moved in a new direction this year by challenging some cherished opinions about what the third world needs.'

These are two ways in which one can view the role of biotechnology in relation to existing tried-and-tested public health measures. One way is to argue that biotechnology is distinct and should not displace currently effective public health measures – such as the provision of clean water, clean air, simple diagnostics, inexpensive medication, vaccines, control of fertility, and good nutrition. The other way is to see biotechnology as improving these very same basic public health measures. Thus, for example, genomics biotechnology generally can produce new tools to improve public health. These tools might include genetically engineered vaccines (such as those being developed against malaria) or diagnostic tools (including use of the polymerase chain reaction for rapid, reliable, robust, and inexpensive diagnosis of infectious disease such as dengue and leishmaniasis; see Daar et al. 2002).

Two powerful new tools, bioinformatics and pharmacogenomics, and their applications are at the very cutting edge of the genomics revolution (Pharmacogenomics Consortium 2002). A recent issue of the *Lancet* describes a community in West Africa that may be unresponsive to antiretroviral therapy because of a specific genetic mutation (Schaeffeler et al. 2001). Millions of dollars could be spent on attempting to treat the people of that community with expensive drugs that would have no effect at all. However, knowing the pharmacogenomics of such populations could save millions of dollars and many lives. In addition, pharmacogenomic knowledge stimulates efforts to discover and develop drugs that *would* work in such populations.

The Canadian Program on Genomics and Global Health: A Case Study

Over the past few years, the University of Toronto has attempted to forge more international links. These have included not only links with other universities in North America and Western Europe but also with those in developing countries. In addition, the university has responded to the need for interdisciplinary research by creating a number of centres, among them the University of Toronto Joint Centre for Bioethics (JCB). In 1999 the centre produced an early concept paper on working out an international program of its own, as well as a strategic plan in which both genomics and closer ties with institutions in developing countries were identified as major priorities.

The seeds of our own work on genomics, biotechnology, and development were planted with a grant from the Ontario Research and Development Challenge Fund to establish the program in applied ethics and biotechnology at the University of Toronto. This was followed by two major research grants. These were from Genome Canada, which was established by the Canadian government to capitalize on the genomics revolution unleashed by the human genome project, as part of its agenda for innovation to enable Canada to a become major player in the knowledge economy (see Canada 2001). Both grants were administered in Ontario, on behalf of Genome Canada, by the Ontario Genomics Institute. Collectively, these programs have become known as the Canadian Program in Genomics and Global Health (CPGGH), at the University of Toronto (see, e.g., Dowdeswell et al. 2003).

Before undertaking our own work, we identified important lessons learned from the experience with GM crops, especially the social response (Singer and Daar 2000). These lessons include the following:

- Health care biotechnology must learn from agriculture that research and development needs to take a global view. 'Designer' tomatoes, for example, do not generate the same level of public support as rice enriched with pro-vitamin A or iron.
- The public's perception of risk must be taken seriously. A dismissive attitude towards risk and risk perception on the part of the scientific or corporate communities was not effective in agricultural biotechnology and will not be so in health biotechnology. Proponents of health biotechnology will need to develop better methods of public engagement and address seriously even hypothetical public health risks.
- Pharmaceutical firms will need to recognize that no matter how good their technology or marketing strategies, attention to social and ethical issues is crucial to their bottom line. At the same time, university scientists, social scientists, and ethicists need to accept industry as a legitimate stakeholder with which to engage in constructive dialogue.

The vision of the Canadian Program in Genomics and Global Health (CPGGH) is to:

1 Harness genomics and biotechnology for global health equity to bridge an emerging genomics divide between developing and developed countries.
2 Explore the convergence of social issues in genomics and biotechnology that arise in the health, agriculture, and environment sectors.
3 Provide a forum for societal debate on ethics and biotechnology among academic institutions, government, the public, the biotechnology industry, and the media.
4 Analyse the social implications of advances in genomics and biotechnology, identifying associated prospects and problems in the early stage of development.
5 Optimize the benefits and minimize the risks of genomics and biotechnology advances through careful social evaluation.
6 Provide consultative advice to Ontario Genomics Institute research projects.
7 Serve as an independent and objective public resource on the ethical and social implications of genomics and biotechnology.

The CPGGH established an international advisory board to represent academia, industry, government, the public, media, and relevant provincial, national, and international non-government organizations (NGOs). The program was launched in June 2001.

For this program we developed a specific interdisciplinary platform (see Fig. 14.1) which has the following components:

- *Problem identification.* Problems for study are identified by the investigators and discussed in depth with members of the advisory board.
- *Case studies.* A case study is 'an empirical inquiry that investigates a contemporary phenomenon within its real-life context.' A case study ensures that real-world problems are the focus of attention, that ethical and legal analyses are based on empirical evidence, and that best practice guidelines are grounded in reality.
- *E³LSI (ethical, environmental, economic, legal and social issues) analysis.* E³LSI analysis consists of foundational conceptual work, as well as the application of the foundational analyses to the specific case studies. Ethical analyses include the identification of values in multi-stake-

CPGGH Process

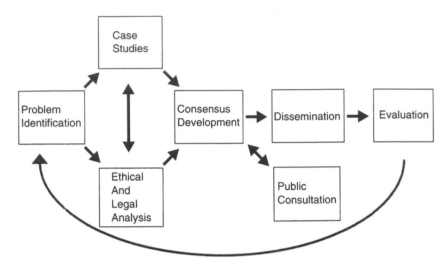

Figure 14.1 Interdisciplinary platform for the Canadian Program on Genomics and Global Health (CPGGH)

holder vaccine controversies, especially the common values brought to light by the consensus-building process.

- *Consensus development.* The case studies and ethical and legal analyses contribute to a process of consensus development. For several of the research projects, we are developing best practice guidelines using a panel that represents academics, government, industry, media, NGOs, and the public. Panel members work together in face-to-face meetings and by electronic communication over an extended period to build consensus. By consensus we do not intend unanimity but rather a collaborative process encompassing communication, deliberation, mutual learning, transparency, and building trust.

- *Public consultation.* Although it is widely recognized that public involvement is critical to the social acceptance of new technologies, there is no single adequately evaluated and widely accepted method for public involvement. We work with internationally recognized experts and use a variety of methods.

- *Dissemination.* Our reports and guidelines are disseminated through the appropriate partners for each project. One of our major goals is

Table 14.1 Projects of the Canadian Program on Genomics and Global Health (CPGGH)

---

 1 Top 10 Biotechnologies for Improving Health in Developing Countries
 2 Genomics as a Global Public Good for Health
 3 Harnessing Genomics and Biotechnology for the U.N. Millennium Development Goals
 4 Global Genomics Initiative – Building a Global Public Dialogue
 5 Genome Innovation Systems in Developing Countries
 6 Bioscience Business Ethics
 7 Ethical Guidelines for Nutrigenomics
 8 Ethical Guidelines for Plant-made Pharmaceuticals
 9 Genetically Modified Animals
10 International Comparisons of Health and Research Ethics Systems
11 Intellectual Property Modelling Group
12 Regulatory Model for Developing Countries
13 Stem Cell Policies In Developing Countries
14 Regenerative medicine
15 Genomics and Public Health Policy Executive Courses
16 Global Genomics Opinion Leaders' Network
17 Stem Cell Curricular Modules for High Schools
18 Public Engagement in Genomics through Plays

---

for the guidelines to be adopted by relevant Canadian and international institutions, including industries. We recognize that 'buy-in' from decision-makers is crucial, and how best to achieve this is also a focus of process refinement. Program deliverables are also disseminated through Web sites, publications in academic journals, and the capacity-strengthening programs. They are accompanied by media releases and op-ed pieces in major Canadian newspapers.

The CPGGH pursues its goals and objectives through various research and capacity-strengthening projects (see Table 14.1).

The Role of Higher Education: Lessons Learned from the CPGGH

Below are some key lessons relevant to the role of higher education that we have learned from our work with the Canadian Program on Genomics and Global Health.

Building Partnerships and Value Networks

It is perhaps in building global partnerships more than through most other activities that long-term sustainability of our type of approach can be achieved. The University of Toronto's Joint Centre for Bioethics, as a result of our engagement with these global equity issues, has been named a WHO collaborating centre for bioethics. This allows us to interact with and tap the enormous connections that WHO has. In April 2002, our centre held a conference in Toronto, jointly with the World Health Organization, to explore ways of implementing the recommendations of the latter's report on Genomics and World Health (WHO 2002a). We identified two areas where we could assist WHO. We can be of help with intellectual property (IP) issues and with the development of a model regulatory regime for genetics/genomics research and its applications in developing countries. We recruited a post-doctoral fellow and seconded her to WHO headquarters in Geneva to conduct research and lay the foundations for our further work in these two areas.

To develop the IP work we are collaborating with the IP Modeling Groups of which we were a founding member, and have joined the centre for Intellectual Property Policy at McGill University (see Gold et al. 2002).

The Joint Centre for Bioethics at the University of Toronto has strong links with the African Centre for Technology Studies (ACTS), which is based in Nairobi, and with its founding director, Calestous Juma, who is now at Harvard University, as well as with its immediate past director John Mugabe, who is now based in Pretoria as the secretary of the New Partnership of Africa's Development (NEPAD) Science and Technology Commission. We developed and implemented the Nairobi executive development course on genomics and public health policy with ACTS. We have also helped establish a functioning network from among the participants of the Nairobi course that is now known as the African Genome Policy Forum. That group has produced its own recommendation on how to harness genomics to improve health in Africa. A staff member from ACTS came to the University of Toronto to do a Master's degree in our collaborative program; her thesis is on South Africa's health biotechnology innovation system.

The JCB worked with the Indian Council for Medical Research. (ICMR) in developing its executive course of genomics and health policy. The participants of that course went on to set up the Indian Genome Policy Forum, which has produced its own recommendations for harnessing genomics/biotechnology to improve health and general national wealth in India. The deputy director of ICMR is now a graduate student at the University of Toronto, in the international Master of Health Sciences program, and is conducting a case study of India's genomics/biotechnology innovation system. The interconnections among opinion leaders that we foster will in time be connected into a global network of opinion leaders that will undoubtedly influence the policies of developing countries in relation to genomics.

Industry

To obtain funds from granting agencies, such as the Ontario Research and Development Challenge Fund, we are often required to raise matching funds from industry. This is one way in which we have to work with industry. However, our view is that industry is a key stakeholder in the unfolding of the genomics revolution. Instead of demonizing industry, we believe it can be engaged constructively. Industry can be both the subject of research and a legitimate participant in formulating good practices and ethical guidelines. Universities can develop rules of engagement and apply these successfully and learn from their mistakes. It is possible to learn to dance with the porcupine (Lewis et al, 2001) Industry does need ethical guidance and if we as bioethicists do no do this, who will (see, e.g., Dhanda 2002).

As the Strong report notes: 'More creative and imaginative ways must be found to make the corporate sector take notice of the importance of these issues, to involve it in the process of agenda setting, and to ensure that it is supportive of, and is a much more substantial contributor to, public debate and investment in Canada's role abroad' (IDRC 1996).

Public Engagement

Nowadays, it is widely recognized that public involvement is critical to the social acceptance of biotechnology. To some, public involvement is simply public education. However, when dealing with complex scientific and technological developments – and especially when regulators need guidance in an environment where there are opposing viewpoints, the stakes appear to be high, and there is no agreement on the meaning of risk and risk evaluation and management – public involvement should really be extended to public engagement. By public engagement we mean both public education and public feedback. The extent to which the feedback then influences policy will vary with the question being examined and the evolution of the public engagement exercise itself.

A variety of methods of public engagement exist. These range from simple opinion surveys, focus groups, cafe discussions, citizen juries, to deliberative polling. There is no single adequately evaluated and widely accepted method for public engagement, and indeed different methods may be appropriate for different issues. Some methods, although expensive to undertake, can actually influence public policy. For example, Canada has recently undertaken a major public engagement exercise on the question of whether Canada is ready to proceed to clinical trials of xenotransplantation. This consisted of a series of citizen forums involving education, discussion, and 'citizen juries.' A report by the Canadian Public Health Association (2001) recommends that Canada not proceed with xenotransplantation involving humans until several critical issues have been addressed. It seems to have influenced the government not to proceed at this stage.

In the JCB's program on consensus building, on a small scale, there is the beginning of public engagement. In some of the projects, the drafts of the guidelines are being disseminated to a wider audience for comment before finalization. We also often interact with the public through public seminars such as those we have held on stem cell research. We also often write op-ed pieces to try to stimulate debate (see, e.g., Daar and Singer, Feb. 2002, April 2002; Daar et al., May 2002; Caulfield et al. 2002; Singer 2002). An innovative approach to public engagement is the use of narrative technique. At our centre, Jeff Nisker is pioneering the use of dramatic theatre to engage the public on issues related to genetic testing.

Benefits for Canada

We believe that this kind of work has benefits to Canada that justify the investments, for example, it:

- Reinforces Canada's reputation as an honest broker.
- Generates good will towards Canada, only one benefit of which is in future trade.
- Allows us to engage with, understand, learn from, and discover with our colleagues in developing countries ways that enhance our understanding and contribute to peace – from which everyone benefits.
- Brings to Canada talented graduate students, who pay fees to our universities, enrich our academic lives, and help build our collaborations and partnerships.
- Trains graduate students who participate in our research projects as part of their thesis requirements.
- Grounds our academic research and output in relation to issues involving developing countries.

- Enables us to identify major challenges that we would not otherwise identify – including challenges that, at least initially, appear to be among Canada's priorities.

The products of our research generate further opportunities for partnerships, collaborations, and research ideas. For example, the reception of our study of the top ten biotechnologies (Daar et al. 2002) led to invitations from the U.N.'s working group on implementation of the Millennium Development Goals (MDGs) to identify how the top ten biotechnologies can be used to help implement the MDGs; and an invitation from the Bill and Melinda Gates Foundation to participate in their effort to identify the top ten grand challenges for global health.

Foreign Policy

The linkage between science, technology, and foreign policy is not obvious at first. However, science and technology are now emerging as major concerns of the foreign policy initiatives of developed countries. We have argued that Canada has a special role in genome diplomacy and have identified key actions for Canada in this regard (Daar et al. 2003).

Conclusion

Great universities have a major role, indeed a duty, to address global inequities, chief among which are the inequities in health. No institutions other than respected universities have all the ingredients for such work. The case example of the University of Toronto's Canadian Program on Genomics and Global Health illustrates how a great university can marshal innovative thinking, interdisciplinary methodology, and a global outlook to begin to address how cutting-edge technology can be applied to the problems of health in developing countries.

Universities have a special role in advocating for the concerns of the less fortunate and in making us understand the rationale for mutual caring (see Benatar et al. 2003). For, as stated by former Canadian Prime Minister Lester B. Pearson: 'There can be no peace, no security, when a few rich countries with a small minority of the world's people alone have access to the brave, and frightening, new world of technology and science, while the large majority live in deprivation and want, shut off from opportunities of full economic development; but with expectations and aspirations aroused beyond the hope of realizing them' (Pearson 1972).

REFERENCES

Ahmed, F. (2000). Hello, I'm Calling from Paulia. *UNESCO Courier.* http://www. unesco.org/courier/2000_07/uk/connex2.htm.

Benatar, S.R., A.S. Daar, and P.A. Singer. (2003). Global Health Ethics: The Rationale for Mutual Caring. *International Affairs* 79(1): 107–38.

British Broadcasting Corporation (BBC). (2002). Mobiles to Leapfrog into the Future. *News,* 30 Sept. http://news.bbc.co.uk/1/hi/technology/2287913.stm.

Canada. House of Commons Standing Committee on Industry. (2001). *A Canadian Innovation Agenda for the Twenty-First Century.* Fifth Report. http://www. parl.gc.ca/InfoComDoc/37/1/INST/Studies/Reports/indu04/06-toc-e.htm.

Canadian Public Health Association. (2001). *Animal to Human Transplantation: Should Canada Proceed?* Ottawa: Author.

Caulfield, T., A.S. Daar B.M. Knoppers, and P.A. Singer. 2 May (2002). MPs Have the Wrong Focus. Globe and Mail, 2 May A21.

Daar, A.S., and J.-F. Mattei. (2000). *Medical Genetics and Biotechnology: Implications for Public Health.* Document WHO/EIP/GPE/00.1. Annex 1 of the Report of the informal consultation on Ethical Issues in Genetics, Cloning and Biotechnology: Possible Future Directions for WHO. Geneva: World Health Organization, 1999. Referenced in Doc. No. WHA53/15, Report on Cloning, WHO Director-General to the 53rd World Health Assembly, Geneva, 2000. http:// www.who.int/wha-1998/WH00/PDF/ea15.pdf.

Daar, A.S., and P.A. Singer. PA (Feb. 2002). Killing with Kindness? *Project Syndicate.* http://www.scidev.net/opinions/index.cfm?fuseaction=redopions& itemid=56&language=1.

Daar, A.S., and P.A. Singer. (25 April, 2002). Human Capital Is Key to Research Ethics. *SciDev.Net.* http://www.scidev.net/

Daar, A.S., T. Caulfield, B.M. Knoppers, and Singer. P.A. (9 May 2002). Ban Cloning, Not Its Life-saving Cousin. *Globe and Mail.* 9 May [Op-Ed].

Daar, A.S., E. Dowdeswell, and P.A. Singer. (2003). Genome Diplomacy: Canada's Role. *Policy Option* 24(8), 56–61.

Daar A.S., H. Thorsteinsdóttir. D.K. Martin, A.C. Smith, S. Nast, and P.A. Singer. PA (2002). Top 10 Biotechnologies for Improving Health in Developing Countries. *Nature Genetics* 32(2): 229–32.

Dhanda, R.K. (2002). *Guiding Icarus: Merging Bioethics with Corporate Interests.* New York: Wiley.

Dowdeswell, E., A.S. Daar, and P.A. Singer. (2003). Bridging the Genomics Divide. *Global Governance* 9, pp. 1–6.

Easton, D. (1991). Divided Knowledge: Across Disciplines, across Cultures: The Division, Integration, and Transfer of Knowledge. *Bulletin of the American Academy of Arts and Sciences* 44(4): 12.

Gazzaniga, M.S. (1998). How to Change the University. *Science* 282: 237.

Gold, E.R., D. Castle, L.M. Cloutier, A.S. Daar, P.J. Smith. (2002). Needed: Models of Biotechnology Intellectual Property. *Trends in Biotechnology* 20(8): 327–9.

International Development Research Centre (IDRC) (1996). Connecting with the World: Priorities for Canadian Internationalism in the 21st Century. Task Force Report. (The strong report.) Ottawa: author. http://www.idrc.ca/strong/index.html.

Kitchens, S. (2002). Big Five fried. Forbes.com. http://www.forbes.com/global/2002/0401/064_print.html.

Lewis, S., P. Baird, R.G. Evans, W.A. Ghali, C.J. Wright, E. Gibson, et al. (2001). Dancing with the Porcupine: Rules for Governing the University–Industry Relationship [editorial]. *Canadian Medical Association Journal* 165(6): 783–5.

Mnyusiwalla, A. A.S. Daar, P.A. Singer. (2003). 'Mind the Gap': Science and Ethics in Nanotechnolgy. *Nanotechnology* 14: R9–R13.

National Science Foundation. (2002). *Converging Technologies for Improving Human Performance: Nanotechnology, Biotechnology, Information Technology and Cognitive Science.* http://wtec.org/ConvergingTechnologies/.

Pearson, L.B. (1972). Address at St Martin-in-the-Fields, London, on the occasion of the presentation to him of the Victor Gollancz Humanity Award. Text available at: http://www.unac.org/en/link/-learn/canada/pearson/gollancz.asp.

Pharmacogenomics Consortium. (2002). *Pharmacogenomics: Ethical and Regulatory Issues in Research and Clinical Practice.* University of Minnesota: University of Minnesota Centre for Bioethics.

Schaeffeler, E., M. Eichelbaum, V. Brinkmann, A. Penger, S. Asante-Poku, U.M. Zanger, and M. Schwab. (2001). Frequency of C3435T Polymorphism of MDR1 Gene in African People. *Lancet* 358(9279): 383–4.

Singer, P.A. (2002). The Public's Right to Know, or Not. *National Post*, 22 Aug. A23.

– and A.S. Daar. (2000). Avoiding Frankendrugs. *Nature Biotechnology* 18(12), p. 1225.

United Nations. (1995). *Role of Microcredit in the Eradication of Poverty – Report of the Secretary-General.* http://www.grameen-info.org/mcredit/unreport.html.

– Human Development Program (UNDP). (2001). *Human Development Report: Making New Technologies Work for Human Development.* New York: Oxford University Press.

– (10 July, 2001). Some Developing Countries Become Hi-Tech Leaders while Others Fall Far Behind. In *Human Development Report 2001.* http://www.undp.org/hdr2001/pr3.pdf.

University of Toronto. (1999). Joint Centre for Bioethics' Vision 2006. Available from http://www.utoronto.ca/jcb/main.html

World Health Organization. (2002a). Genomics and World Health: Report of the Advisory Committee on Health Research. Geneva: author. http://www3.who.int/whosis/genomics/genomics_report.cfm#.

– (2002b). WHO Report Calls for Genetic Medicine Benefits for All: Genome Research Can Save Millions in Developing World.Press Release. http://www.who.int/mediacentre/releases/release34/en/.

CHAPTER 15

Contribution of Higher Education to Research and Innovation: Balancing the 'Social Contract' of Universities with Their Drive for Scholarly Excellence

Calvin R. Stiller

The evolution of a knowledge-based economy has focused the attention of both the government and the private sector on universities as never before. Universities are now recognized as the primary source of the renewable resources – knowledge and discovery – that will determine an economy's competitiveness. Knowledge is a vital component in this process of research, innovation, and subsequent economic growth. As a result of the complex network of relationships among universities, government, and industry, the optimum model of a public – private partnership has yet to be determined. The new social contract that universities are expected to deliver on, by both a demanding public and government, needs thoughtful design if the growing requirements of universities are to be met. We must recognize that investing in basic research at our universities for the sole purpose of attracting the greatest minds, and creating the most vibrant centres for research, is not only vitally important for our society, but lies at the heart of this new social contract.

The Role of Government Policy in University Funding

The economy is no longer based on manufacturing, but on knowledge, with the emphasis on technology to maintain or enhance economic performance. The role of the university has become central. Traditionally, the function of universities has been to develop knowledge and to train students who become the scientists and engineers responsible for research and innovation. Indeed, the role of universities in knowledge production is well known, and the shift from traditional, discipline-based university research (Mode 1) to multidisciplinary research with a focus on application (Mode 2) has been written about in detail. Now it is being proposed that both these foundations for research have to coexist in a complementary, rather than a competing way (Calvert and Patel 2002). Regardless of one's position, the research role of the university has been used, abused, or ignored at the whim of government, university administrations, the military, and the private sector over the past century, depending on the need to buttress arguments for greater or lesser funding as well as greater or lesser independence.

Currently, government funds research at universities because this adds to the economic wealth of the surrounding community and to the country in general. By increasing funds for research, the government helps to expand the pool of useful information, thereby expanding opportunities for innovation. This is clearly evident, for example, in the close link between academic research and biotechnology. Universities, for their part, seek more funding from government for their research and staff because they will be unable to function competitively if they are not funded competitively. Unable to attract the best minds, universities cannot maintain both their research infrastructure and their high-calibre student population, which are both necessary to consolidate the economic spin-offs of the university.

If taken in a limited context without considering the total framework of the university's role, including the components necessary to achieve success in this model, we run the risk of inadvertently planting the seeds of failure. As a result of the growth in science-based technologies, however, there is now a new social contract between Canadian universities and government as it applies to research. The new social contract needs clarity – reasonable expectations, clear and measurable goals, and identified vehicles that can deliver on that contract.

Previously, studies have attempted to demonstrate the economic benefits of basic research funding by citing impressive return-on-investment ratios. Although newer models in growth theory attempt to use a variable of 'technical progress' to measure the growth created by technological development (Salter and Martin 2001), there is no accepted, suitable measurement. Although we can observe the impact of academic centres on regional economic growth, there is no robust equation for measuring input towards basic research and output in terms of economic growth or performance. By assessing only the return on investment, we are limiting our analysis of the total benefits from this relationship.

Having said this, however, Salter and Martin's review (2001) of the literature estimates that the rate of return to privately funded research and development ranges between 20 and 50 per cent. These rates of return depend on firms acquiring the knowledge and information that is produced by universities or research institutes, and then successfully applying this information to their innovative activities.

The rate of return on publicly funded research and development, although somewhat less, is still impressive at 28 per cent (Mansfield 1991). Mansfield studied seventy-six firms. He found that 5 per cent of their total sales depended on academic research that had been undertaken within the previous fifteen years. In a follow-up study, Mansfield (1998) estimated that 15 per cent of new products and 11 per cent of new processes could not have been developed without academic research.

Patents have also been considered an indication of academic output – a 'proxy indicator' of the link between university and industry (Narin, Hamilton, and Olivastro 1997). Narin's study (1977), regarding his analysis of scientific publications cited in American patents, is well known. He used this method to trace the impact of academic research and knowledge to the private sector. What is less well known is that this study also showed an increasing number of scientific references being cited. During a six-year period, there was a tripling in the number of citations to academic research.

There is more to this equation, however, than simply the transfer of protected knowledge to industry. As a result of the complex relationship between research and innovation, an appropriate algorithm would be a dynamic 'signal/signal transduction/receptor/feedback' process. The university uniquely provides a continuing source of new information, while generating smart, educated employees who populate the companies. They comprise the 'absorptive capacity,' those people who are capable of interpreting and applying the information.

It does not stop there. New, spin-off companies use professors from several universities – just as the intellectual property (IP) usually comes from several universities – to serve on their scientific advisory boards (SAB) as consultants (Fig.15.1). Their role is to further interpret, massage, reinterpret, and suggest application of the new information coming now from both the company and the university. It is this collective 'new knowledge' that is the real currency of the private sector. Universities also play an increasing role in carrying out contract research for these new companies. They can accommodate the need for large infrastructure, such as equipment, new instrumentation processes, animal models, and human testing.

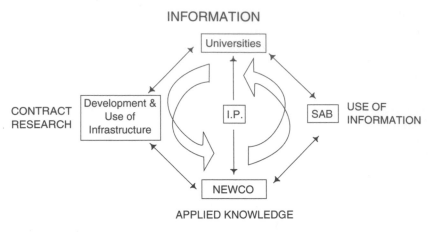

Figure 15.1 Cycle of Knowledge and Commercialization

In this dynamic interface, which is more like a network, the emerging economy requires the 'whole' university to be present, excellent, engaged, and renewed – people, ideas, information, instrumentation, wisdom, knowledge, networks, credentials, and objectivity. All components are needed for signal/signal transduction/receptor function and feedback so that society can gain the benefits from its investment in research.

Previously, it was thought that the benefits from publicly funded research could be easily measured because research was seen as the first step in a linear model – research provided economically useful information for industry to exploit in the way of new technology. Now, we realize that this is a limited approach. Because of the complex relationship between research and innovation, science and technology, it is difficult to measure all the benefits, including the economic returns, from research. This is further complicated because the flow between research and the private sector is bi-directional.

Even though we do not have the necessary direct measurements of input/output, one only has to go to the satellite view of North America to observe where the primary centres of economic growth from new knowledge have occurred. Boston and Stanford light up. Equally, they light up when you ask for indications of high academic performance and scientific impact. Parenthetically, they also light up because of the existence of a developed venture capital market.

Current work in industrial geography is assessing the importance of proximity between the private sector and the university / public research institute on the economic development in that region. High-tech clusters demonstrate the importance of research infrastructure. I would add, however, that a critical component is venture capital. The primary cause of failure of these start-ups is lack of capital, not inadequate science. Science is critical, but capital is the fuel for the engine.

Although difficult to quantify, the economic benefits from government investment in research at our universities are clear. The danger, however, is that government designs its programs to meet that goal. It has been shown that, not only are early timing and appropriate funding important, but also how this support is given. Short-term, narrow drives to force universities to commercialize technology have rarely been successful (Geuna 1999). Government stimulates innovation the most when it allows researchers the freedom to pursue new avenues of enquiry (Jacobsson 2002).

Investing in basic research at our universities for the sole purpose of attracting the greatest minds, and creating the most vibrant centres for research, is not only vitally important for our society: it lies at the very heart of the new social contract. Without globally acknowledged basic research foundations in our universities, the argument for commercialization cannot be made. One begets the other, even though there may be no direct link. The genotype is outstanding scientists and basic research in a protected environment. The phenotype is a university that has receptors for capturing commercial value, transporting it to 'incubators,' and then exporting it to the private sector.

Why Should Government Invest in Universities – Is It a Burden to Be Borne or an Opportunity to Gain?

Funding of medical research in Canada steadily declined from 1989 to 1995 despite campaigns and lobbying, including from citizen groups. In the mid-1990s, Dr Henry Friesen embarked on a metamorphosis of the Medical Research Council of Canada by presenting medical research as a key political, social, and economic strategy for Canada.

First, he changed the focus from 'medical' to 'health,' and he convinced academia and government that the only hope of meeting the future health needs of the country lay in research. Second, Friesen advanced the economic proposition and encouraged the launch of the Canadian Medical Discoveries Fund, a venture capital fund to commercialize Canadian discoveries. In the next two federal budgets, Finance Minister Paul Martin cited the fund as an example of why government should invest in medical research. During a six-year period, the amount of risk capital invested in biotechnology doubled year by year in Canada, rising from a steady state of Can\$ 50 million per year (from 1991 to 1995) to over Can\$ 2.1 billion in 2000.

Coincident with this, a significant increase occurred in federal funding through the Canadian Institutes for Health Research, along with the creation of new national pools, including the Canadian Foundation for Innovation (CFI) and Genome Canada. As well, there was unprecedented provincial funding for research through the Ontario Research and Development Challenge Fund and the Ontario Innovation Trust. These latter funds, which were established using a business partnership template, recognized for the first time the real cost of research at our universities by including overhead costs. Breaking that barrier alone was a significant advance in redressing a longstanding inequity in expecting our universities to be enthusiastic and full partners in the 'economic engine model' for our communities.

The successful linkage, in the minds of government, between research and jobs and the creation of wealth creation was a two-edged sword. It certainly helped in driving the research agenda, yet it was in danger of becoming the only model for new funding. I would argue that this economic engine model is a vital supplement, indeed a sibling, of the primary model of funding fundamental research at our universities.

It is no longer a case of arguing whether university research has a Mode 1 or Mode 2 basis. Rather, it is a matter of recognizing that a 'triple helix' (see Martin and Etzkowitz 2000) has been formed between universities, government, and industry. It should be the aim of government to balance these two models, by funding research through the Canadian Institutes for Health Research and also investing in research through the programs designed to partner with the private sector. Indeed, one could make the argument, and I do, that the former should be accomplished through stable funding envelopes and the latter through market-sensitive tax incentives.

It is the role of the universities to internally organize themselves to protect fundamental science, research, and teaching, while devising the external relationships (with clear intramural conduits) so that the private sector captures, develops, and exploits the research for the benefit of Canadians. This helix approach can foster strategic development, fund 'big science' projects, and network without disrupting the invaluable investigation-initiated scholarly pursuit of truth and discovery that takes place in the university setting.

Because of the linkage between research and higher education, the government can ensure a flow of skilled graduates by stimulating students to pursue higher education. We need to remember that 'talent, not technology' is vital to this process (Salter 2000). In addition to the government's role in promoting higher education, Scott et al. (2002) discuss the work of Guellec and Van Pottelsberghe, citing their suggestions on how government can assist by funding research and development. In addition to funding universities to conduct research, government can perform its own research in public laboratories, fund businesses directly to undertake research, and provide tax-based incentives.

It is my view that federal funding should focus on 'council-funded research,' basic research, multidisciplinary research, and the creation of networks and special initiatives in emerging sciences. Provincial governments should focus on building partnerships with federal and local gov ernments, as well as the private sector, to commercialize research and reap the benefits of its subsequent economic activity. In the end, we should recognize the unique roles that each partner – government, university, and the private sector – plays in this three-way partnership of university-based entrepreneurship.

In a knowledge-based economy, the engine is the university, and the fuel for that engine must come from government and the private sector. The vehicle will, by necessity, be a hybrid public-private vehicle that will increase our capability to create and respond to new opportunities. The transfer of academic research into industrial practice is best achieved when universities are given the necessary resources to conduct high-quality research (Geuna 1999) without placing limitations on the research. It is incumbent on all of us to steer this vehicle in the right direction with speed, but mindful of the first requirement – to protect the precious cargo of new knowledge and new discovery!

REFERENCES

Calvert, J., and P. Patel. (2002). *University-Industry Research Collaborations In the U.K.* Brighton: Science and Technology Policy Research.

Geuna, A. (1999). *The Economics of Knowledge Production.* London: Edward Elgar.

Jacobsson, S. (200). Universities and Industrial Transformation: An Interpretive and Selective Literature Study with Special Emphasis on Sweden. Electronic

Working Paper Series No. 81. Science and Technology Policy Research, University of Sussex.

Mansfield, E. (1991). Academic Research and Industrial Innovation. *Research Policy* 20: 1–12.

– (1998). Academic Research and Industrial Innovation: An Update of Empirical Findings. *Research Policy* 26: 773–6.

Martin, B.R., and H. Etzkowitz. (2000). The Origin and Evolution of the University Species. *Journal for Science and Technology Studies* 13(3-4): 9–34.

Narin, F., K. Hamilton, and D. Olivastro. (1997). The Increasing Linkage between U.S. Technology and Public Science. *Research Policy* 26: 317–30.

Narin, F., and D. Olivastro. (1992). Status Report: Linkage between Technology and Science. *Research Policy* 21: 237–49.

Salter, A., P. D'Este, B. Martin, A. Geuna, A. Scott, K. Pavitt, P. Patel, and P. Nightingale. (2000). *Talent, Not Technology: Publicly Funded Research and Innovation in the U.K.* Brighton: Science and Technology Policy Research.

Salter, A., and B. Martin. (2001). The Economic Benefits of Publicly Funded Basic Research: A Critical Review. *Research Policy* 30: 509–32.

Scott, A., G. Steyn, A. Geuna, S. Brusoni, E. Steinmueller. (2002). *The Economic Returns to Basic Research and the Benefits of University-Industry Relationships.* Stockholm, Sweden: Report for the Office of Science and Technology.

CHAPTER 16

The Academic-Commercial Interface in a Knowledge-Driven Economy: A View from MaRS

John R. Evans

Experience since the Second World War illustrates the profound impact of technologies derived from basic university research. Since the war the United States has led the world in public investment in university research and development through a variety of federal agencies. Benefits have been highly visible, for example, in the military and in health but, more generally, economic studies have demonstrated that over half the growth of the United States economy during the past half-century can be attributed to advances in technology, many of which originated in the universities. Economic analysis suggests a high annual return (of the order of 20 per cent) to the organization that invests in the research, 50 per cent to society and the nation at large, and a still greater rate of return for global society as a whole. These proportions indicate that regional investments are not exclusively parochial in their benefits. Local success leads to a ripple of benefits to society nationally and globally.

While the United States was making these forward-looking public investments in science and technology, the Canadian economy continued to rely heavily on natural resources and on branch plant manufacturing. Significant contributions in information technology, telecommunications, and aerospace have been made but in general Canada has lagged behind the advanced industrialized countries and particularly far behind the United States. In scientific research Canada has also been slow in recognizing the potential of new waves of innovative technologies and has been forced into the position of playing catch-up rather than riding the crest of new waves of innovation.

It is only in the past decade that a full appreciation has emerged of the importance of knowledge-based technologies as the major platform for future economic growth. To compete in global markets successfully Canada must invest in the most basic research as well as applied technology, establish an attractive institutional environment for research, compete successfully for the very best minds, and overcome the deficit of Canadian receptor firms necessary for commercialization.

Major waves of innovation come infrequently. It is crucial to catch them early. Currently biotechnology and life sciences research, the fastest growing segment of the knowledge-intensive economy, represents such an opportunity for investment at the crest of the wave. Global biotechnology is expanding four times faster than the average economic growth in the G-7 countries. In Canada, the biotechnology and biopharmaceutical sector is one of the fastest growing segments, outpacing aerospace and communications technologies, and creating highly skilled jobs directly and more indirect jobs than the industry average. Biotechnology is of course much more than the development of new pharmaceuticals. Biotechnology also represents convergence of the new innovations in genomics, proteomics, and other aspects of the life sciences with the natural sciences and engineering in a wide variety of measurement devices, control systems, and infomatics.

The life sciences, however, are just one example. It is the full spectrum of scientific research at universities and affiliated hospital research institutions that should occupy centre-stage in promoting future economic growth in Canada. It should do so directly through the generation of knowledge and indirectly through the training of highly skilled personnel. These functions are not new. What is new is the scale of investment by private and public sectors, the need to meet global standards of performance, the intensity of international competition for talented faculty and students, and the expectation that research results will be transformed into commercial products and services.

Since 1997 governments in Canada have recognized the central role of academic institutions in future economic development and have provided greatly increased research support through the granting councils, and infrastructure funds through the Canada Foundation for Innovation and the Canada Research Chairs.

Implicitly, if not explicitly, governments and universities have entered into a public research contract. In response to university commitments to excellence in research, and best efforts to commercialize research results governments have undertaken to sustain research investment at a level sufficient to move Canada from fifteenth to among the top five industrialized countries.

The universities' commitment in the public research contract is not just commercialization in general. It is a commitment to commercialize in Canada – to ensure national economic return on the substantial public research investment by strengthening existing industries in Canada and by carving out new niches to produce and deliver goods and services which will compete effectively in domestic and international markets.

Should highly trained personnel and intellectual property for export be all that the massive public research investment in Canadian universities produced, it would be a totally unsatisfactory national economic return, and the level of research investment would be unsustainable. The commitment is to generate wealth in Canada and create highly skilled job opportunities in Canada for its highly educated workforce.

For Canadians to be 'among the first to generate new knowledge and put it to use' presents a formidable challenge to our universities and will require new ways of thinking, acting, and organizing. First, universities must be able to attract and retain the outstanding human capital, faculty and students, and provide the supportive environment essential for excellent research. Second, to promote commercialization of discovery, the academic institutions will need to celebrate a genuine culture of entrepreneurship, foster industrial linkages, and facilitate access for entrepreneurs to technology transfer processes to assess and enhance the commercial potential of the intellectual property. The technology transfer processes require highly skilled personnel and a level of financial support normally not funded by universities or conventional research grants.

The university gains significantly from the commercialization of its intellectual property through income from licence and equity invest ments, through early access to exclusive technologies, and state-of-the-art equipment, and through broadening career opportunities for faculty, students, and technical staff.

At the same time, there are risks from the increased intensity of academic and commercial research activities which coexist in time, place, and sources of support. Most universities now recognize the need for proactive, independent, and transparent processes to prevent conflicts at the academic-commercial interface and to ensure that the benefits anticipated for faculty, students, and the institution do not come at the expense of fundamental academic purposes.

Going forward, universities will be primary engines to drive economic growth. Successful commercialization, however, will depend on complementary factors not under the universities' control. Two of the most important are, first, venture financing for the development process necessary to bring innovations to market and, second, creation of a supportive environment for entrepreneurs to drive the innovation process. Weaknesses in both currently handicap commercialization in Canada. Rectifying these deficiencies is critical to creating dynamic opportunities to advance our scientific discoveries close to home and to counter both external and internal brain drain.

Financing Commercialization

Studies from the United States, Europe, and Canada underline the overriding importance of venture capital in transforming academic discovery into commercial reality. For example, it is increasingly recognized that venture capital can be more effective in stimulating patenting than traditional corporate research and development (R&D) and is responsible for a greater share of industrial innovations.

In a recent speech in which he reviews European innovation and competitiveness, Roland Berger laments the failure of European economies to match U.S. practices of massive capital investment in the future – in education, R&D, capital stock, and capital markets. He states that Europe is 'suffering capital drain due to the attractiveness of the U.S. capital markets to global investors – the U.S. is significantly more inclined to take risks and considerably more willing to leave the past behind' (personal communication).

Canada should take note of the analyses. A recent Canadian study of small and medium-sized enterprises, concludes that venture capital markets in Canada are a decade behind the United States, in part because of past regulatory restrictions on banks and pension plan investments. This lag has meant that institutional investors are less familiar with venture capital portfolios and have tended to be more risk averse. In addition, Canada has been less developed than the United States in providing access to seed capital for young and risky growth firms in the technology and health science fields with the consequence that the pipeline of prospects for venture capital investment is also underdeveloped (Canadian Federation of Independent Business 2002).

Biotechnology companies in Canada have fewer financing vehicles available at each stage of their development compared with their counterparts in the United States. The lack of angel financing often aborts development at the technology transfer stage. Limitation of access from the other sources of financing to fund the long product development process forces firms either to license out products too early at low royalty rates or to go public prematurely. As a result, the firms forgo higher royalty rates and milestone payments from pharmaceutical partners or more significant economic gain from a later initial public offering (IPO).

The average size of capital deals in the year 2000 in Canada was U.S.$ 2.6 million versus U.S.$ 14.5 million in the United States. Canadian firms, therefore, are competing in the same global arena with but a fraction of the resources to execute the necessary processes of bringing a new chemical entity to market.

The biotechnology sector has a large proportion of fragile start-up companies which have a slender pipeline of early stage products and face long development programs of ten years or more before they go to market, yet have financial resources rarely adequate for more than twelve to eighteen months of development. There is an urgent need to expand investment in life sciences in Canada through tax incentives and other mechanisms. At the present time, their share of capital investment is 2 per cent in Canada compared with 12 per cent in the United States. Canadian access to the more mature U.S. venture capital funding pools is impeded by cross-border withholding taxes on investment income.

In Canada, greater access to financing is vital to all stages of commercialization of discoveries: pre-seed and seed funding by angel investors greatly expanded venture capital for firms up to the IPO stage, and access to public capital markets. At each stage government incentives such as co-funding, tax concessions, or flow-though shares are important to increase the amount of funds available and the risk tolerance of the investors. These incentives are particularly critical in the current market downturn.

Nurturing Commercialization

The second critical factor in commercialization is the creation of a supportive environment for start-up and early stage firms – an environment in which fledgling firms have ready access to venture financing appropriate to their stage of development but also access to experienced management, technical and business support services, and interaction with other entrepreneurs in start-up and established firms.

The cluster strategy advanced by Michael Porter and Roger Martin (2001) appears to be a powerful means to meet this need. They propose that the geographical co-location of business and financial and academic enterprises, which feed on each others' ideas and experience, will facilitate each others' development. As they suggest, innovation, competitiveness, and prosperity arise out of geographical proximity of highly skilled human capital.

There seems to be an emerging consensus on the value of clusters. The U.S. National Venture Capital Association endorses clusters from a venture capital standpoint noting that monitoring costs are lowered and there is greater confidence in the ability of an individual firm to tap into a local research and development network.

In *The Path to Prosperity* report' the Canadian Federation of Independent Business (2002) emphasizes a shortage in Canada of clusters of high-tech and health science activity compared with the United States. The report notes that priority investment to enhance commercialization of academic research discoveries lies in the development of clusters that can become a magnet for the diversity of talent necessary for commercialization and a useful address in the global science and technology world.

The government of the United Kingdom has just announced plans to fund regional development clusters of innovative businesses and incubators to enhance innovation and productivity through shared knowledge and to reduce costs by jointly sourcing services and suppliers.

In a study by Cortright and Mayer, published by the Brookings Institution Center on Urban and Metropolitan Policy (2002), the powerful impact of regional bioscience clusters on commercialization in the United States is documented. From a review of over fifty-one regions they found that bioscience development was increasingly concentrated in just nine metropolitan centres. A large base of high-quality biomedical research and a leading research university or medical centre were essential features but what distinguished the nine from the remainder of the fifty-one regions was the striking growth in share of new biotech firms and the very high concentration of capital flows from biotech and general venture funds and from pharmaceutical research alliances. The nine regions accounted for 80 per cent of all U.S. venture capital for biopharmaceuticals, represented 92 per cent of the most active biotechnology venture capital firms, and accounted for 96 per cent of the dollar value of pharmaceutical company research alliances.

The Brookings Institution report contends that this concentration reflects the agglomeration economics or critical mass of having a large number of biotechnology firms, workers, and investors all in a single location. These areas attract large numbers of professionals – both managers and research scientists – with previous experience in commercial biotechnology. The areas also have concentrations of specialized financial expertise in the form of venture capitalists. Once established, these clusters of activity sustain and even attract additional talent and additional money, especially in the case of alliances with pharmaceutical firm (Cortright and Mayer 2002).

There appears to be strong consensus that the concept of clusters is powerful. With convergence, critical mass and appropriate mix of constituents and with actively managed networking, the clusters facilitate entrepreneurial development by bringing together excellent scientific research and entrepreneurial firms, by providing access to financing and experienced venture management, and by providing access to technical and business support services. Once established, the clusters demonstrate internal momentum which gives them the edge in attracting additional talent and financial resources.

The Brookings study concludes that metropolitan areas looking to reap benefits from commercial biotechnology may find policies to stimulate venture capital and to engage local entrepreneurship, easily the most important steps towards the development of a successful cluster.

MaRS

Let me turn now to 'the view from MaRS.' MaRS is an example of clusters at varying stages of development across Canada, six of which have major emphasis on biotechnology.

MaRS, or the Medical and Related Sciences Discovery District, is an independent, not-for-profit corporation designed to achieve the benefits of a cluster. The purpose is to enhance commercialization of intellectual property from the world-class research capability of the neighbouring universities and hospital research institutes. MARS is an attempt to achieve the benefits of a cluster, as defined by Porter and Martin, through geographical co-location of businesses and financial and academic enterprises that feed on each others' ideas and expertise and as a consequence facilitate each others' development. MARS's goal is to become an important address in the global science and technology world and a magnet to attract diversity of talent, services, and, in particular, venture capital.

How Will the MaRS Cluster Add Value?

It will promote an active network interaction among scientists from diverse disciplines, businesses at different stages of development, and sources of financing, in particular, venture capital. It is important to create a pool of personnel experienced in commercialization.

MaRS should facilitate access to technical and business support service onsite or in neighbouring academic institutions, for example, sophisticated analytic services and bioinfomatics without the distraction and expense for small firms of attempting to build infrastructure in-house.

The immediate proximity to university and hospital research facilities will permit investigators to participate actively in the commercialization of their discoveries outside the academic institutions without having to give up their academic posts. This is a key factor in attracting and retaining outstanding scientists.

MaRS could also enhance regional critical mass and specialization of technology transfer capability by acting as a platform to coordinate the efforts of the talented individuals based at the university and hospital research institutes.

Most importantly, MaRS will active as a magnet for venture capital and other sources of financing by facilitating effective communication among interested parties and by establishing specific programs on-site.

Toronto is a great site to promote the cluster convergence of critical elements because:

- Toronto represents the largest concentration of medical and scientific research in Canada and ranks in the top five in North America in biomedical sciences.
- Toronto is the strongest financial centre in Canada and is also the principle site of national media.
- Toronto is home to 50 per cent of Canada's pharmaceutical industries, 60 per cent of its medical device firms and more than 100 biotech companies.
- Toronto is also a hub of communications and transportation linkages, domestically and internationally, and the home of provincial government ministries.
- Toronto is a great place to live – an important determinant of where today's scientists and entrepreneurs want to work.

From hundreds of start-ups based on research in the universities and hospitals MaRS will provide the opportunity to establish close relationships to supporting firms and services and possibly partnership with big pharmaceutical companies. A few of those start-ups will grow in that environment to become billion dollar companies.

The MaRS cluster will house outposts that may be attractive to faculty and students in management and law, as well as to scholars in a variety of disciplines critical to a public understanding of new developments in science and technology. The students and small firms might benefit from the interaction.

Spatial proximity will enhance the competitive dynamics of the cluster promoting demand from customers eager to achieve comparative advantage through early adoption of innovations and rivalry among firms competing to supply creative innovations.

The MaRS physical facilities have a strategic location, being adjacent to a broad array of scientific research at the University of Toronto and the hospital research institutes as well as the Ontario government buildings and Canada's principal financial district. On 24 June 2002 the City of Toronto designated the two square kilometer area including the University of Toronto, affiliated teaching hospitals, and more than thirty research institutes as Toronto's Discovery District. MaRS is at the centre of this district.

The reach of MaRS, however, can be extended to the Ontario Highway 401 corridor of universities and hospital research facilities through a virtual network facilitated by a fibre optic communications system. With a critical mass of businesses, research, and services at the physical locations of MaRS in Toronto, it should be possible to establish an effective networking relationship with other nodes of scientific commercialization.

The MaRS physical centre, located at University Avenue and College Street in Toronto, will be developed in two or more phases. Phase One consisting of approximately 600,000 square feet of research and office space, is scheduled for occupancy in late 2004. The University Avenue end of the site has the potential for a later addition of 700,000 square feet of space.

Core financing has been provided by generous capital grants from the Province of Ontario and the federal government to match donations in cash and kind from private citizens, corporations, and the University of Toronto. The city, through the Toronto Economic Development Corporation (TEDCO), has also been a financial sponsor.

Conclusion

Universities will be primary engines to drive economic growth. Successful commercialization, however, will depend on complementary factors that include, first, venture financing for the development process necessary to bring innovations to market and, second, creation of a supportive environment for entrepreneurs to drive the innovation process. Weaknesses in both currently handicap commercialization in Canada.

Rectifying these deficiencies is critical to creating dynamic opportunities to advance our scientific discoveries close to home and to counter both the external and internal brain drain.

When MaRS is up and running it is expected to enhance commercialization of scientific discoveries. It represents an initiative to put into practice the advantages of an actively networked cluster. It will be 'mission accomplished' if MaRS becomes an internationally recognized address for accelerating the path from discovery to commercialization in Canada. Success will contribute to Canada's international competitiveness by creating highly skilled jobs, generating wealth, and ensuring that Canadians share in expanded social and economic returns made possible by the substantial public investment in academic research.

REFERENCES

Canadian Federation of Independent Business, Canadian Manufacturers and Exporters, and RBC Financial Group. (2002). The Path to Prosperity: Canada's Small and Medium-sized Enterprises. Toronto: author.

Cortright, Joseph, and Heike Mayer. (2002). *Signs of Life: The Growth of Biotechnology Centers in the U.S.* Washington, D.C.: Brookings Institution, Center on Urban and Metropolitan Policy.

Martin, Roger, and Michael Porter. (2001). *Canadian Competitiveness: A Decade after the Crossroads.* Unpublished report Rotman School of Management, University of Toronto.

CHAPTER 17

Innovation U: New Practices, Enabling Cultures

Louis G. Tornatzky

Over the past decade, research universities have become settings for an often-spirited debate about their core mission and activities. Increasingly challenged has been the traditional mission of the institution: research and scholarship, teaching and education, and college and community service. An alternative vision, with greater emphasis on the externally 'engaged' institution is in the process of becoming legitimated.

The impetus for these changes has come from several quarters. For one, historical champions of the land grant university have urged a reexamination of the basic premises and foci of the service and extension roles (Kellogg Commission 2000). In effect, a process is under way to redefine the land grant mission so that it extends to industrial partners and clients and encompasses dramatically different approaches to moving new knowledge into society. That is, more societal benefit will accrue from selling knowledge rather than from giving it away. Second, state governments and regional economic development organizations have come to see universities as something more than a source of trained students, but as potentially active and important assets to be used in improving public policies and economic opportunities (Tornatzky 2000). Third, sophisticated companies, both large and small, see the research university as a critical resource in building knowledge-intensive businesses, and they are drawn to communities that are centres of research and technology (DeVol 1999). Oddly enough, parents and families have also fueled this discussion, as it becomes increasingly clear that states and regions with an absence of technology industry end up exporting most of their science and engineering graduates to other parts of the country (Tornatzky et al. 1998).

This chapter describes the results of a modest research effort designed to document the efforts of a small group of research universities to be externally engaged in the service of technology-based economic development. It is organized into four sections. First, we will briefly reprise the methods and approach of the research. Second, we will describe the types of novel practices and policies being implemented in our sample of institutions. Third, and critically important, we will describe some of the *cultural* underpinnings of these efforts. Finally, we will speculate about the future of these organizational innovations.

Reprise of the Project

The study (reported in Tornatzky et al. 2002) was a two-year effort, supported by the National Science Foundation and part of an eight-year program of benchmarking research (Tornatzky 2001) that focused on research universities. That program had developed a systematic and quantitative approach to ranking and rating universities on their technology transfer performance, and in parallel defining what 'best-in-class' universities were doing differently in terms of practices, programs, and policies that might account for their higher level of performance.

The current study followed the same general strategy, but our team wanted to look more broadly at university-industry-community relationships and involvement in regional economic development. Based on our knowledge of the research and practice literature, we defined several domains of relevant activities. We looked at the following as domains: industry-research partnerships, technology transfer, entrepreneurial development, industry-focused education and training, career services and placement, formal partnerships with state or regional economic development organizations, and use of industry input to campus programs. We were also interested in other precursors or concomitants of the more operational partnering: rewards, mission, and organizational culture.

We then persuaded forty national experts – researchers, consultants, practitioners, and policy buffs – to act as a panel of judges and choose exemplary universities in terms of external partnering. We asked the panel members to consider our definitions and descriptions of the partnering domains, and in parallel to review a list of the top 164 U.S. universities in terms of annual research expenditures. The panelists' task was to nominate or vote for those institutions that they thought exemplified successful involvement across the range of partnering domains. Our team simply added up the votes from the forty judges, and identified the top 10 per cent of vote getters as defining our case study sample of 'best-in-class' institutions. Some false positives appeared among the ratings, in that upon closer examination and preliminary contact with a nominated university, it became quickly apparent that it had departed from an earlier commitment to the agenda of external engagement; two universities were eliminated from the final study sample because of resource and time constraints. Thus, given our methodology, it would be inappropriate to assume that no other universities shared some of the characteristics of our sample of case study institutions. We know that many of them do, and in the absence of a true comparison or control group, we do not know the frequency of those characteristics in the population. Nonetheless, we have assumed that the practices of 'engagement' described here are more concentrated in our sample than in the average university.

We spent eighteen months laboriously gathering information from the twelve institutions in our final sample. The raw data derived from dozens of phone and in-person interviews, review of several linear feet of internal reports, planning documents, and program propaganda, and much iterative feedback from our informants. Each draft chapter was reviewed several times by different people at each institution to make sure the final version was factually correct and up to date as of the time it went to press.

What We Learned: Novel Practices, Programs, and Policies

Aside from organizational innovations that were domain-specific, these institutions were notable in other ways. For one, each of the schools seemed to be actively involved – and achieving successes – in most or all of the practice domains. While most first-class research universities can point to successful involvement in one or two areas, it is not the norm to be pervasively involved across the range of partnering activities. In addition, these seemingly disparate partnering activities tended to be joined in a systemic approach. That is, they were typically organized and conceived as integrated and complementary, with a lot of cross-referrals, contiguous offices, and use of coordinating councils or other governance structures that were orthogonal to the established academic structure.

Industry Research Partnering

The research and development (R&D) work done in collaboration with companies was extensive, customer-friendly, and accepted among the study sample. The scope of industry-sponsored work was significant as a fraction of total research expenditures (7 per cent is the approximate national norm), and in terms of organizational values and rewards the money was 'the same colour' as that from the National Science Foundation or the National Institutes of Health. In other words, getting industry research support was not necessarily fatal to a tenure or promotion bid, and often helped. Often the cooperative research relationships led to, or derived from, technology transfer relationships, again illustrating the integrative aspects of the partnering activities. Some illustrations:

- Penn State has roughly 17 per cent of its research portfolio funded by industry. It has an industrial research office to foster industry research relationships and function as a single initial contact point for companies. There is an industry-friendly directory of faculty expertise and interests, and procedures are in place to package industry relationships (e.g., master agreements). An adjacent research park, with both industry and university tenants, facilitates industry-university interaction.
- Purdue has 12.5 per cent of its research funded by industry. It also has an industry research office, an Internet-based faculty directory (*Connect Indiana*), a system of contract facilitation and master agreements, and an extremely large research park.
- Georgia Tech, with 22.5 per cent of its research supported by industry, is the champion in this arena, both among our sample and nationally. It too has an industry contract office to facilitate one-stop shopping, as well as adjacent facilities that bring industry and academics together. Georgia Tech has been very successful in launching centres and institutes with extensive and intensive industry involvement. The Georgia Research Alliance, which has a mix of industry and government money and expertise, has played a significant brokering and financial role in all of these activities.

Technology Transfer

All of the twelve institutions are adept at patenting, licensing, and commercialization, and rank in the top quartile or better on virtually all performance indicators of technology transfer. In addition, extensive attention is paid to the 'economic geography' of technology transfer. That is, the extent to which technology transfer involves state-based companies, thus contributing significant value to the state economy. Most have developed significant expertise in doing start-up deals (and encouraging faculty therein), and technology transfer seems to be closely linked to other engagement domains. Some other details and examples are the following:

- There is a can-do approach to managing conflicts of interest and commitment, or as one informant described it: 'Don't cross the line, but you can get real close.'
- Several of the institutions, often in partnership with state government, have orchestrated access to pre-seed money to enable the development of prototypes and conduct proof-of-concept studies. For example, Purdue operates the Trask Technology Innovation Awards program, which provides grants of up to U.S.$100,000 to faculty inventors to develop the commercial potential of their technologies.
- Virtually all of the offices have departed from a strategy that emphasized maximizing royalty returns on licensing deals to an approach that concentrates on moving the technology out the door, often in the form of start-up arrangements.
- There are easily understood 'roadmaps' for faculty via which they can understand the policies, rules, and procedures of the technology transfer function (Virginia Tech is a good example).
- Several of the university technology transfer offices have strong working relationships with local business incubation programs and services, many of which are located in university research parks (e.g., all of the following universities – Penn State, Purdue, Georgia Tech, Ohio State, Wisconsin, North Carolina State).
- There is extensive faculty education and training on intellectual property and technology transfer topics, often running concurrently in unit and institutional levels (e.g., Carnegie-Mellon). Virginia Tech runs an annual all-day workshop on intellectual property issues.
- Staffing of the technology transfer programs is at or above national benchmark levels in terms of professionals per unit of research expenditures, with a range of expertise represented (e.g., doing start-ups).
- The technology transfer function is highly visible, legitimate, and linked to other external partnering activities. At Ohio State it is part of the technology partners cluster of linked organization.

Entrepreneurial Development

Virtually all of the twelve universities that we studied are actively involved in fostering local entrepreneurial ventures through technology business incubators (Tornatzky et al, 1996), educational programs, and community outreach. Typically these activities are an adjunct to or partner of the technology transfer function. Some examples are the following:

- Purdue claims the largest square footage of incubation space anywhere in the United States, with three incubators in its research park. The facilities are made available to faculty inventors, and there is extensive enabling policy to encourage their involvement. In addition, Purdue operates the Trask Pre-Seed Capital Investment Program, which provides grants of up to U.S.$250,000 to faculty start-up companies.
- Georgia Tech has developed 125,000 square feet of incubator space, graduated nearly a hundred companies, and attracted hundreds of millions of dollars in investment capital.
- Utah's Centers of Excellence program , which provides grants for pre-commercial development, has led to the establishment of over 120 companies and the creation of over 2,000 jobs.
- The University of California at San Diego operates the Connect Program which tends to be externally focused on the San Diego high-technology entrepreneurial network. It conducts a wide variety of outreach, education, and networking programs, and supports itself entirely by fees and soft money.
- There is an extensive, award-winning program in entrepreneurial education at Carnegie-Mellon University, with graduate, undergraduate, and continuing education courses being offered.

Extension

Several of the twelve universities had adapted their historic extension role to providing technical assistance to hundreds of industrial companies – as kind of a new land grant model. In some cases, the extension services are organized around key state industries. For example:

- The Industrial Extension Service at North Carolina State is more than thirty years old. It provides services to hundreds of clients annually and has the active involvement of the college of engineering faculty and staff.
- PENNTAP is an industrial extension operation based at Penn State. It was established in 1965, and had 600 engagements with client companies in its most recent program year.

- Georgia Tech has the oldest and largest extension service, with seventy staff members in eighteen regional offices, and over 1,500 client engagements annually.
- In the 1960s, Texas A&M pioneered the development of its Engineering Experiment Station, which was a deliberate take-off from its land grant tradition, but designed to serve industrial companies.

Industry-Responsive Training and Education

All of the universities that we studied were involved in extensive, non-traditional, educational offerings. These catered to local industry needs and addressed new technologies and management issues of technology-based companies. Some examples are:

- Georgia Tech reaches 18,000 participants annually with a diverse program of short courses and certificate programs, which in turn, is linked to its industry extension service that operates in several branch offices around the state.
- Purdue delivers an extensive customer base of non-traditional students via its network of branch campuses. It makes extensive use of assessments of industry-focused training needs assessments in crafting coursework at regional centres.
- The program at the University of California at San Diego reaches 35,000 people annually, with an emphasis on technology-related courses and programs that are aligned with the San Diego economy.

Formal Partnering with State and Local Agencies

Several of our twelve universities are involved in strategic and operational partnering roles with state economic development organizations. Informed state policy makers recognize the importance of university technology assets. For example:

- There are longstanding relationships between Georgia Tech, the State of Georgia, and the Georgia Research alliance. As a result, Georgia Tech becomes, in effect, the operator of several of the program components of the state's technology-oriented economic development strategy. Through other programs of the Economic Development Institute, Georgia Tech also assists in training and development of strategy for local economic development organizations.

- Penn State is a partner and an operator of various Commonwealth of Pennsylvania programs (e.g., PENNTAP, Ben Franklin Partnership).
- Through its public services program and Economic Development Assistance Center, Virginia Tech provides program development assistance, training, and planning help to local economic development organizations throughout the state.

Culture and Rewards: The Engine that Drives the Train

While this compendium of program and practice examples extracted from the *Innovation U* book (Tornatzky et al, 2002) is indeed impressive, what was even more apparent to our research team was the extent to which each of the twelve institutions had adapted their organizational cultures to legitimate their new roles. We have come to the conclusion that this was *the most important element* in technology-focused external partnering and engagement. Some of the expressions of such cultural support include the following:

- In virtually all of the institutions, senior leadership was 'out front' and visible in support of and championing the programs. One would find sprinkled throughout university publications rich in quotations from presidents and chancellors about the critical importance of these new roles for the institution. Many were from chief executive officers (CEOs) who had had experiences in their own career that predisposed them to stress the new partnering roles.
- At several levels within the institutions there was language in mission, vision, and goal statements that supported the external partnering roles. Often this language was prominent in recent university-wide strategic plans as well.
- Several of the universities had annual awards or recognition programs that spotlighted the accomplishments of individuals and units in technology commercialization, entrepreneurship, industry research partnering, and related activities. The symbolic value of these events generally far exceeded the dollar value of the formal awards, as they tended to be covered by regional media and attended by state political leaders.
- New language in promotion and tenure criteria formally legitimated the role of various partnering activity accomplishments in a portfolio (e.g., patents).
- New positions, with wide visibility and authority, were created (e.g.,

Vice-president for university outreach, director of office of industry partnerships) that legitimated and extended the external partnering role.

- University Web sites were replete with links and language pointing to university roles, services, and accomplishments in external partnering.
- High visibility hires tended to have partnering experience and interest among the selection criteria they matched, and institutions with a long history in external partnering tended to have a cadre of leadership with like minds on the wisdom and legitimacy of these activities.

Issues of Sustainability

Given the perspectives and biases of the research team – with much of our careers focused on helping and urging universities to be more externally engaged – we felt that the organizational innovations described in the *Innovation U* book and summarized in this chapter are a positive development for the academic community. Needless to say, there are others in the academic community who would argue that these developments are unfortunate and will degrade or defocus the institution. Given those circumstances, it might be useful to close with some speculation about what might allow these new roles for the university to continue and flourish, and conversely what might threaten their survival.

Continuation of Leadership

Institutional leadership and support is a key factor. Unfortunately, successful university CEOs are a hot commodity, and the typical career path involves moving from one university to another every few years. In our own research – and even among our study sample for this project – we have seen how fragile many of these partner initiatives are, and how easily they can unravel. To sustain these new university roles, it is important that they do not rely on one or two influential leaders, but are supported by a whole cadre of deans, chairs, and prominent faculty members.

The General Difficulty of Universities in Maintaining Focus

By their nature, universities are diffuse and somewhat disorganized social systems. It is difficult for them to maintain focus outside of their traditional roles, unless extraordinary sustained efforts are expended. This is just the nature of the beast.

Issues of Partisan Politics

Many of activities described here involve some degree of direct collaboration with state government. For example, if state political leadership is pushing an agenda of technology-based development, the state universities can benefit from new resources and government support. The potential danger is that the state development agenda may not have bipartisan support, which can expose the university to buffeting and shifting financial and political backing as administrations change.

Organizational Restructuring

Partnership activities are not necessarily consistent with the typical organizational structures of universities. We found that the more established and stable partnering activities tended to be housed and managed in novel types of organizational structures and governance relationships. To the extent that early efforts are launched in an ad hoc manner, and do not go through a process of careful organizational re-structuring, their long-term survival may be chancy.

University Traditionalism

Last, but clearly not least, is that most academics and academic leaders are lukewarm about the partnering approaches described here. To the extent that they can outlast the champions of organizational change and innovation, these new forms of engagement may not be long-lived.

REFERENCES
DeVol, R. (1999). *America's High-Tech Economy: Growth, Development, and Risks for Metropolitan Areas*. Santa Monica, CA: Milken Institute.
Kellogg Commission on the Future of the State and Land-Grant Universities. (2000). *Renewing the Covenant: Learning, Discovery, and Engagement in a New Age and Different World*. Washington, DC: National Association of State Universities and Land Grant Colleges.
Tornatzky, L. (2000). *Building State Economies by Promoting University-Industry Technology Transfer*. Washington, DC: National Governors Association.
– (2001). Benchmarking University-Industry Technology Transfer: A Six-Year Perspective. *Journal of Technology Transfer* 26: 269–77.
– Y. Batts, N. McCrea, M. Lewis, and L. Quittman. (1996). *The Art and Craft of*

Technology Business Incubation. Research Triangle Park, NC: Southern Growth
Policies Board.
- D. Gray, S. Tarant, and J. Howe. (1998). *Where Have All the Students Gone? Interstate Migration of Recent Science and Engineering Graduates.* Research Triangle
Park, NC: Southern Growth Policies Board.
- P. Waugaman, and D. Gray. (2001). *University-Industry Technology Transfer: Models of Alternative Practice, Policy, and Program.* Research Triangle Park, NC:
Southern Growth Policies Board.
- (2002). *Innovation U: New University Roles in a Knowledge Economy.* Research Triangle Park, NC: Southern Growth Policies Board.

Contributors

Robert Birgeneau was president and professor of physics at the University of Toronto from 2000 to 2004. In 2004 he became chancellor of the University of California, Berkeley. He carries out research on the effects of disorder, dimensionality, and correlations in materials, especially in quantum many body solids. He is also broadly interested in science policy and the role of research and education in advanced societies.

David Bloom is the Clarence James Gamble professor of economics and demography of the department of population and international health at Harvard University's School of Public Health. He is also research associate at the U.S. National Bureau of Economic Research in Cambridge, Massachusetts.

Abdallah S. Daar is professor of public health sciences and professor of surgery at the University of Toronto. He is director of the program in applied ethics and biotechnology at the University of Toronto Joint Centre for Bioethics and director for ethics and policy, McLaughlin Centre for Molecular Medicine, University of Toronto.

James Duderstadt is president emeritus and university professor of science and engineering at the University of Michigan. His teaching, research interests, and national service activities span a wide range of subjects including nuclear energy, information technology, science policy, and education policy.

Eva Egron-Polak is secretary-general of the International Association of Universities, a UNESCO-based non-governmental organization. She worked for more than fifteen years in various positions at the Association of Universities and Colleges of Canada (AUCC), including vice-president for international and Canadian programs.

John Evans is chairman of the Canada Foundation for Innovation, the MaRS (Medical and Related Sciences Discovery District) board, and Torstar Corporation. He was founding dean of the McMaster University Faculty of Medicine, and he was president of the University of Toronto from 1972 to 1978.

Ruth Hayhoe is professor of comparative higher education at the Ontario Institute for Studies in Education at the University of Toronto. From 1997 to 2002, she headed the Hong Kong Institute of Education and is now president emerita. She is the author of numerous books and articles on Chinese higher education and Chinese educational relations with Western countries.

Glen A. Jones is professor of higher education and associate dean, academic at the Ontario Institute for Studies in Education at the University of Toronto. He has published extensively on higher education systems, policy, and governance.

Patricia L. McCarney is associate vice-president, international research and development at the University of Toronto, and associate professor of political science and director of the Global Cities Programme at the Munk Centre for International Studies. Her teaching and research is in the field of comparative development, urban governance, and global cities in comparative perspective.

Ramamurthy Natarajan is chairman of the All India Council for Technical Education, New Delhi. Previously he had served as director, Indian Institute of Technology, Madras, for six years. He obtained his doctoral, as well as master's degrees from the University of Waterloo. Ontario. He is a fellow of the Indian National Academy of Engineering, the Institution of Engineers (India), the Indian Institution of Plant Engineers, the Indian Society for Technical Education, the Indian Institution of Materials Management, and the Madras Science Foundation.

Shirley Neuman is professor of English at the University of Toronto. A leading scholar in Canadian literature, she studies autobiography as a literary genre. Prior to joining the faculty at the University of Toronto, she was professor of English and women's studies and dean of the College of Literature, Science and the Arts at the University of Michigan.

Maureen O'Neil is president of the International Development Research Centre. She serves on the board of directors of the International Institute for Democracy and Electoral Assistance and is a member of the international board of governors of the Centre for International Governance Innovation (CIGI), as well as chair of the hemispheric advisory board of the Institute for Connectivity in the Americas.

Beth Savan teaches in the environmental programs at Innis College, University of Toronto, and is an adjunct professor in the geography department and in the master's in planning program. She has recently managed major collaborative projects linking university scholars with both government agencies and non-governmental organizations. She has published widely in the areas of community sustainability, community-based research, bias and self-deception in scientific research, and community-based environmental monitoring.

Peter Scott is vice-chancellor of Kingston University in the United Kingdom. Prior to this position, he served as pro vice-chancellor for external affairs at the University of Leeds, where he was also professor of education and director of the Centre for Policy Studies in Education. Before going to Leeds in 1992, he was editor of the *Times Higher Education Supplement* for sixteen years.

Peter A. Singer is the Sun Life Financial chair in bioethics and director of the University of Toronto's Joint Centre for Bioethics, program director of the Canadian Program on Genomics and Global Health, professor of medicine at the University of Toronto, and a distinguished investigator of the Canadian Institutes of Health Research.

Michael L. Skolnik holds the William G. Davis chair in community college leadership and is a professor in the higher education program at the Ontario Institute for Studies in Education of the University of Toronto. A former Rhodes Scholar at Oxford University, Professor Skolnik has published extensively on the organization and governance of universities and colleges and on the economics of higher education.

Calvin Stiller is chair of the Ontario Research and Development Challenge Fund and director of the Ontario Innovation Trust. He is a professor in the department of medicine at the University of Western Ontario and was co-director of Immunology at the John P. Robarts Research Institute. Dr Stiller established the multi-organ transplant service in London, Ontario, and served as the unit's chief from 1984 to 1996 . He currently is chair and chief executive officer of the Canadian Medical Discoveries Fund.

George Subotzky is the director of the Centre for the Study of Higher Education at the University of the Western Cape, in Cape Town, South Africa. His current research interests include knowledge production and development; gender equity in higher education; globalization, marketization, and the changing higher education workplace; and organisational change in higher education.

Louis Tornatzky is vice-president for business planning and development at Select University Technologies in California, and concurrently a senior fellow with the Southern Technology Council as well as a senior adviser with New Economic Strategies in Washington, DC.

David Wolfe is professor of political science at the University of Toronto and co-director of the program on globalization and regional innovation systems, which is the node for one of five subnetworks of the Innovation Systems Research Network of which Professor Wolfe is national coordinator. He is also the principal investigator on its major research initiative entitled 'Innovation Systems and Economic Development: The Role of Local and Regional Clusters in Canada.'